# The Revolutionary War

**Other Books of Interest from St. Augustine's Press**

Jeremy Black, *Britain's Imperial Histories*

Jeremy Black, *Defoe's Britain*

Jeremy Black, *Smollett's Britain*

Jeremy Black, *The Importance of Being Poirot*

Jeremy Black, *The Age of Nightmare*

Jeremy Black, *In Fielding's Wake*

Jeremy Black, *The Civil War*

Donald S. Prudlo and Paul J. Voss, *Merchant Saint: The Church, the Market, and the First Lay Canonization*

Harvey Flaumenhaft, *The Framework of the Federalist: Visualizing the Structure of the Argumentation*

Kenneth Weisbrode, *Real Influencers: Fourteen Disappearing Acts that Left Fingerprints on History*

Marvin R. O'Connell, *Telling Stories that Matter: Memoirs and Essays*

George J. Marlin, *Modern Monsters: Political Ideologues and Their War Against the Catholic Church*

John von Heyking, *Comprehensive Judgment and Absolute Selflessness: Winston Churchill on Politics as Friendship*

Klaus Vondung, *The Pursuit of Unity and Perfection in History*

Gene Fendt, *Camus' Plague: Myth for Our World*

Jeffrey J. Langan (Translator), *The French Revolution Confronts Pius VI*

Roger Scruton, *The Meaning of Conservatism: Revised 3rd Edition*

Roger Scruton, *On Hunting*

Douglas J. Slawson, *The World and Work of Father John J. Burke: A Mystic in Action*

Winston Churchill, *My Early Life*

Winston Churchill, *Savrola*

Winston Churchill, *The River War*

# The Revolutionary War

JEREMY BLACK

ST. AUGUSTINE'S PRESS
South Bend, Indiana

Manufactured in the United States of America.

1 2 3 4 5 6 30 29 28 27 26 25

**Library of Congress Control Number: 2025939489**

Paperback ISBN: 978-1-58731-693-7
Ebook ISBN: 978-1-58731-694-4

∞ The paper used in this publication meets the minimum requirements of the American National Standard for Information Sciences – Permanence of Paper for Printed Materials, ANSI Z39.48-1984.

St. Augustine's Press
www.staugustine.net

For
Jonathan Dent

## Table of Contents

# PREFACE

A key episode in global history, the formative one in that of America, and an important and fascinating conflict in military history, the American Revolution deserves attention from the global as well as the American perspective. *War for America. The Fight for Independence 1775–1783* (Stroud, 1991) was my major earlier effort in this field. It remains a good operational account of the war, but work, by others and myself since, ensure that it is necessary to revisit the subject and to reconsider not only the specifics of assessment but also the more general way of analyzing and presenting the struggle. It would be marvelous if readers had the time to read both accounts, as well as shorter pieces I have written in the meanwhile, but that would be a foolish assumption. As a result, although this book is a "new write," I have repeated some material, especially quotations from primary sources.

At every stage, we must remember that people risked and lost their lives and also suffered much. There can be a mistaken tendency to underplay these points when focusing on a "should have done" account of military options. In practice, conflict in the Thirteen Colonies was very trying, and not least in the circumstances of civil war. The nature of the campaigning was hard.

Heavily-encumbered British regular units found that thickly-wooded and hilly terrain posed problems, as did entrenched positions. The troops faced a difficult physical environment. Advancing from the St Lawrence toward Lake Champlain in June 1776, Lieutenant William Digby of the 53rd Regiment complained of "the great heat," adding in July:

> The weather was intensely hot, scarce bearable in a camp, where the tents rather increased than diminished it, and the great number of men in so small a space, made it very disagreeable, though we all went as thinly clothed as possible, wearing large loose trousers, to prevent the bite of the mosquito.[1]

Brigadier-General Alexander Leslie wrote to his brother from Staten Island in July 1777 after his return from:

> Our marching and counter-marching in the Jerseys ... the weather was much against us, for we had it very hot and a good deal of rain, and no tents.... We embark tomorrow.... I hope it is north, for the climate will be our enemy if we go southward.[2]

Heatstroke was a problem for soldiers at the battle of Monmouth Courthouse, New Jersey, on 28 June 1778, and in the South the British and their opponents suffered greatly from malaria and also from yellow fever.[3] John Hayes, an army surgeon, observed of the British troops in South Carolina:

> A country full of marshes and small rivers, woods and insects, and a Sun so powerful in heat, with dews at night most astonishing and to which the soldier must be always exposed, are causes not to be combatted .... sickness therefore was general and of the bilious kind mostly tending to a putrescency.[4]

The climate was particularly difficult as most units had not been accustomed to such climes. The successful siege of Spanish-held Havana in 1762 as well as the Caribbean campaigning of the Seven Years' War had provided much experience, but many of the troops involved had died of disease. This also was an issue in the American Revolution, notably so with smallpox but also with reference to dysentery, scurvy, scabies and other results of poor sanitation and malnutrition. Respiratory illnesses were a consequence of the close proximity of troops.

Historians' problems are far gentler, but worthy of mention. Nomenclature is a key one. 'Patriot' is a problematic term, as the Loyalists and the neutralists were also Patriots. Indeed, the term 'Patriots' used for the revolutionaries is somewhat smug and self-reverential. Possibly Rebels or Secessionists might be a better term than 'Patriots'.

Since 1990, when I wrote the first book, I have had many opportunities to speak on the subject in lectures and seminars, and I would like to thank those who invited me and participated. Throughout, I have been treated with great kindness, and travelling to America to speak has been a great pleasure since 1988, sometimes on up to six trips annually, only interrupted in two years, 1989 and 2021. Having spoken from Hawaii to Maine, I owe a big thank you. Repeated opportunities to speak for conferences held by the Continuing Education Department of the University of Virginia at Charlottesville, Oxford, Williamsburg, and Yorktown proved particularly important. I have also profited from the chance to speak on the war in many other places, in Britain, Continental Europe, and further afield. While writing this book, I had the opportunity to give the opening keynote for SCETL's Annual Conference at Arizona State University, and to speak at the University of Florida, Hillsdale College, the Center for Constitutional Studies at Utah Valley University, the American Museum at Bath, and Oundle School.

I am most grateful to many colleagues and friends for their comments on an earlier draft. Their help is much appreciated. They are not responsible for any errors that remain.

This book is dedicated to Jonathan Dent with many thanks for a valued friendship dating back to 1978.

## LIST OF ABBREVIATIONS

| | |
|---|---|
| Add | Additional Manuscripts |
| AE | Paris, Ministère des Archives Etrangères |
| Ang | Angleterre |
| BL | London, British Library, Department of Manuscripts |
| Cobbett | W. Cobbett (ed.), *Parliamentary History of England* (36 vols, London, 1806-20) |
| CP | Correspondence Politique |
| FO | Foreign Office |
| Fortescue | Sir John Fortescue (ed.), *The Correspondence of King George the Third* (6 vols, London, 1927-8). |
| Franklin | L.W. Labaree et al (eds), *The Papers of Benjamin Franklin* (New Haven, Conn., 1959-) |
| Halifax | Halifax, Calderdale District Archives |
| HM | San Marino California, Huntington Library, HM series |
| HMC | Historical Manuscripts Commission |
| Jefferson | J.P. Boyd et al (eds), The Papers of Thomas Jefferson (Princeton, NJ, 1950-) |
| LC | Washington, Library of Congress, Manuscript Division |
| Me | Nottingham, University Library, Mellish papers |
| Munich | Munich, Bayerisches Hauptstaatsarchiv, Gesandtschaft London. |
| NA | London, National Archives |
| NAS | Edinburgh, National Archives of Scotland |
| NeC | Nottingham, University Library, Newcastle, Clumber papers |
| NRO | Ashington, Northumberland Record Office |
| PCC | Washington, Papers of the Continental Congress |
| RA | Windsor Castle, Royal Archives |
| SP | State Papers |
| WO | War Office Papers |
| WW | Sheffield, Wentworth Woodhouse papers |

# 1. INTRODUCTION

"It was not fair to shoot at us from behind trees;
If they had stand open as they ought before our great
guns we should have beat them with ease [...].

Of their firing from behind fences, he makes a great pother,
Ev'ry fence has two sides; they [the Americans] made
use of one, and we only forgot to use the other."

*The King's Own Regulars*, American Revolutionaries' song of 1775

Civil war in the British empire in 1775 was scarcely predictable a decade earlier, no more than the French Revolution in 1779. There was no sense of inevitable breakdown between rule by the British Crown and the wishes, still less actions, of much of the population in the Thirteen Colonies. This was unlike the situation for many in America in the decade prior to the second Civil War, the one that began in 1861, and notably so once fighting began in Kansas in the mid-1850s. In part, this contrast was because the British empire was stronger and more coherent in the aftermath of eventual victory in the Seven Years' War (1756–63) than the uneasy American federation that split in 1861 (and that was only to be reunited after a conflict far more bloody and traumatic, but far less transformative, than the War of Independence).

A very different war appeared in prospect in the North Atlantic, with France and Spain preparing to block what they feared might be a surprise British attack, and, thus considered holding invasion forces ready to menace England and Ireland. By keeping most of the British navy in European waters, this was seen by the Spanish government as the best way to protect the Spanish empire from attack. Charles III of Spain emphasized the strength of his navy to the French ambassador.[1] Yet there was no British plan to attack, and no outbreak of hostilities. Had there been, the American war might have easily been overshadowed, and the

British in no position to send the force to America that was indeed later dispatched in 1776.

As with all conflicts, there are a variety of perspectives on the cause, or rather causes, of the Revolution, with different and developing accounts, as well both from the time and subsequently. The Revolution was to be explained in ideological terms (themselves very varied), but also from those of self-interest, as well as from the short to the long-term, and from the inevitable to the accidental (and with all variants thereof). It is easy to confuse short-term precipitants with long-term causes.

These variants reflect both contrasting assumptions and differing assessments of the evidence; but there is a common problem in an assumption of progressivism. In short, the American Revolutionaries—namely, the Patriots—are seen as in some way more advanced militarily and politically than their British opponents; But also as more moral, although this has been qualified by the presence and role of slavery in the colonies. This framed approach appears to render inevitable both the political and military outcomes, with this inevitability reading from the political to the military, and vice versa. In that context, if political in emphasis, any discussion is generally devoted to causes and consequences; or, if military in focus, to the established narrative. In each case, inevitability is somehow the explanation and certainly is scarcely a "hidden hand" of history. What we see here is a clear teleology at play, even if discussions can vary in content between the military and the political.

That, unfortunately, simplifies the necessary discussion. Instead, it is appropriate at every stage of the narrative to build in an interaction with an analysis that links the progress of the conflict not to some clearcut criterion of (inevitable) success, but to shifting contexts and policies, and with both sides having agency. Moreover, the latter ensures that there is an interactive character to causation, albeit without that being necessarily symmetrical, for the context was different for each with quite varied pressures at play.

The two sides came from the same heritage. In part, the origins of the American Revolution understandably looked back to seventeenth-century (and earlier) British traditions of resistance to unreasonable royal demands, a long-established process in which resistance to taxation and to the structures and demands it represented were to the fore. New taxes were resented both for their pressure on living standards and due to the politics they seemed to represent.

In some respects, and this was more 'modern' or recent than earlier opposition to taxation, the Revolution was a second version of the First English Civil War of 1642–6, and that had been not only a rejection of royal power (and increasingly authority), but also a war of religion within Protestantism. In the American Revolution, again as with the previous conflict, non-Anglicans/Episcopalians played the key role in resistance. Indeed, the Bible was used by preachers to help instill a military patriotism aimed against George III.[2]

In turn, the principal source of support from within the colonies for royal authority came from Anglicans; and George's support for authority and order was seen in large part, by both him and others, as influenced by religious considerations. Providence was seen as at play, providing a teleology of necessity, while 'the just vengeance of Heaven' extending to a disaster for Boston, could be sought by supporters of George.[3] In 1780, Adam Ferguson, a former army chaplain, and, as an Edinburgh Professor, a pillar of the Scottish Enlightenment, who had been secretary to the unsuccessful Carlisle Peace Commission, pressed the justice of the "national cause" against France and Spain, adding: "Every well meaning clergyman ought to stuff his sermon with it on the approaching Fast Day."[4]

In contrast, Catholicism was essentially a tangential issue, and more so than had been the case during the First Civil War when suspicion of Charles I (r. 1625–49) in terms of pro-Catholic policies had been at a high rate. Similar suspicions in 1775–6 related largely to the Quebec Act of 1774 and fears based upon British acceptance of *Quebecois* Catholicism. However, although the basis for anxiety, notably in nearby New England, this fear could not act as a feasible basis for any sustained depiction of George's policies in the Thirteen Colonies.

In terms of political ideology, and as a marked contrast to the alignments in the 1640s, many colonists resisted Parliament's efforts to project its sovereign authority across the Atlantic; these efforts, however, were seen as natural in Britain in order to secure the coherence of the empire. The debate over the terms of the empire that grew out of the Seven Years' War had in North America become an effort to limit the exercise of state power, or rather that of the central (imperial) government, by defining and asserting the allegedly natural and constitutional rights of individuals and groups within the body politic.

These disagreements over the colonial bond both tempered the authority of government and cut to the core of the nature of the empire—namely, reciprocal benefit controlled by the state, as expressed through the sovereignty of the Crown. The degree to which this could be seen as represented by the Westminster Parliament varied, not least because there was the question of the autonomy of other representative assemblies, no longer a Parliament in Edinburgh then so not only the Parliament in Dublin but also colonial assemblies. The North American colonies were not like Wales, represented in and under the authority of the Westminster Parliament, and with no separate constitutional presence.

Unlike in the 1640s, the disagreement over the colonial bond in the 1760s and 1770s had a geographical dimension, one with reference not to colonies as a whole but to a number of them and only to a portion of their populations. Indeed, a central failure of the Patriots was their inability to attract wider support, not only from the colonial population in the Thirteen Colonies but also from farther afield both in North America and in the British world as a whole.

This represented a contrast with the 1640s, where there was a degree of alignment across the British Isles. Instead, the similarity was more with the Civil War in which, whatever the degree of sympathy, the Confederates had limited support beyond the South and the Border states.

The established understanding of empire was challenged by autonomous tendencies in the colonies, that, in turn, led to uneasiness in the metropole. Joseph Yorke, a well-connected diplomat and MP, remarked in 1763, "I cannot bear the thought of the North Americans selling powder [gunpowder] to the savages to murder the King's troops whilst they look on," a reference to Pontiac's War of 1763–4.[5] Many Patriots, however, saw governmental policies and assumed attitudes as the causes of the breach of constitutional conventions and political practices.

Tension in the 1760s and 1770s also arose from other developments within the colonies, not least the disruptive consequences of rapid population growth,[6] both from the existing settler population and by immigration from the British Isles, which led to sensitivity about the availability of land. Control over land was bound up in governmental relations with Native Americans, and thus with the supposed destiny of the colonies, but also with the very nature of authority. In 1771, for example, the Cherokee, who owed money to a consortium of traders, ceded a large amount of land along tributaries of the Savannah River in Georgia. Governor James Wright argued, however, that such a cession could legally be conducted only with the government. This occurred in 1773 when the land was formally ceded to Georgia, which reimbursed the traders, intending to compensate itself by selling the land to settlers.[7]

More generally, the relative share of the colonial population in the British empire increased, but without any comparable increase in the fiscal support provided by the colonists. That was at a time when the fiscal burden of the Seven Years' War pressed hard because it had been fought in large part on credit. Furthermore, the Great Awakening, a powerful Protestant revival movement, ensured that rumors about the possible establishment of an Anglican episcopacy in North America, in contrast to the previous position in which George II had denied a bishop passage to America, were greeted with particular hostility among the large number of non-Anglicans, a number that grew greatly with immigration. Protestant concerns also made the granting of rights to French-speaking Catholics under the Quebec Act of 1774 a matter of particular sensitivity, as it compromised notions of Protestant nationhood, and threatened settler opportunities to expand west of the Appalachians. As so often happens, individual episodes could and should be understood in a variety of lights, which must encourage care in analysis.

There was a range of challenges to established patterns and practices of authority and social influence; and these necessarily involved the prestige and authority of Crown. This was certainly true of opposition in Massachusetts to Thomas Hutchinson, the Governor, in the early 1770s.[8] And not only there. William Eddis, the royal customs officer in Baltimore, noted in 1772 that "an idea of equality seems generally to prevail."[9]

More specifically, the imposition of a series of fiscal duties, notably the Stamp Act of 1765 and the Townshend Duties of 1767, led not only to a questioning of government objectives, purposes and methods, but also to mob action that wrecked these measures and helped launch a path in which violence became normative. The lack then of troops in the East Coast cities, as compared to on the frontier facing the Native Americans, removed the capacity for a firm response and contrasted with the general stress in the Early Republic on military expenditure on coastal fortification, although that was directed against the prospect of British attack, rather than in order to maintain political control.

In turn, the British government sent troops in the face of disturbances in Boston in 1768. However, the troops had no clear duties and their presence increased tension, leading, on 5 March 1770, to the "Boston Massacre," in which five Bostonians were killed by troops acting in self-defense. Although seen by many Americans as proof of the militarization of authority, in practice this action accorded with conventional conduct during crises and with policing methods in Britain, and generally elsewhere. George III pressed for firm action in the face of the Gordon Riots in London in 1780, "for I am convinced till the magistrates have ordered some military execution of the rioters, this town will not be restored to order."[10] Non-violent policing is very much a later concept. However, Sir John Wentworth suggested in November 1770, after a tour of the colonies as Surveyor-General of the King's Woods in North America, that the use of force was counter-productive and was losing support.[11] In the face of mob action he was to flee his house in June 1775.

The role of Patriots not in the élite leads some modern scholars to emphasize the social dimension of the pre-Revolution, as of the Revolution; but, rather than identifying any opposition between these groups, it might be better to suggest "that the Founding Fathers spoke for the ordinary people."[12] The social politics was certainly very different to that of the *Mischianza* held by the British army in Philadelphia on 18 May 1778 with its mock tournament of knights, or, for that matter, the officer corps that included several aristocrats—notably Charles, 2nd Earl Cornwallis and Hugh, Earl Percy.

This American social politics pressed harder because the war was followed by economic difficulties that exacerbated the more general lack of liquidity in the colonies, notably in New England that by which lacked an equivalent to lucrative plantation good exports. The lack of liquidity was also seen in the prevalence of debt both within the colonies and to British creditors, particularly merchants.

The net effect was that of a state of flux, and one in which each aspect of flux underlined an awareness of that in other fields, including the demographic, social, political, and economic. This situation was accentuated by and contributed to an atmosphere in which rumor was to the fore and paranoia increased anxieties. There was also the more general instability of frontier regions, not least in response to an attempt to establish governance. This was a matter both of the Thirteen Colonies as a whole as a frontier region and of their interiors as a less stable such region. Thus, just as the Civil War was preceded by conflict in Kansas in the mid-1850s, so in North Carolina in 1766–70, the colony's government was resisted by backcountry farmers who sought to "regulate" local officials. However, the Regulators' attack on regressive taxation and a lack of consultation was unsuccessful and they were defeated in battle. To think of long-settled places such as Boston, New York, and Williamsburg as if "frontier" might seem questionable, but as far as the authority and power of a central government based in London was concerned, they certainly were in this category. There was a counterpart with the uncertainty involved in the management of Ireland, although it is also important not to ignore the degree to which British society and politics were scarcely placid.[13]

This situation was enhanced by the ethnic and religious variety of the colonies, and by the extent to which aspects of power—if not control—other than that of the state were weaker or less coherent, notably that of religious establishments close to the Crown and of a social hierarchy that clearly looked to it. There was a very different landed aristocracy in the Thirteen Colonies to that in Britain and, more particularly, one that lacked comparable political and constitutional weight (as well as grounding in influence in society as a whole). This was particularly the case in New England and in the Southern interior.

Chance certainly played a role in the coming of the Revolution, but so did attitudes. In part, this was a matter of the interplay of colonial assertion with a metropolitan failure to understand the situation. In Britain, to a considerable extent, the difficulty of retaining the link was ignored or underrated, first politically and then militarily. Thus, a London pamphlet of 1756 urging the import of iron from America rather than Sweden, the established source, confronted the objection that:

> [I]t would occasion a vast increase of people and wealth, and consequently of power in those countries, that in time might become rivals to their mother country, prejudice her interests, and become at last independent of her. But however plausible this objection may appear, there can be no just foundation for it, since [...] it will be always in our power to subject them by our fleets, and still more by refusing them supplies of many of the necessaries of life.[14]

The geopolitical transformation in North America and the North Atlantic world from 1758 was an important background to the Revolution. Until then, and more particularly in the early 1750s, the British colonies had been threatened (and truly *felt* threatened) by the combination of a France that was expanding in the North American interior, in particular along the Canada–St. Louis–Louisiana axis, and its Native American allies. This was a situation that, alongside Virginian expansion westward, led to conflict in the Ohio Valley in 1754. Thus, the dynamism of the settler community was matched by that of the French. There was no equivalent in the conflict that broke out in 1775 despite the attempt to present the British as in some way matching the earlier French threat focused on Quebec and Native Americans.

Fear of France had earlier helped lead to a determination to strengthen trans-Atlantic cooperation with Britain, a determination that was encouraged by a growing economic interdependence as trade grew. This determination benefited from a major change in British politics from 1754 and even more so in 1755 as the Pelhamite hegemony was challenged by politicians committed to an imperial policy—notably, in 1755, a group aligned with William, Duke of Cumberland, third and sole surviving son of George II, and, as Commander-in-Chief, the director of army patronage. These included George, 2nd Earl of Halifax, the President of the Board of Trade, uncle of Lord North under whom he was a cabinet minister in 1770–1, and Henry Fox, the Secretary at War.

Subsequently, the key role in supporting imperial expansion was that of William Pitt the Elder, who acted as a dominant figure when a Secretary of State in 1756–61 and was later 1st Earl of Chatham.

Following earlier failures,[15] the conquest of Canada in 1758–60 (a conscious strategic decision by Pitt sustained in three years of campaigning) transformed the geopolitical situation. This was not least because the French also lost Louisiana to Spain in the subsequent Peace of Paris, which ensured that that colony could not be the basis for a revived North American policy on the part of France. Indeed, in the 1760s, France put more energy into other transoceanic operations, for example developing the colony of Cayenne in South America, as well as into rebuilding the fleet that had been heavily defeated by the British in 1759 at the battles of Lagos and Quiberon Bay.

As Britain's North American colonies moved away from anxiety about France, they gradually ceased to feel themselves in the front line. This was a point that was fully apparent in 1770–71 when Britain had come close to going to war with France and Spain in the Falkland Islands Crisis, only for the Bourbon powers to back down. In this crisis there was no threat to these colonies.

This situation provided a geopolitical background for rising tensions between Britain and the North American colonies whereas, given they were exposed to French and Spanish attacks from their nearby colonies, those in the West Indies remained fearful. However, the eventual outcomes, in the form, successively, of conflict (1775), struggle for independence (1776), French intervention (1778), and the eventual partition of British North America (1783), were all unpredictable, as were their interactions.

The Boston "Tea Party" on 16 December 1773, a rejection of the recent Tea Act passed by Parliament, dramatized the breakdown of imperial authority for at least some of the colonists. This was to be a breakdown that was the first stage of a more general collapse in European control in the New World, a collapse that helps make the American Revolution appear normative (although this was only to be apparent in hindsight). This collapse also involved very different contexts, notably the slave revolution on Saint-Domingue in 1791, which eventually led in 1804 to the establishment of Haiti, the second republic in the New World.

Moreover, the century onward from 1768 also saw, as an underestimated factor, a series of unsuccessful rebellions. These began with the Louisiana Rebellion of 1768–9 in favor of the overthrow of Spain and a return to French rule (there was no equivalent in Quebec). The rebellions continued, some pitted against particular policies and some in favor of independence—the most prominent of the latter being the American Civil War that broke out in 1861, which had a very different outcome to the successful Latin American Wars of Independence in the early nineteenth century.

These rebellions, successful and unsuccessful, provide a very different context to the American War of Independence than that which is offered by comparing it with the other uprisings in the British world in the eighteenth century. These latter uprisings were an aspect of the long-term contesting, and thus bedding down, of the "Glorious Revolution" settlement.

Repeated failures inevitably invite attention to the reasons, other than contingent elements, for the successes of others. Failures could be large-scale, as with the rebellion in 1780–3 that meant to overthrow Spanish colonial rule in Peru in opposition to the Bourbon reforms that were parallel to those of George III, but this also included elements of Inca revivalism. There was no equivalent to the latter with the American Revolution.

In this period in the Thirteen Colonies, the process of reaching and endlessly redefining a consensus that underlay and often constituted government, including colonial rule, broke down.[16] Yet rather than suggesting any inevitable clash, it is necessary to underline the continued similarities between the societies of Britain and British North America, and also the colonists' self-identification as British. In contrast, in Louisiana there was little positive engagement with Spanish rule.

Alongside the teleological approach, it is important to explain why the process of breakdown did not occur for the large numbers of colonists who remained loyal, a situation also seen elsewhere. Indeed, any discussion of the move toward revolution and new American identity (and whether or not this discussion is presented in terms of inevitability) must take note of the widespread practice of Loyalism. This was also a kind of Patriotism and American identity, and Loyalists were willing to fight and die for their values. In the case of the battle of King's Mountain in 1781, many indeed did.

Hostility to central government was strongest from the colonies where there was a lower rate of recent immigration, especially New England and Virginia, whereas, in contrast, colonies with higher percentages of immigrants, such as New York, contained more Loyalists. This was particularly true of East and West Florida, whose European population almost changed with the end of Spanish rule after cession to Britain in 1763, and also of Nova Scotia after the end of French rule.

Meeting George III on 1 July 1774, Hutchinson recorded that the King had "so perfect a knowledge of the state of his dominions."[17] This, however, was not the same as an appreciation of their dynamics. More generally, a lack of understanding of American colonial society and aspirations, on the part of the imperial government (not least by George and by Frederick, Lord North, as First Lord of the Treasury, the head of the ministry from 1770 to 1782) played a major role in the developing crisis. America was far less understood than Ireland, and unsurprisingly so given its distance, size, and diversity. Anyway, George, who had limited understanding of dissent other than in terms of disobedience, did not grasp the degree to which the individual colonies were collaborating with each other in response to successive crises, and therefore did not discern that joint action on their part was increasingly an option.

This failure of appreciation was exacerbated in 1774 by the view that concessions would be seen as weakness and only lead to fresh demands. This was politically commonplace, and a particular reaction to the crisis leading to the repeal of the unpopular Stamp Act in 1766 after widespread agitation; but it also contrasted with a greater understanding for politics and policies within Britain of the value of conciliation, as with the repeal of the Cider Tax in 1766. George was accurate in 1796 when he observed, "My mind is not of a nature to be guided by the object of obtaining a little applause [...] rectitude of conduct is my sole aim."[18] On 22 March 1774, D'Aiguillon, the French Foreign Minister, mentioned for the first time American problems for British rule to David, 7th Viscount Stormont, the British envoy, an experienced diplomat. The latter replied that the troubles were "of such a nature as spirit, firmness and temper would certainly cure." He added for the benefit of the British

Secretary of State for the Southern Department's reflection that "in such emergencies the middle way is no way at all [...] procrastination and irresolution have produced numberless evils, but never cured one," a lesson that the Stamp Act crisis was held to have demonstrated.[19] Stormont was to be Secretary of State for the Northern Department himself in 1779–82, playing a key role in managing British foreign policy.

The legislation of 1774, the Coercive or Intolerable Acts, terms used to describe what was legal (even if unpopular) legislation, was designed to provide exemplary punishment and a remedy for disorder. This stemmed from a belief that the latter arose from the actions of a small number rather than from widespread disaffection; in short, it was admonition that conspiracy and agitation were at issue, not revolution. This was a commonplace response to opposition.

The Coercive Acts, the Boston Port Act, closing the port, and moving the customs house for overseas trade until the East India Company was reimbursed for the tea, were designed to protect trade and customs officials from harassment; the Massachusetts Charter Act meant to strengthen the executive, particularly by reducing the elective character of the legislature; and the Administration of Justice and Quartering Acts intended to make it easier to enforce order.

However specific and pragmatic, these measures were apparently pregnant with autocratic possibilities and struck colonists across the Thirteen Colonies as an infringement of charter rights that threatened the liberties of all colonies and the rights of all colonists, by which they did not mean slaves.[20] The legislation was also criticized by the Opposition in Britain as excessive.

More generally, criticism of government policy made by the Opposition in Britain, criticism that was sustained and could be readily read in America through the press, helped encourage the Patriots in America both by supporting and helping shape or, at least, give resonance to their narrative and analysis, and also by encouraging a sense that there was significant support in Britain for the Patriot cause. This was indeed the case, and notably in the early stages, and it was easy to see how a measure of resolution could be anticipated in terms of the fall of the ministry and its replacement by a more accommodating one.

Ministries had fallen repeatedly from 1762 to 1770, and it was understandable that this, rather than the need to fight for independence, should appear a viable outcome and, indeed, the likely one. If John, 3rd Earl of Bute, who had conspicuously enjoyed George's favor, should fall in 1763, or George Grenville, the supporter of the Stamp Act, could go in 1765, why not North in 1774 or 1775? Moreover, as past falls had shown, strong victories in elections did not preclude subsequent removals—the electoral victories of 1754, 1761, and 1768 all being rapidly thus followed. A major question of the trans-Atlantic crisis of 1774–6 is why this outcome failed to occur. Like much that did not occur, however, this possible outcome has received insufficient attention.

Indeed, the Coercive Acts were passed in Parliament by overwhelming majorities. The Boston Port Bill was unopposed in Parliament, and the opposition motion to repeal the Tea Duty was defeated in the House of Commons, 182 votes to 49, a divided result that reflected the support given to the government by independent MPs. George, who was pleased by the Coercive Acts, was delighted by Parliament's backing for the legislation. Personalizing blame on George, as read in the Declaration of Independence, was therefore mistaken given he actually represented a broad tranche of opinion. Indeed, a French report of 1784 that described Britain as a democracy under the form of monarchy, as well as a republic tending toward monarchy, argued that foreign policy was a key dimension, with the monarch representing the nation and negotiating for it, and the nation requiring that he did so in accordance with its interests.[21] This was at least the theory, although in 1775 policy toward the American colonies (which was not foreign policy) revealed division in the nation, with many in Britain (as in the colonies) opposing any movement toward violence.

Parliament, as was legal (for example being done in 1747 and 1790), was dissolved in 1774 (a year earlier than was made necessary by the Septennial Act) partly to capitalize in the general election on the popularity of the Coercive Acts in Britain. American issues, nevertheless, played only a modest role in the general election of 1774, which corresponded with a relative lack of engagement by most political commentators.[22] These results sustained the position of the North ministry, and the confidence of the government.[23] Another election was not obligatory until 1781, although another it was held in 1780 and produced another clear majority for the government. There was no equivalent to the political crisis for the Walpole ministry (at the time fighting Spain) stirred up by the poor results of the 1741 general election, results that led to its downfall the following year.

As another instance of the failure to consider the significance of what did not occur, 1774 saw a slackening of international tension. Anglo-Bourbon relations had been poor after the Seven Years' War, culminating with the Falkland Isles Crisis in 1770 when war had nearly broken out with France and Spain. Instead, the latter two backed down, which led to the downfall of hostile French ministers. Indeed, in 1772–3, at a time of international crisis due to Russian expansion in Poland and threats to Sweden, there was an attempt by France for better relations. The British government was divided on this point, but ultimately the Swedish crisis led to a decision against any such French alignment.

This decision can be seen as of fundamental significance for the American Revolution. Alliances did not mean that allies could not be abandoned—for example, France not coming to the help of Austria when it was attacked by Prussia in 1778. Yet, had an Anglo-French alignment existed and been effective in 1772–3, it is possible that France would have been more reluctant to break with Britain. But it was not so: the French monarch and ministry in 1778 were different than those in place during 1772–3.

Another key point was that international tensions decreased and in 1774–7, more particularly 1774–6, this gave the British a significant window of opportunity to adopt a firmer policy in America. In 1774–5, this policy was supported with insufficient strength. But from 1776 onward this situation changed dramatically.

Alongside the stability, indeed stabilization, of the ministry in Britain, a marked contrast to the situation in 1761–70, the situation in the British Atlantic certainly deteriorated in 1774, with increasing hostility in the colonies to British authority. More troops were sent to Massachusetts, while General Thomas Gage, the Commander-in-Chief in America, was appointed governor and ordered to use force to restore royal authority, a significant militarization of policy. Shocked by the Boston Tea Party, the king supported the firm line, as he saw the *status quo* as no longer an option, matters as beyond compromise, and leniency as destructive to order and good government. This was symptomatic of a more general psychological rift. George saw the colonists as disobedient children, whereas the Patriots regarded him as a bad father, a theme apparent in the Declaration of Independence and one that contrasts with the "modern" expectations of Revolution ideology. In some respects, indeed, this Revolution was a struggle over the nature and image of monarchy, rather than a rejection of the latter. This point can be taken further by seeing the option of a president as a different form of monarch.

The collapse of authority, which led in the winter of 1774–5 to the seizure of government munition stores in Newport, Charleston, and Portsmouth,[24] seemed to George to threaten Britain's position as a great power. In September 1774, George, who like the American Patriots was prone to dramatic language, wrote to North: "The dye is now cast, the colonies must either submit or triumph," adding, two months later, "The New England governments are in a state of rebellion [...] blows must decide whether they are to be subject to this country or independent."[25] In 1637–42, the crisis in England had begun with one in Scotland and then been precipitated anew by crisis in Ireland. In 1774–5, there appeared to be a comparable danger that crisis in North America might precipitate further problems elsewhere in the empire, including in the British Isles.

New England was regarded as the center of opposition and the focus for government action; the extent of opposition elsewhere was minimized and thereby discounted, a view criticized in Parliament on 11 March 1775 by Edmund Burke, a vocal Rockinghamite Whig MP,[26] when he presented a plan for reconciliation to restore "the former unsuspecting confidence of the colonies in the mother country." Having emphasized the value of America to the empire, Burke argued against any reliance on force:

> The use of force alone is but *temporary*. It may subdue for a moment, but it does not remove the necessity of subduing again; and a nation is not governed which is perpetually to be conquered.

This captured the different strategies that were advanced in responding to America, strategies that spanned conflict and politics, the latter remaining the key context and rationale for any understanding, use, and evaluation of force.

Burke was eloquent but in opposition. Abigail Adams remarked, "The die is cast."[27] George was against any suspension of the Coercive Acts, a course pressed by Gage,[28] and thought that concessions would be seen as weakness. This conviction was strengthened by George's belief that the repeal of the Stamp Act in 1766 by the Rockingham ministry in the face of vociferous discontent had caused many of the problems in North America,[29] and also by the extent to which Parliament supported firmness and the maintenance of its authority and the rule of law, a position already taken with the Declaratory Act of 1766.

In contrast, on 20 January 1775, Chatham (formerly Pitt the Elder) pressed in the House of Lords for the withdrawal of the troops sent to intimidate Boston and warned about the danger of France exploiting the situation.[30] This was sensible but out of line with government attitudes.

There was no chance of George following the advice of Thomas Jefferson, in his critical *A Summary View of the Rights of British America* (1774), and thereby vetoing parliamentary legislation that affected American rights and interests. Jefferson called on George to accept a theory of kingship that was actually in accordance with many of the king's assumptions, but to an end he could not accept:

> That these are our grievances which we have thus laid before his majesty, with that freedom of language and sentiment which becomes a free people claiming their rights, as derived from the laws of nature, and not as the gift of their chief magistrate. Let those flatter who fear; it is not an American art [...] kings are the servants, not the proprietors of the people. Open your breast, sire, to liberal and expanded thought. Let not the name of George the third be a blot in the page of history. You are surrounded by British counsellors, but remember that they are parties [...]. It behoves you, therefore to think and to act for yourself and your people.[31]

Jefferson offered a view of the empire as a series of parts, each with rights, under the care of the Crown. This was an approach for the empire but on new terms, something also advocated by Irish Patriots and British radicals, such as John Cartwright.[32] It was to be taken up for the "White" colonies in the nineteenth century, when the growth of "responsible government" meant that colonial governors were henceforth to become politically "responsible" to locally-elected legislatures, rather than to London. At the time, although the Colonial Laws Validity Act of 1865 declared colonial legislation that clashed with that from Westminster invalid, the Act was only rarely invoked. Alongside signs of unity in action—such as, from 1887, the Colonial and Imperial conferences that helped give the Dominions a voice in imperial policy—there was also recognition of self-government under the Crown. An Imperial conference in 1926 defined the Commonwealth as "the group of self-governing communities composed of Great Britain and the Dominions," and this formed the basis for the Statute of Westminster (1931), which determined that Commonwealth countries could now amend or repeal "any existing or future act of the United Kingdom Parliament [...] in so far as the same is part of the law of this Dominion." A "common allegiance to the Crown" was seen as characteristic of the "freely associated members of the British Commonwealth of Nations."

In a way, this was what Jefferson meant when he urged George to "deal out to all equal and impartial right," but such a system, let alone the strong republican central authority proposed by John Adams,[33] were not politically practical in the 1770s. The Westminster Parliament, British ministers, and indeed George himself would not have accepted an increase in royal power that would have stemmed from the King "holding the balance" of the empire, as he arbitrated between its parts. To them, royal authority was a matter of the Crown-in-Parliament, and this could not be separated without losses to both. For a more powerful Crown—based possibly on the monarch using his power in one part of the empire to influence, even coerce, another part—risked becoming a tyranny and then losing support and becoming weaker.[34]

Reading the mid-seventeenth crisis in these terms was significant, with Charles (r. 1625–49) regarded as one seeking to use control in Ireland so as to dominate England (as was feared by the Parliamentarians in response to the control of troops to deal with the Irish rising of 1641). This was a period in which the politically informed were suffused in accounts of the history of the previous two centuries, and figures not otherwise now generally known for this achievement were also prominent historians of the period—notably Oliver Goldsmith, David Hume, Tobias Smollett, and John Wesley. As a young man, George had been brought up with much attention given to British history and, as an adult he showed that he retained this knowledge and related assumptions—for example, when he commented on the tomb in Gloucester Cathedral of Edward II who had been overthrown in 1326 as a result of misgovernment and murdered the following year.

Alongside the emphasis on specific points of agreement and disagreement, mutual suspicion was a key problem, a product of a loss of the sense of political community between Britain and the American colonies.[35] The rhetoric of defiance became more heated, with Patrick Henry declaring on 23 March to the Second Virginia Convention at Richmond: "There is no retreat but in submission and slavery! [...] The war is actually begun [...] give me liberty or give me death!" Henry was of course a slaveowner. He was to be Governor of Virginia from 1776 to 1779.

The Jeffersonian prospectus was also inappropriate, in that it implied that the same policies would not have been adopted if George were conscious of his duties to all his subjects. Instead, the King's view of the necessary interdependence of the empire was not something opposed to the British government's fiscal policies—most particularly so in the case of the American markets for Indian tea. This practice of interdependence, however, was unacceptable to the Patriots.

Again, as an instance of counterfactuals, it is worth considering whether attitudes might have been different had Pontiac's War of 1763–4, or other episodes of Native American opposition, been more serious, widespread, and sustained, and therefore had there been more of a need for British troops (as was real in the Caribbean in the face of fears of rebellion by the enslaved). This was a fundamental demonstration of imperial interdependence, but this notion in North America was overthrown in 1775 by Patriots (yet not by Loyalists).

At any rate, George's stress on the need for order and, in particular, on the importance of defending it when challenged, would have ensured problems in responding in the manner the American Patriots wanted (whatever the role of Parliament) and even if it were only a question of supporting existing authorities within the colonies. This was also later true of Ireland in the 1790s, where the willingness of the United Irishmen to seek a federal relationship with Britain[36] flew in the face of the political realities of the Anglo-Irish relationship. Ironically, but unsurprisingly, the American Patriots would also try to maintain their authority over other colonists. This was seen during the emergency of what became a civil war, at the expense of Loyalists, and also in the Patriot invasion of Canada in 1775–6. This use of force to retain authority was also subsequently employed, as in the use of troops and militia to suppress the Whiskey Rebellion in western Pennsylvania in 1794, in what was a response to a tax imposed on a domestic product by the federal government. This was ironic given the extent to which the American Revolution began as a large-scale tax agitation, and then uprising.

Eventually, the British government would adopt the path of imperial conciliation. It did so unsuccessfully in America in 1778, when the Carlisle Commission was sent to try to negotiate a settlement, but by then the Revolution was entrenched and there was a debt of blood, as well as an incipient promise of French support.

In contrast, the government was successful, at least in terms of defusing an immediate problem, in 1782–3, when British legislative authority was renounced in favor of the Dublin Parliament, and differently in 1801 with the Union with Ireland that was based on legislation in 1800. Similarly, in England in 1779, the legal position of Dissenters, which had not been eased in 1772–3, changed when they were allowed to merely assent to the Scriptures in order to become undergraduates or clerics, rather than having to subscribe to the Articles of the Church of England.[37]

Although earlier compromises in the case of the American colonies were floated, it might, however, have been difficult to win widespread support in America, at least on the part of the Patriots. In addition, there was no consensus in Britain in favor of a compromise, or rather one different from the idea of the colonial link, which had been discussed by George Grenville in January 1766 when defending the Stamp Act: "Protection and obedience are reciprocal. Great Britain protects America; America is bound to yield obedience [...]. The nation has run itself into an immense debt to give them their protection."

In February 1775, North proposed that, in return for a colony being willing to provide for its defense and civil government, it would be exempt from parliamentary taxation. This, however, was an offer given too late, as it was incompatible with the position of the Continental Congress, which had first convened in Philadelphia on 5 September 1774 with delegates from twelve of the colonies (not Georgia or the Floridas). Though presenting itself as a loyal body, the Congress, which was inherently revolutionary as it sought to establish a union between colonies able to mount a trade embargo of Britain, and lacked any legality in terms of the imperial constitution, in other words, the respective rights of Britain and the colonies. At the same time, there was a background of colonial cooperation, with the Albany Congress of 1754 bringing together representatives of seven of the colonies to discuss the crisis arising from hostilities with France, and the Stamp Act Congress of 1765 urging joint opposition to the Stamp Act. The Continental Congress claimed that the colonies should raise revenues as they thought appropriate, a rejection of Parliament's right to legislate. Congress formally rejected North's proposal in July 1775.

The emptiness of the imperial ethos for many Americans had been revealed for a decade as paranoia and in symbolic and practical acts of defiance. In 1775, the spiral of violence led instead to a more charged atmosphere and then full-scale conflict, with the militarization of authority by the British government clashing with attempts by the Patriots to defy the latter. Fighting began on 19 April, when the British tried to seize a cache of arms reported to be at Concord, a town 16 miles from Boston, beyond the village of Lexington. Raising the question of what might have happened had a different route been taken, the British found about 70 militia at the village drawn up in two lines. Outnumbered, the militia began to disperse. But a shot was fired—it is not clear by whom—and the British opened volley fire, scattering the militia, eight of whom were killed. The British pressed on to Concord and searched there for military supplies only to meet with greater and more determined opposition.

The shedding of blood outraged much of New England. The immediate response was vigorous action against that British column, which met serious harassing fire on its retreat, leading to far heavier casualties than the Patriots suffered. In addition, a substantial Patriot force, largely dependent on their own muskets, soon encircled Boston. This *ad hoc* army was commanded by Artemas Ward. Elsewhere in the Thirteen Colonies, British authority collapsed: Due to the concentration of troops in Massachusetts, governors elsewhere were defenseless, although it is unclear what the dispersal of troops into "penny packets" could have achieved militarily.[38] Massachusetts was in revolution. In August, a royal proclamation, for which the king had pressed, declared that George's American subjects were "engaged in open and avowed rebellion."[39]

## 2. THE NATURE OF REVOLUTIONARY WAR

> "These people show a spirit and conduct against us they never showed against the French, and everybody has judged of them from their former appearance and behaviour when joined with the King's forces in the last war [Seven Years' War] [...]. They are now spirited up by a rage and enthusiasm as great as ever people were possessed of and you must proceed in earnest or give the business up. A small body acting in one spot will not avail, you must have large armies making diversions on different sides, to divide their force. The loss we have sustained is greater than we can bear. Small armies cannot afford such losses, especially when the advantage gained tends to little more than the gaining of a post."
>
> General Gage, 1775[1]

Ignoring the advice of Gage, the initial and general British perception of the rebellion was more of a large-scale riot. The concept of a massive popular rebellion—and one that was tantamount to a nation in arms—was alien to British ministers. Their closest experience, a very direct one for Lord George Germain, the Secretary of State for the Colonies from 1775 to 1782, was the confrontation with the Jacobite uprising in Scotland in 1745–6. This too was a serious rising and one that immediately threatened the situation elsewhere in the British Isles (unlike the American Revolution, which only threatened Canada). The event of 1745 was certainly not a revolution by a nation as a whole; it was rather another iteration of civil conflict within Scotland. In the Thirteen Colonies, the Revolution likewise revealed division, as the idea of a nation under arms did not match the reality posed by the Loyalists.

Yet, 1775 also began the first example of a large-scale transoceanic conflict fought between a European colonial power and subjects of European descent. It was also a major example of a revolutionary war and became in 1776 a struggle for independence in which the notion of the citizenry under arms played a significant role—not least because there was no turn to a rival dynastic legitimacy as had been the case with the Stuart challenge to the Hanoverians in 1745–6. In specific military terms, dynastic legitimacy meant command by Charles Edward Stuart, the Jacobite heir, whereas in the American case there were the emerging issues and opportunities offered by having to choose a commander. This also meant a question of the legitimacy of the choice in the shape of the very body making that selection along with its powers. Thus, the very military aspects of launching a non-dynastic revolution meant an embrace of what is "modern" in terms of command arrangements.

The new state, indeed, was accompanied by a new army that was more egalitarian and dynamic than any in Europe. Many of the commanders of the leading Patriot force—namely, the Continental Army—were from the wealthier section of society—notably George Washington, the commander—and the army matched many of the socio-professional assumptions of the British. While drawing on differing military practices and showing considerable flexibility,[2] Washington, who was temperamentally both a warrior and a gentleman,[3] believed that the army could be strengthened by an appropriate officer corps; he saw "gentlemen" officers as crucial to the discipline and subordination he believed necessary, and the conditions of service between officers and soldiers was great—notably with respect to discipline, healthcare, memorialization, and imprisonment.[4]

Yet, the social range of the Patriot leadership was far greater than that in European armies, with possibly as many as quarter of the Continental Army's officers in the Maryland Land from non-elite backgrounds,[5] and the British could satirize this as in the song "Capt. Ephraim Or the Yankee Entertainment," which began:

> Brother Ephraim sold his cow
> And bought him a Commission,
> Then he went to Canada
> [...]
> He proved an errant Coward.[6]

Moreover, discipline was different. A key contrast was the "contractual" nature of service, with those who wished to leave the army readily able to do so, and frequently, indeed, taking their weapons with them. This was not an army subject to the same type of military discipline seen with its opponent. The social composition of this army may have been similar to that of British regular troops, but this was an army of citizens, not subjects, and considerable autonomy was given in particular to junior officers.[7] To a degree, however, this was a necessity given the scale of area contested, the need to reconcile regular and militia systems and practices, and the particular limitations of campaign communications.[8]

In practice, however, this was neither particularly radical nor conservative. The idea of a citizens' militia drew on deep roots in Western culture—notably that of the Classical world, of medieval and early-modern republics, and of more recent British history (not least in the mid-1750s when a militia was seen as a defense for a revived British nation).[9] These ideas were realized in North America. There was no true radicalism, no women serving, nor Blacks made officers. Yet, in terms of the Western values of the age, including those of relatively enlightened Britain, the appointment as officers of men of humble background represented a dramatic instance of a "levelling spirit."[10] Within the British armed forces, the nearest equivalent was with the appointment and promotion processes of the navy and the Ordnance (artillery). The regular regiments—most notably the cavalry—were very different.

However, that did not mean a lack of combat worthiness on the part of British units. Many of the officers who served in America had impressive combat experience, either in Europe or in the Western Hemisphere in the Seven Years' War—the two groups known by contemporaries as the Germans and the Americans. This contributed to the range in assumptions and experience of the British officer corps as well as to their tendency to factionalism. Furthermore, conflict throughout the 32 years after the War of American Independence ended in 1783 illustrated that commanders from an aristocratic background were nonetheless highly effective— seen most notably with Arthur, Duke of Wellington (although his brother-in-law proved a disaster at New Orleans in 1815), but also possibly more surprisingly for American readers, for Charles, 2nd Earl Cornwallis. This loser at Yorktown in 1781 was victorious in India in 1792 over Tipu Sultan of Mysore, and in Ireland in 1798 over rebels (supported by French invaders).

Differences in social background may well have been important to the character of the conflict, and notably so with the successful Patriot use of militia; and these differences are certainly significant to the American account of the war. Nevertheless, the degree to which this character was an explanation of Patriot capability—let alone success—is open for discussion. Conversely, failure created a lasting impression of the obsolescence of the British army—one that was particularly significant because it is still strongly held in America. This idea contrasts with the account of the Royal Navy despite its limited success in this war prior to 1782. There is no "investment" in naval matters in the American public account or "myth" comparable to that in land warfare, and nothing that matches the focus on ship-to-ship conflict in the War of 1812.

Military effectiveness is in part a matter of context. The problems facing British forces in India in the same period are instructive but also suggest that it was not necessary to have the public culture and social politics of the American Patriots in order to defeat the British, as the Marathas did in 1779 and Mysore in 1780 and 1782. The political dimension of the war in North America was very different for the British to their earlier conflicts there with France, Spain, and/or Native Americans, but that difference did not determine the outcome, although it helped explain cause, context, and consequences.

The decision to form a Continental Army was not simply a matter of military options: It was a political act. The army, a force that would not dissolve at the end of the year, even if individual terms of service came to an end, symbolized (in contrast to the militia) the united nature of the struggle by the Thirteen Colonies. It was a vital move in the effort to win foreign recognition and support. It was not necessary to have such an army in order for individual colonies/states to assist each other militarily. Militia alone could do this, as could volunteers. Prior to the Revolution, military units had been deployed outside the boundaries of individual colonies against Native Americans and French and Spanish forces. During the Revolution, militia units under the control of state governments were sent to assist other states, as indeed they were sent to the Continental Army.

Yet by having such an army military decisions were in large part taken out of the ambit of state government and their particular concerns.

Instead, these decisions became an issue in the relationship between these governments and the federal government. This was a relationship that was already vexed due to its novelty and the resulting need to devise new solutions, but to do so under the pressures of war. Concerns about British plans increased the pressures from state governments over the allocation of military resources.

An emphasis on the Continental Army, a would-be defined force able to employ conventional methods, does not contradict the idea of revolutionary warfare as popular insurrection, for the latter in practice did not imply any particular military formulation, let alone formation. Indeed, revolutions, as later with those of France, Russia, and China, in practice sought the military stabilization and strength of a defined force, but also pursued conventional operations. In contrast, the idea of revolutionary warfare as insurgency and, more particularly, guerrilla conflict is most appropriate for the situation from the 1960s, and in large part represents the impact of the Vietnam War on American and other assumptions.

This, in turn, was read back onto earlier revolutions, notably that which erupted in America, a process encouraged by contemporary interest in comparing these two events. This is unhelpful in both political and military terms. In the case of the latter, the American Revolution generally saw symmetrical warfare, and unsurprisingly so as the two sides were similarly armed on land. The Royal Navy in 1775–83 was as close a comparison as is possible with American air power in the Vietnam War but lacked the range of the latter. Moreover, there was an overlap in the background of commanders and combatants, whereas the American Revolution saw each side in control of areas in a fashion that was different to South Vietnam. Politically, the American Revolution was actually a civil war, much like the conflict in South Vietnam between the Viet Cong and government forces. The American military in the Vietnam War was an alien force, more akin to the French in the American Revolution than to the British.

There would be guerrilla conflict in the Revolution, indeed this kind of conflict helped make the war a revolution. It was particularly pronounced in New Jersey from 1777 and in the South onward from 1781. On the one hand, this conflict was locally important and bore significant national consequences, as well as demonstrated the limited control of the formal military and governmental structures, and thereby of any strategy understood in those terms.[11]

On the other hand, such conflict no more characterized the Revolutionary War as a whole, than the similar but more sustained irregular conflict in Appalachia did for the Civil War of 1861–5. If anything, the contrast with conventional warfare was more pronounced at sea where the absence of a significant naval (as opposed to maritime) Patriot presence and practice meant a reliance on single ships operating as raiders. The British, in contrast, from 1778 faced fleet opposition at sea from the French, and this situation corresponded to conventional operations between the two powers.

On land, in contrast to at sea, there was greater similarity between the Patriots and the French, notably as (by French entry) the Continental Army had had some continuity. The French were more skillful with artillery, an area of weakness for the Continental Army. The French were also more proficient in siegecraft, although this was not to the fore in operations until Yorktown in 1781, which was a siege of exposed field entrenchments rather than a fort.

The Patriots and Loyalists drew heavily on an imperial military practice learned from operating within the British system over the previous century against French and Spanish forces, and even against Native Americans. There had been service in expeditions commanded by British officers and/or alongside British units. Many Americans, both Patriots and Loyalists, had also served within these units—for example, the Patriot Major-General Charles Lee.

This is instructive because the British had plenty of experience in fighting in North America, notably in conquering Canada from France in 1758–60. This success represented a learning curve for, earlier in 1754–7, the British by contrast had failed there, a situation highlighted in 1758 when the initial British success involved the capture of Louisbourg, an operation against a port that drew heavily on the Royal Navy. This was true also, on a far smaller scale, with Pontiac's War in 1763–4, with Native American ambush victories in the early stages followed by an effective British response. This raises the question of why there was not a comparable learning curve for the British in the War of

American Independence, a different war of independence from that involving Pontiac. (Yet the contrast between Bunker Hill and Brandywine can be seen in terms of a learning curve.)

In the War of Independence, the British were helped by the extent to which the conflict saw familiar weaponry and tactics. The rifles used by Patriots were damaging—and notably so on the British retreat from Lexington and Concord in 1775, and at the battles of Long Island in 1776 and Saratoga in 1777. However, the rifle's slow rate of fire and inability to carry a bayonet gravely reduced its value as a battlefield weapon (unless being fired from cover, in other words as a skirmishing weapon). Rather than assuming that rifles were necessarily better than muskets, it is worth noting the comments in 1849 of Sir Charles Napier, the British Commander in Chief in India: "As an old rifleman myself I cannot be supposed to have any prejudice against the rifle, but as a weapon of war [...] it is inferior to the musket." His reasons included the rifle taking longer to load and being heavier, the musket/bayonet combination being more effective than the rifle at the close quarters in which bayonets were useful, and the rifle fouling more than muskets after firing.[12] These were all factors during the War of Independence. Patriot firepower, more generally, could be reduced, even countered, by a number of British techniques. These included outflanking, closing, the use of artillery, and the deployment of riflemen in the British forces— notably the Hessian *Jägers*. In 1779, skirmishing in the Hudson Valley near Stoney Point show the latter as effective:

> The two first days the militia were importunately troublesome by coming down in small bodies, and firing upon our *Jäger* post, but five or six of them having dropped by our rifle shot, they thought fit to disappear, and have given us no further disturbance.[13]

More generally , the British and the Loyalists proved effective in some of the skirmishing warfare, for example near New York in 1778.[14] There was no automatic Patriot advantage, which is an argument or implication in some of the discussion of the war.

On the British side in the War of Independence, there was consideration of innovation in weaponry, but no significant change: Patrick

Ferguson's breech-loading rifle was accurate but seen as likely to use ammunition too rapidly. In 1779, Major-General Charles Rainsford submitted a plan for a mixed cavalry-light infantry force with arms "rifled, or otherwise well made, with sights like the German rifled barrel, and bayonets like the infantry,"[15] but that proved to be only an idea. Instead, the standard British deployment remained close-order, the regulations for the First Battalion of the Norfolk Regiment in 1780 stating: "In firing great care to be taken that the battalion is in close order, that the men level well, and ram down their cartridges, as a slow well-directed fire is far preferable to an hasty irregular straggling one."[16]

In contrast to the essential continuity in infantry weaponry, Lieutenant-General Thomas Desaguliers, Colonel Commandant of the Royal Artillery from 1762 until 1780 and Chief Firemaster (Superintendent) of the Woolwich arsenal from 1748 until 1780, made advances in the science of gunnery, the manufacture of cannon, the capabilities of mortars, and horse artillery. In 1773, a new horizontal boring machine was introduced at Woolwich, improving the manufacture of cannon there. Yet, there was no equivalent to the use of rockets and shrapnel that would follow during the French Revolutionary and Napoleonic Wars.

It would be misleading to see the British as tactically hidebound. They adapted well to the challenge of the war usually firing a single volley before closing quickly, and showing considerable flexibility in formations and tactics.[17] Based on the Seven Years' War, in which the army had shown considerable flexibility in America,[18] the British had implemented from 1770 onward a light infantry system whereby one of the companies of each regiment was designated as a 'light company.' These were the most agile men who were the best shots. They could fight as either skirmishers in an extended line, as a regular two or three line unit, or as flankers; but this form of war was in its infancy, and given the weaponry of the day concentrated volley fire from a linear formation remained the best way to inflict significant damage on an opposing force in battle. It was also a good way to sustain unit cohesion and morale, to survive contact with the enemy, and to provide a formation able to respond to orders (and thus to adapt to changes on the battlefield). These were necessary as there were stages in many of the battles of the War of Independence wherein it was necessary to respond to the moves of opponents, to regroup and to attack anew. This was very much the case, for example, for the British with their eventual successes at Guilford Court House (1781) and at Eutaw Springs (1781). The use of linear formations and volleys therefore was far from anachronistic and was not bound to fail at the expense of looser formations and individually-aimed shots. Overall, the British responded well to the circumstances in America, deploying themselves accordingly.[19]

Similarly, although cavalry played a relatively modest part in the conflict, both sides were able to use it effectively, notably in the Carolinas and in Westchester County.[20] The problem of transporting and sustaining cavalry across the Atlantic affected the British. Their main role was scouting and raiding. The war saw developments that later became widespread across the British Empire. Light cavalry units were raised from the existing population to supplement the regular British forces. There was also the mixed "Legion" of light cavalry and light infantry, Tarleton's being the best known. These innovative mixed formations later included the Indian Army's Corps of Guides raised in 1846. The Patriot side also had few cavalry—notably that under "Light Horse Harry," Henry Lee III, the father of Robert E. Lee—while the French sent over some as well. The availability and feeding of good quality horses was a major issue. In October 1780, Germain was pressed on "the great want" of cavalry in America.[21]

The innovative nature of the British war machine was seen with the Royal Navy during the conflict, not least in the coppering of ships' bottoms so as to reduce the impact of infestation by maritime creatures (notably the teredo worm and barnacles) and the slowing effect these inflicted. There were also a series of incremental changes in firepower that contributed to the major British naval victory of the war, that in 1782 over the French off the Saintes in the Caribbean. Thanks to these changes, the British delivered more firepower and at a faster rate than the French.

The idea that the British army was hidebound is seriously flawed. It was not this issue that caused the British problems but, instead, the serious strategic difficulties posed by the essentially political nature of the struggle—a problem that rendered the understanding of strategy essentially unfixed. Much of the later discussion of British strategy, and notably of its weaknesses, has focused in fact on the operational level of the war—most notably the failure to break free from a defensive focus on Boston in 1775, to sustain the pace of pressure in 1776, to coordinate the moves of forces in 1777, to retain a position in Philadelphia in 1778, to fix and engage the Patriots in 1779, to give adequate depth to the Southern strategy in 1780, and to maintain the initiative in 1781 (although different assessments are possible for each of these).

In contrast, there has been less of an emphasis on the real strategic conundrum, that of winning and utilizing the political dimension of the conflict. This is an instance of the contrast between the War of Independence and the Civil War of 1861–5: Although both were political (not least as civil wars), the former was more so in that there were not the geographical blocs of support and resulting problems seen in the latter. Strategic problems for the British ranged from the difficulties of defining and pursuing a viable outcome to the struggle in America, to those issues arising from French entry into the war in 1778. As a key instance of the need for focus on more than just the fighting and the operational level, the major role of the Patriot militia created a problem for the British. This is not due to the use of rifles. Instead, this was a problem both in operational terms (for example by restricting the range of the British supply-gatherers) and in the political context of the conflict, especially in harrying Loyalists.

At the outset of the Revolution, militia units overcame royal governors and defeated supporting Loyalists. In December 1775, John, 4th Earl of Dunmore, the last royal Governor of Virginia, was defeated by Virginia militia at Great Bridge, with his North Carolina counterpart, Josiah Martin, following two months later at the battle of Moore's Creek Bridge. The British failure to crush the rebellion in 1775 gave the Patriots time to organize themselves politically and militarily, to extend the rebellion greatly, and to weaken the Loyalists. These successes helped give the Patriots strategic depth, lessening the importance of British operations, first in New England and subsequently in the Middle Colonies. Yet, British victory in either would not have ensured automatic compliance further south. Furthermore, the militia might provide at least temporary reinforcements for the Continental Army and could also sustain the struggle if the latter was absent from a region or defeated.

The Patriot focus was offensive in 1775 and early 1776 but then switched to defensive, both in order to protect gains already made and also to respond to British capability and attacks. The response involved a range of preparations and expedients. Thus, a great chain was stretched across the Hudson at West Point, erected to block British vessels. This was one of the longest and largest iron chains ever forged and a considerable technological triumph.[22]

However, a defensive posture and position warfare provided the British targets for attack, and the opportunity to provoke battle. This was similar to the opportunities provided the Mughal Emperor Aurangzeb in the 1690s and 1700s by the Maratha defense of forts, which meant that the Marathas switched from the manoeuvrist potential of their cavalry. Washington's defense of New York in 1776 and Philadelphia in 1777, and Benjamin Lincoln's attack on Savannah in 1779 and defense of Charleston in 1780, all provided the British with opportunities to engage. British troop numbers were limited and under pressure—notably from French entry in 1778—such that casualties were a significant problem, as with losses at Guilford Court House in 1781. Yet, in essence the British were not forced into attritional assaults; New York in 1776 was scarcely Stalingrad in 1942.

The major contrast was Bunker Hill in 1775, as the Patriot defense led to heavy British casualties, affected the British operational spectrum thereafter until 1776, and, crucially, had the major strategic consequence of ensuring that the British lost the ability to prevent the Patriots from developing and consolidating their advantages, and from extending the Revolution into Canada. Indeed, the latter represented what in some respects was the most dangerous moment of the Revolution for Britain—namely, that in which the export of the Revolution threatened a wider transformation of the British Atlantic world. There was no sense that the scale of the war or the scope of change were fixed. The different trajectory of the French Revolution, and, therefore, of the French Revolutionary War, serves as a further reminder of unexpected courses of development—military, political, and ideological—with the resulting strategic recontextualizations.

## 3. THE STRATEGIES AND POLITICS OF THE WAR

From the American perspective, the abrupt novelty of politics was that of the creation of a new state. The seminal moment and document of the new state was a declaration of independence that was issued in 1776, which was different to the innovative constitutional documents dating from the crises in the seventeenth century. As a result of the quest for independence, there emerged a need to conceptualize, as well as implement, a new strategy and—to employ another word also not in use in this period in a modern sense—a novel geopolitics.

Yet, although 1776 brought this major change, there was a need for the Patriots to formulate a strategy from the outset of the struggle, a strategy focused on changing British policy. This need was continued after the war ended in 1783 because it was widely believed that the British might attempt to strike back and reverse independence. Linked to this was the necessity of affecting British strategy, which arose in part because the revolutionary war ended not in triumph, rather in a compromise exemplified by the partition of British North America. This situation was very different to the subsequent fate of the French, Portuguese, and Spanish empires in the Americas: France and Spain retained control of Caribbean islands (and France of Cayenne), but Britain's presence was scarcely limited to Newfoundland, Prince Edward Island, Bermuda, and the British Caribbean—it extended across what Canada then amounted to. Indeed, the failure of the American invasion attempt meant that this partition was in play onward from 1776.

These points were to be played down in the subsequent memorialization of the war in America, a situation also seen after the War of 1812. However, the reality of the post-war world not only featured independence, but also a continued British presence in neighboring Canada (again, as a result of the failure of American invasion). Moreover, this presence was linked to the well-founded belief that this presence encouraged Native American opposition to American expansion, which was very much the case up to 1815, but not thereafter.

The conspectus for the Revolution might appear clear, but choices over strategy were centrally involved, as was true also in the case, from 1792, of republican France, who experienced a political struggle at that time also over the identity of the new state. These struggles encompassed constitutional formulation, political practice, force structure, ideology, and geopolitical alignment. For example, the powerful Patriot ideological-political preference for militia was highly significant. To abstract strategy from this context is not only unhelpful but misleading. In the case of America, the Continental Army, created in 1775 to defend what might be seen as "American liberty," represented a new political identity and social practice. This helped to sustain the cohesion of the army and even the continuation of the Revolutionary cause when the war went badly, as happened in the winter of 1777–8 when the army camped at Valley Forge while the British benefited from the comforts of Philadelphia.

The formation of this army was indeed a political act: The army, a force that would not dissolve at the end of the year (even if individual terms of service came to an end) symbolized the united nature of the struggle by the Thirteen States, and thus limited the role of state governments in military decisions. In theory, creating the Continental Army made the planning of strategy easier, allowing generals to discern the clashing demands from the individual states for action and assistance. In June 1775, the Second Continental Congress transformed the New England force outside Boston into a national army. George Washington, who combined military experience with knowledge of politics in the Virginia House of Burgesses, was selected as commander, and the relationship between Congress and general was thereby defined: Congress was to determine policy and Washington to follow its orders. In practice, the creation of the army, although essential to the dissemination of a new notion of nationhood, did not free military operations from the view of state governments, nor from the political disputes of the Continental Congress. The role of Congress in military appointments did not ensure that politics, seniority and state quotas would not play a major role in hindering merit.[1]

At the same time, there was to be much tension between the needs of the army and the views of the public, tension that in part focused on the place of the militia or, rather, militias. In December 1780, General Nathanael Greene, the new commander of Patriot forces in the South, wrote to a friend, General Henry Knox, who was responsible for the Patriot artillery:

> With the militia, everybody is a general and the powers of government are so feeble that it is with the utmost difficulty you can restrain them from plundering one another. The people don't want spirit and enterprise but they must go to war in their own way or not at all. Nothing can save this country but a good permanent army conducted with great prudence and caution; for the impatience of the people to drive off the enemy would precipitate an officer into a thousand misfortunes, and the mode of conducting the war which is most to the liking of the inhabitants is the least likely to effect their salvation.

Greene wrote to Governor Lee of Maryland:

> It is unfortunate for the public that the two great departments in which they are so deeply interested, Legislation and the Army, cannot be made to coincide better, but the pressing wants of the Army cannot admit of the slow deliberation of Legislation, without being subject to many inconveniences nor can a Legislature with the best intentions always keep pace with the emergencies of war: and thus the common interest suffers from the different principles which influence and govern the two great national concerns.[2]

In running the army, Washington had to confront a marked particularism that revealed itself in hostility to serving in the same unit with men from another colony, as well as, separately, a strong identification between men and their officers, and furthermore the opposition to reenlistment among men concerned with their farmsteads and families. (This would all be confronted again in the Civil War.)

Appointed Major-General by Congress in June 1775, Charles Lee, a British-born veteran of the Seven Years' War—in which he had served as a British officer in North America (1754–60) and Portugal (1762), where he served under Burgoyne—and as a former Major-General in the Polish army when it resisted Russian invasion, unlike Washington advocated radical solutions, and was to be a controversial character both at that time and subsequently (all this a reminder of different paths that could have been taken to that of Washington).[3] These solutions amounted to a militarization of society and the creation of a national army under central control:

> 1$^{st}$. A solemn league and covenant defensive and offensive to be taken by every man in America, particularly by those in or near the seaport towns; all those who refuse, to have their estates confiscated for the public use, and their persons removed to the interior part of the country with a small pension reserved for their subsistence.
> 2$^{dly}$. New York to be well fortified and garrisoned or totally destroyed.
> 3dly. No regiments to be raised for any particular local purposes, but one general great Continental Army adequate to every purpose. South Carolina may be excepted from its distance [...].
> 4$^{thly}$. The regiments to be exchanged. Those who are raised in one province to serve in another rather than in their own, viz. the New Englanders in New York, the New Yorkers in New England, and so on. This system will undoubtedly make them better soldiers.
> 5$^{thly}$. A general militia to be established and the regular regiments to be formed by drafts from the militia or their substitutes.
> 6$^{thly}$. A certain portion of lands to be assigned to every soldier who serves one campaign, a double portion who serves two, and so on.[4]

Such notions obviously conflicted with the profoundly local nature of American political culture, a product of the separate and different governmental, political, social, religious, and demographic development of the colonies. Lee's ideas also clashed with the respect for the law and for individuals and property rights that, with the obvious exceptions of Native Americans and Loyalists and, even more, enslaved Blacks, was central to this culture. This reality compromised any idea of a total mobilization of national resources. Such a mobilization was not to be achieved by legislation through the developing new political system. In effect, the individual colonies were to achieve independence first, and then later cooperated on their own terms through a federal structure. Each colony or state had military and economic resources of its own, such that a British victory in one part of America had only a limited effect elsewhere. Compared to the Jacobites, the Patriots benefited from having more space and resources, a diffuse leadership and more military and political autonomy—although the last was also seen in a willingness by many to fight for local goals and security[5] —but not further afield.

Aside from the nature of the military organization, there was also the different, albeit fundamental, strategic dimension posed by goals. Most particularly this related to the relationship with George III and Britain. Whereas fighting began in April 1775, there was no declaration of independence until July 1776. There was also the question of whether there would be a positive response to negotiations with Britain and, if so, what consequences might accompany it. This political dimension underlined the number of possible strategic "players." In the event, there was to be no civil war in the Thirteen Colonies over peace terms, as there would be in the Irish Free State in 1922–3 after British rule ended in 1922.

The social dimension also involved many "players," a situation accentuated by the novelty of the political situation, in both its goals and methods. The overthrow of royal authority in 1775 witnessed large-scale activity by those not yet in the political-military system, and this was a key element of the strategic context, both in so far as those who fought were concerned, but also more generally.[6] In New York in 1775:

> the news of the attack at Boston, reached us on Sunday the 23rd and that very day the populace seized the City arms and unloaded two vessels bound with provisions to the troops of

> Boston. In the course of the week they formed themselves into companies under officers of their own choosing, distributed the arms, called a provincial Congress, demanded the keys of the Custom House and shut up the port, trained their men publicly, convened the citizens by beat of drum, drew the cannon into the interior country and formed an association of defence in perfect league with the rest of the continent.

By 7 June, over 2,000 men were reported to be training daily in New York and, on 10 June, it was claimed that "if a stranger was to land here, he would be at a loss whether to pronounce this a city immersed in commerce, or a great garrisoned town."[7]

The equestrian statue of George III in New York, erected at Bowling Green in 1770 in accordance with a commission from the New York Assembly approved in 1768 to the London workshop of Joseph Wilton, was pulled down by the "Sons of Freedom" on 9 July, and the melted-down lead was used to cast bullets. This followed the reading aloud that day of the Declaration of Independence to the Continental Army troops mustered nearby.[8] In contrast, the statue of Pitt, erected in 1770 in Charleston, was not taken down until 1794.[9]

A mixture of popular zeal, the determination of the Revolutionaries, and the weakness of their opponents decided the fate of most of the colonies in late 1775. Intimidation by mob action proved an effective strategy and gave the Patriots strategic depth in subsequent operations. The disorientating experience of the agencies of law and authority being taken over by those who were willing to connive at, or support, violence affected many who were unhappy about developments. To resist this situation, the royal governors had little from which to draw.

In part, there was also the issue of assumptions. Foremost came the British tendency to treat the events in 1775 as a local rebellion, rather than a large-scale event that was a revolutionary civil war, an assessment that accorded with the governmental wish to restrict the resources deployed.[10] In operational terms, British generals and admirals were not keen to disperse their strength, amphibious operations were hard to execute successfully, and units that were landed might have found it difficult to obtain supplies and would have risked defeat at the hands of larger Patriot forces (with the retreat from Concord being repeated up and down the eastern seaboard).

It is, and was, not difficult, however, to feel that the opportunities the British had were missed and that the British failed to make adequate use of their sea power and available troops. An anonymous British pamphlet of 1776 complained, with reason, that the Patriots had been given "the advantage of gaining time to form a union of counsels, to adjust plans of action, to turn their resources into the most convenient channels, to train their men in regular discipline, and to draw to their camp ammunition and stores, and all the necessary implements of war."[11] All of these tasks took time and were best achieved when not under immediate pressure.

Arguably, the same problems that were to face the British in the South in 1780–1 would have affected earlier operations there—namely, to make a sufficiently widespread impact, it would have been necessary for Britain to dispatch substantial forces, but they would not necessarily have been able to dominate the situation and some units might have been defeated. As it turned out, the widespread activity of the Patriots in 1775–6 helped direct the strategic context, even though they failed to do so in Canada where, crucially, the Patriots lacked the popular support they would otherwise come to rely on. Prefiguring the impact of the later alliance with France in 1778, the invasion of Canada was seen in Britain as changing the very strategy of the struggle by:

> the commencing of an offensive war with the sovereign [...]. Opposition to government had hitherto been conducted on the apparent design, and avowed principle only, of supporting and defending certain rights and immunities of the people, which were supposed, or pretended, to be unjustly invaded. Opposition, or even resistance, in such a case [...] is thought by many to be entirely consistent with the principles of the British constitution.[12]

The invasion of Canada was inconsistent with these principles, however they were understood, for example the "Glorious Revolution" of 1688–

9 that had overthrown James II. Yet, conversely, putting aside principles, this invasion might be related to the determination after William III's seizure of power in England to extend control to Scotland and, even more so, Ireland.

In 1776, the Declaration of Independence reflected the stiffening of Patriot resolve, prefiguring, in a different context, the change in Union strategy during the Civil War in 1863 toward a harsher conduct of the war and the new goal of slave emancipation. At the same time, this process was highly divisive. In 1776, Loyalists were harried, as seen in the disarming of Maryland Loyalists in the spring and also the end of the *modus vivendi* that had enabled British warships off New York to continue to receive provisions while they, in turn, did not attack the city. Earlier, British warships had to leave Norfolk.

The new Patriot government slowly became better-prepared to wage war, a Board of Ordnance being instituted on 12 June 1776. However, in the event, this was to prove a considerable hindrance to Washington, for such bodies affected his ability to deal directly with individual states.

A sense of reaction was important to the politics of Patriot strategic preparation. Thus, on 30 December 1776, John Hancock, the President of Congress, announced in a circular that:

> the strength and progress of the enemy [...] have rendered it not only necessary that the American force should be augmented beyond what Congress had heretofore designed, but that it should be brought into the field with all possible expedition.[13]

Yet, what such rhetoric could and might mean in practice was less clear. Political determination and military preparedness proved difficult to synchronize, with the latter not materially rendered by the rhetoric of the former. Although also with non-revolutionary states, this was a repeated problem with revolutions, as in the case of the unsuccessful Dutch Patriots in 1787. The latter provided an instance of the fragility of revolution and, consequently, the need to be cautious in assuming some supposed inevitability about the success of a revolutionary cause, a point soon after demonstrated with the suppression of such movements in the Austrian Netherlands (Belgium) and in the Prince-Bishopric of Liège. A key element for the Dutch in 1787 was the greater forcefulness of the hostile international intervention—that is, the Prussians taking action whereas, unlike in 1778, the French ally of the Patriots did not do so. It is instructive to consider whether a similar move by France in 1787 might have led to success for the Patriots in the United Provinces (Dutch Republic).

Moreover, the military context was scarcely consistent in the case of preparedness, both between cases but also within them. In the first case, in the 1700s, the Hungarians rebelling against the Habsburgs/Austria and the Afghans rebelling more successfully against the Safavids/Persia both required different levels of military adaptation than is seen in the case of the Patriots.

Yet there was no uniform nature of preparedness in the case of the Patriots, for whom preparedness was often very limited, but also varied. The context, most clearly, was very different in Canada to the position in the Thirteen Colonies. An account from the Patriot headquarters outside Quebec on 28 March 1776 listed:

> a catalogue of complaints. Indifferent physicians and surgeons […] a few cannon without any quantity of powder or ball will never take a fortress if by a cannonade it is to be done […]. Suppose you had a good train of ordinance with plenty of ammunition, we have not an artillery man to serve them […] a well-furnished military chest [money] is the soul of an army […]. Without it nothing can be done. For want of it, inevitable ruin must attend us […]. The slowness of our operations is one means of a great backwardness in the Canadians engaging […] we were promised that cash should be sent after us. None is yet arrived. Without it, recruiting goes on badly all over the world and particularly in Canada […]. Bricks without straw we cannot make.[14]

The Patriots were relatively easily driven from Canada in 1776, in that, although effort was required by Britain, the campaign was comparatively short and low in casualties. Examined differently, the need to drive the Patriots from Canada distracted resources from the British offensive in the Thirteen Colonies.

Fresh Patriot attempts on Canada were suggested and concern expressed by British generals.[15] However, invasion plans drawn up in 1778, 1780, and 1781 were not followed through for a variety of reasons, including a lack of French support reflecting strategic priorities in the West Indies, far more pressing opportunities and problems for the Patriots in the Thirteen Colonies, and the logistical difficulties of operating in this largely barren region. Canadian emigrés, such as Moses Hazen, pressed unsuccessfully for action, but the military task was formidable. An invasion would have entailed sieges of strong positions by forces enjoying scant local support and dependent on distant sources of supply. Having already failed once at Quebec, there was no reason to assume success in a subsequent attempt. Ironically, and underlining the problems of judging strategic capability and achievement, the Patriots in the long-run probably profited from being driven out of Canada. Such extended lines of communication and supply, and the commitment of manpower required, would have bled the Continental Army dry and might even have led to mutinies. It would have been very difficult to relocate troops in Canada, not least in the event of British operations in Virginia southward.

Washington, however, reflected on the failure to take Canada: "Hence I shall know the events of war are exceedingly doubtful, and that capricious fortune often blasts over most flattering hopes."[16] This, indeed was a major blow to what had at times been a dangerous overconfidence in political circles about the military challenge posed by Britain.

More generally, the situation deteriorated for the Patriots when a British amphibious force took New York in 1776. In addition, acute supply problems at that moment were exacerbated by widespread demoralization. The Patriots pursued a reactive strategy in 1776, and low morale and desertion were major problems.

One of the most insistent themes in the correspondence of the generals on both sides, however, was the weakness of their forces, a theme that was to grow stronger as the war progressed. This was a weakness that interacted with the contingent nature of local support, one in which compromise rather than conviction was to the fore. A sense of weakness could be crippling, discouraging generals from acting, even when their opponents were in no real position to obstruct them. This situation benefited the Patriots rather than the British, both as the latter had to reverse the situation established by the Patriots in 1775–6 and because the British could not fall back on a militia/volunteer support comparable to that enjoyed by the Patriots. General Sir William Howe, the British commander in North America from 1776 to 1778, reflected:

> I do not apprehend a successful termination to the war from the advantages His Majesty's troops can gain while the enemy is able to avoid, or unwilling to hazard a decisive action, which might reduce the leaders in rebellion to make an overture for peace; or, that this is to be expected, unless a respectable addition to the army is sent from Europe to act early in the ensuing year [...]. If this measure is judged to be inexpedient, or cannot be carried into execution, the event of the war will be very doubtful.
>
> Were any one of the three principal objects, vis New York, Rhode Island or Philadelphia given up to strengthen the defence of the other two, one corps to act offensively might be found, in the meantime such a cession would operate on the minds of the people strongly against His Majesty's interests [...] in the apparent temper of the Americans a considerable addition to the present force will be requisite for effecting any essential change in their disposition and the re-establishment of the King's authority.[17]

This letter captured the impact of popular determination as a factor in the war. This determination had been seen earlier in 1777 in the successful resistance to the British army under General Burgoyne advancing south from Canada: Militia played a major role in the failure of this British force, notably at the battle of Bennington, although units sent from the Continental Army were also important. Burgoyne's surrender at Saratoga enhanced the significance of the popular determination by raising the morale of the Revolutionaries, offsetting the effect of Howe's capture of Philadelphia. So it was also with the impact on the opinion of the French government. Indeed, in March 1777, Hans Stanley, an astute pro-government British MP, had pointed out that "success had always depended much upon opinion."[18]

The role of public opinion gave the Patriots a key advantage, one that was not countered by the deficiencies of their military, even though the latter had clear operational consequences and helped forge a reactive character on Patriot strategy. Washington, for example, was unable to prevent Howe from consolidating his position in Philadelphia in late 1777. The Patriot army was still faced with many of the problems of expiring enlistments and inadequate supplies that had dogged it from the outset.[19] There were also serious command problems and major rivalries. Washington's correspondence was replete with reference to insufficient manpower and supplies. There was also a lack of coherence. For example, Major-General Dickinson ignored Washington's request to bring his militia force from northern New Jersey because he feared that the state would be invaded by the British from Staten Island. This was a commonplace tension.

Washington had to confront criticism that he was not more active and enterprising as a commander, but his army was in a terrible situation at the end of 1777 and the British situation very different than when confined to Boston in late 1775. At the same time, cautious command combined with the fighting spirit of the troops had helped deny the British the decisive victory that might convince opinion—in America, Britain, and the Continent—that Britain was winning and would ultimately triumph.

This situation did not preclude operational choices that can be seen as strategic in their implications. For example, Valley Forge was selected as the Patriot wintering position for 1777–8 so as to mount an attack on nearby British-held Philadelphia as well as to shadow any British moves from there. This can be compared with the positions outside Boston in the winter of 1775–6.

Moreover, Washington hoped that the rich Pennsylvania countryside would provide his men at Valley Forge with food and forage, since what passed as Continental army logistics were weak at best, and New Jersey was bare. (In 1863, the wealth of this countryside also encouraged Robert E. Lee when he moved north.)

The decisions taken by the Council of War of the Continental Army provide opportunities for seeing how strategy was discussed. For example, in April 1778, Washington asked his leading officers whether they advised an attack on Philadelphia, an attack on New York, or remaining in camp while the army was prepared for a later confrontation. The response was divided. Anthony Wayne argued that any attack was better than remaining on the defensive and allowing the British to implement their plans, but Washington decided to remain at Valley Forge and to await developments.[20]

These materialized in the shape of British withdrawal from Philadelphia in June 1778, a withdrawal that led to a confused engagement near Monmouth Court House on the 28th of that same month. The battle did not unfold as Washington had intended, but the ability to provide an attractive gloss reflected the role of war as a source of news wielded to sustain morale: Patriot regulars could be presented as seeing off British regulars and not as retreating in disorder as happened in previous engagements. The battle also led to a serious dispute between Washington and Charles Lee. Interesting and instructive in and of itself, this dispute also reflected, as it continues to reflect, the difficulties faced when trying to offer an agreed narrative of battles and, similarly, an agreed analysis. This importantly helps explain why it is possible to assess relative capabilities and effectiveness very differently.

More generally, much of the Patriot strategy was affected by their repeatedly proven inability to defend their own fortified positions—for example Fort Washington in 1776 and Charleston in 1780—and by their changing ability, in turn, to confront the British in defended, fortified positions held by the latter, which culminated in success at Yorktown in 1781 but not against New York in 1782.

As a separate axis of capability and success, it proved challenging for Washington to extend his relative success in the middle colonies, at least in containing the British to the South where the political context was one in which Loyalism was more prominent. There would be no recovery of Savannah, which was lost in 1778 (comparable to that of Philadelphia, lost in 1777 but regained in 1778).

The extension of the war to the South, after a British expeditionary force captured Savannah in December 1778, exposed serious problems in the Patriot army there. As with Canada, although very differently, the

Patriots found offensive operations difficult to sustain. In November 1778, Congress instructed Benjamin Lincoln, the commander in the South, to invade east Florida and destroy the threat posed by the British garrison in St. Augustine. Nevertheless, support for this expedition from the states was inadequate and no advance was launched, which was just as well given the problems faced earlier by colonial militia attacking St. Augustine when it was in Spanish hands. Aside from resistance, both logistics and disease were key factors.

Yet again, however, the key element was opinion. Despite the problems faced, there was a growing confidence on the Patriot side in 1778 concerning the likely military outcome of the war, a confidence that can be seen in the letters of Delegates to Congress. This confidence owed much to international recognition.[21]

As a reminder, however, that the war was fought at different levels and in a variety of spheres, opinion in the shape of local support became the key element in the war in the South after Patriot defeats in 1779–80 left Nathanael Greene, the commander there from late 1780, able to carry on only partisan warfare. Daniel Morgan was given command of a section of the army and was sent to "spirit up the people" in upper South Carolina, to hinder the collection of supplies by the British, and to attack their flank or rear if they advanced into North Carolina.[22] In addition, Greene found himself obliged to rely heavily on the activities of partisan bands under such leaders as Thomas Sumter and Francis Marion. The use of partisans was an obvious response to the Patriot defeats at Charleston and Camden, the uncontrollable vastness of the South, and the need to counter Loyalist activity and British moves. From the British perspective, forces had to traverse vast distances often through wild, inhospitable terrain, rendering forces vulnerable to enemy tactics of *petite guerre*, by which small, highly mobile detachments carried out fleeting attacks and ambushes on the flanks of their larger adversary. This encouraged reconnaissance mapping.[23] The consequence in the South in 1781 was a vicious local war, which paralleled that in Westchester County New York in the same period.

This conflict could later be presented as guerrilla warfare, and with the implication that such an innovation was a product of a different political culture and one that represented a counter to, and (in some way, development on) *ancien régime* professionalism. However, such conflict had already been seen in Europe, for example used in Hungary. Rather than being learned from conflict with the Turks, or in North America as a response to Native Americans or the local environment, guerrilla warfare, in practice, was a sort of collection of instinctive tactics focused on ambushes and based on the weakness of one side and its own knowledge of the ground. Thus, the Piedmontese employed Waldensian militia in small units with remarkable results against the French, especially in the War of the Austrian Succession on the Alpine front in the 1740s, and guerrilla attacks further affected French operations by cutting supply lines. The same tactics were applied in the County of Nice by the local population against the occupying French from 1792 to 1796.

As a related point, far from "small war" techniques being colonial warfare tactics and spreading from North America to Europe, as sometimes argued, these techniques were important throughout, and not only in the Western world.[24] Indeed, Washington and other Patriot commanders were familiar with the European manuals on partisan war. To a degree, this was an example of a rising power learning from the older powers, America now learning from European practice and experience. Thus, there was a combination of forced experience, a knowledge of past practice, and adaptation to one's particular circumstances, all being important in the American context. A similar process was seen in the employment of artillery.

The war in the South was to play a major role in the subsequent Patriot understanding and presentation of their success in terms of irregular warfare. However, in 1780 and 1781, Washington, a conventional general, was far more hopeful of using French forces, land and sea. His initial target was New York. Its fall would be a fateful blow to the British military position in North America and might well lead to the effective end of the war, a step the Patriots desperately required. This would be much more significant than the recapture of Philadelphia. The loss of New York would leave the British without a secure anchorage for their fleet south of Halifax, Nova Scotia, and the Patriots could then turn south to besiege Charleston and Savannah, thus reconquering America from north to south. Nevertheless, Washington was sufficiently flexible enough to appreciate that cooperation with the French came first and that it would be possible to focus on a different target, which turned out to be Cornwallis' army on the Chesapeake.

After the British defeat at Yorktown in October 1781, the same strategy came to the fore. Washington appreciated that his success there was largely due to French assistance, and he hoped to persuade de Grasse, the French admiral, to cooperate in a speedy attack on Charleston or, failing that, on Wilmington, North Carolina. Instead, de Grasse sailed directly from American waters for the Caribbean. There was no immediate follow-up to Yorktown.

In 1782, Washington hoped to combine again with the French, either attacking New York or Charleston. In the event of French support, Washington was also interested in an invasion of Canada. A major British naval victory over the French off the Iles des Saintes in the Caribbean on 12 April 1782 eliminated that possibility, although anyway the French took the view that Washington was not ready for an attack on New York. In the event, the Patriots had to wait for the British to evacuate Charleston and New York as part of the peace settlement. St. Augustine was also evacuated, but to the benefit of Spain. These outcomes indicated the dependence of Patriot success on international support, and the varied consequences, a point further seen if the fate of North America from West Florida to Nova Scotia in 1783 is considered.

The earlier role of contingency in Patriot strategy prior to French entry emerges clearly both in general terms and in specifics. Following the disasters of 1776, Washington recognized that for many the Continental Army was itself the Revolution. Thereafter, he did not take risks unless victory was all but guaranteed. Had the British been more successful, the Patriots might well have resorted to more revolutionary military methods, such as guerrilla warfare and the strategy advocated by Charles Lee. Indeed, in part as an echo, Greene achieved good outcomes in the South in combining partisan bands with the maneuvers of a field army.

Alternatively, and pursuing a very different strategy, the Patriots might have continued to rely on field armies, as the French Revolutionaries were to do in the 1790s, but (again, as the French revolutionaries did) those who attained power in America could have taken a harsher—indeed far harsher— attitude toward states' rights and private property.

The consequence might have been a very different American public culture, one that stressed the national state more than the individual citizen or the individual state, and emphasized obligations over rights.

For the British, in contrast to the Seven Years' War, the political context, both domestic and international, was very different in the War of American Independence. This point underlines the extent to which, whereas any focus on war-winning involves understanding strategy (or, rather, operationalizing it), in terms of military activity, in fact, the key to strategy is the political purposes that are pursued. In short, strategy is a process of understanding problems and determining goals, and not the details of the plans by which these goals are implemented by military means. There was a need on the part of Britain to respond to Patriot strategy, but the prime requirement was the attempt to impose itself on the situation in North America such that there would be no basis for a Patriot strategy. To employ modern terms, counter-insurgency was designed to ensure that there was no prospect for insurgency, but this was true at strategic, operational, and tactical levels. Resistance had to be ended. Otherwise, as Rockingham had suggested in February 1775, any victory would "require a large force to be constantly continued there to keep the Continent in subjection."[25]

British strategy in the War of Independence must be understood in this light because this strategy was very different to that seen during the Seven Years' War. Indeed, the contrast, which reflects the particular types of conflict, very much established the significance of politics. In the latter case, the British focus had been on conquest in North America from France, and not on pacification there. The latter was clearly subservient to the former, although different policies were enacted for the purpose of pacification. These included an eighteenth-century equivalent of ethnic cleansing in the expulsion of the Acadians (French settlers) from Nova Scotia, New Brunswick, and Prince Edward Island in 1755–64, as well as the very different post-conquest accommodation of the Catholics of Québec, which looked toward the Quebec Act of 1774. This accommodation proved highly successful, unlike the policies followed in the case of the British colonies further south. Indeed, the difficulties the government encountered in the latter made it more necessary to press for the accommodation of Québec.

In the War of Independence, pacification was the British strategy, and the question was how best to secure it. The purpose of the war was clear, the return of the Patriots to their loyalty, and the method chosen was significantly different to that taken in response to the serious Jacobite rebellions in Scotland and northern England in 1715–16 and, far more, 1745–6. In these cases, as later in the face of the Irish rebellion in 1798, the remedy had been more clearly military. (However, in making that argument, it is necessary to note post-war policies for their stability through reorganization, most obviously in the introduction of radically new governmental and political systems for the Scottish Highlands and Ireland.)

In the case of America, although military occupation was again a factor and one that compromised British popularity,[26] there was not this sequencing. Instead, there was a willingness to consider, not only pacification alongside conflict, but also new political systems as an aspect of this pacification, although the likely nature of these systems was unclear. Indeed, in one sense, pacification began at the outset in 1775 with the misconceived and mishandled British attempt to seize arms in New England. It continued with the unsuccessful attempt to overawe resistance at Bunker Hill, for the display of British forces there in preparation for their attack indeed had an intimidating character. In contrast, the most prominent instances of a very different type of pacification were the instructions to the Howe Brothers, the commanders appointed in 1776, to negotiate as well as fight, and, even more clearly, the dispatch of the Carlisle Commission in 1778, again with instructions to negotiate (each of which were approaches rejected by the Patriots). Moreover, the restoration of colonial government in the South was a concrete step indicating, during the war, what the British were seeking to achieve and how they were planning to do it.

Alongside that, and more insistently, were the practices of British commanders. Although the Patriots were traitors, they were treated with great leniency, and suggestions of harsher treatment were generally ignored. This point underlines the extent to which conduct in the field both reflects strategy but also affects the development of strategic culture. In most cases during the century, rebels were treated far more harshly. So will it be, eventually, with the treatment of Confederate citizens and

Southern society in the Civil War of 1861–5, as opposed to that of 1775–83 which is not generally presented as a civil war. In practice, there was no comparable move in the War of Independence toward the "hard" approach seen in Union conduct in the Civil War, and certainly not at the official level and as systemic policy. Indeed, the Southern strategy in 1778–82 very much involved an attempt for conciliation.

The focus on pacification provides an essential continuity to British strategy, but there were of course differences in emphasis. An attempt at overall evaluation faces the classic problem that history occurs forward, 1775 preceding 1776, but is analyzed from posterity, with 1775 understood in the light of 1776. This approach is unhelpful, however, not least because the course of the war was affected by two key discontinuities that changed the parameters for contemporaries. The usual one given is the internationalization of the war, notably with France's formal entry in 1778 on the Patriot side. However, prior to that, the declaration of American independence in 1776 transformed the strategic situation. Alongside these discontinuities came military unpredictabilities, such as the initially successful, but eventually totally unsuccessful, Patriot invasion of Canada in 1775–6, and the total British operational failures at Saratoga (1777) and Yorktown (1781). These events were not secondary to the military operationalization of strategy but, instead, helped direct it. The wider political dimension was also greatly affected by events, both military and diplomatic.

Thus, the southern strategy, both military and political—the focus on regaining the southern colonies that dominated British policy from late 1778 when a British amphibious force swiftly captured Savannah—arose in large part from the impact of formal French entry into the war earlier in the year. This entry ended the unusual situation in which Britain was at war solely in North America, and therefore able to concentrate attention and resources on it. Moreover, from French entry, Britain was essentially pushed into a bifurcated struggle involving separate strategies. A struggle for pacification continued in the Thirteen Colonies (albeit being greatly complicated by the French military presence there on land and at sea and by the prospect of a larger presence), while a straightforward military struggle with France began elsewhere, especially in the West Indies, India, and West Africa. Again, this apparently clear distinction can be qualified by noting that Britain had political, as well as military, options to consider in both cases, as well as offensive and defensive aspects to strategy.

The general impression is of inevitable and progressive moves toward such a bifurcated war, although, in practice, the political dimension again came first. This was rendered more complex by the need to consider the goals and moves of various powers, including unpredictable responses to the actions of others. Thus, aside from Britain's relations with the states with which it eventually came to war—France in 1778, Spain in 1779, and the Dutch in 1780—there were relations with neutral powers, both friendly and unfriendly, Russia being prominent among the latter. These relations were, in part, linked to the military operationalization of strategy, notably with the British commitment to commercial blockade as a means to employ, retain, and strengthen naval strength, and with the possibility that alliances and agreements in Europe would yield troops for North America. This was a key goal as, lacking conscription, Britain was very short of troops. Moreover, subsidy treaties provided trained troops. These elements ensured that the conflict was European in part, irrespective of whether European powers declared war on Britain.

As another instance of unpredictability, the European crisis of 1778, which led to the War of the Bavarian Succession of 1778–9 between Prussia and France's ally, Austria, created diplomatic opportunities for Britain and, indeed, it was seen in this light. There has since also been scholarly discussion on the lines that a more interventionist European policy would have distracted France from taking part in the American war, with major consequences for British options there. This point neglects a fundamental aspect of British strategy in the 1770s. Britain was acting as a satisfied or status quo power, obviously keen to retain and safeguard its position, but not interested in gaining fresh territory.

Representing a satisfied power, British ministers were also wary of becoming involved in Continental European power politics. Here the American war fitted into a pattern that had begun with George III's rejection of the Prussian alliance in 1761–2. This was a rejection that proved highly contentious in British domestic politics, both ministerial and public, and one associated with the critique of George's domestic attitudes that would become significant in Britain and its colonies. Both were seen as aspects of novelty on the part of George. His wariness regarding close Continental links had continued with his subsequent refusal in the 1760s to accept the Russian requirements for an alliance, as well as with the rebuff of French approaches for joint action against, and in response to, the First Partition of Poland by Austria, Prussia, and Russia in 1772.

Thus, there was to be no recurrence during the War of Independence of the situation in the Seven Years' War—namely, war in alliance with a Continental power. However unintentional, this latter situation had proved particularly potent, both in terms of domestic politics and of international relations, or it had been shaped thus by William Pitt the Elder with his presentation of British policy in terms of conquering Canada in Europe. In the War of American Independence, there would be no alliance with Prussia (nor anyone else) to distract France, and thus in military terms no commitment of the British army to the Continent, as occurred onward from 1758. Even more, subsidized German troops, such as those deployed in 1757 in an unsuccessful attempt to defend the Electorate of Hanover, would not be used for "German" or European power political purposes.

Instead, some troops would be retained in Europe—Hanoverians, for example, were sent to serve in the Gibraltar garrison. Most, however, notably Hessians, were sent to America where at peak strength they comprised nearly forty percent of the British army. Britain's fundamental strategy thus rested on a policy coherence that had military consequences: Passivity in Europe combined with the preservation of status in America.

Reviewing the strategies on offer, it is reasonable to consider the "What if?" of Austrian or Prussian pressure on France, or the possibility of this pressure deterring the French from helping the Americans from 1778 and thereby justifying a British commitment to Continental power politics. Such counterfactuals were very much to the fore in contemporary public discussion of strategy and provided a prime means by which this discussion was conducted. Counterfactuals were also crucial in the speculation by rulers and ministers concerning the likely international permutations of events, permutations rendered particularly important by the roles of coalition warfare and diversionary campaigning.

Separately, counterfactuals also provide a means to assess both the choices made in the past and the sphere for choice in general. The latter is significant, as understanding strategy in large part requires appreciating the parameters established by ideas, assumptions, and issues, as well as those relating to capabilities, opportunities, and needs. This distinction is related to differences between idealist and realist concepts in modern international relations theory, but is not coterminous with it.

Returning to the 1770s, it is pertinent to ask whether an alliance with a Continental power would have led not to benefits, but instead to a highly-damaging British commitment to one side or the other in the War of the Bavarian Succession. The Seven Years' War, in which Britain had allied with Prussia, was scarcely encouraging in this respect, as it was, at least initially, far from clear that Britain's involvement in the conflict on the Continent at the time would work out as favorably as in fact happened. Given the use made of this example, both at the time and subsequently, notably by supporters of interventionism, this point provides a key instance of the nature of strategic thought and culture as recovered memory and in political contention.

In addition, had Britain allied with Austria or Prussia in the War of the Bavarian Succession, then Hanover would presumably have been exposed to attack by its opponent. Hanover was vulnerable, as was repeatedly demonstrated, indeed far more so than the British Isles as there was no need to gain naval dominance. Had Hanover been overrun (as had been threatened by the French in 1741, was later achieved by them in 1757, and was to occur anew in 1803) then its recovery might have jeopardized the military, diplomatic, and political options of the British government both in Europe and more generally. Furthermore, the War of the Bavarian Succession was restricted to two campaigning seasons, 1778 and 1779, but might have been longer (like the Seven Years' War) or speedily resumed (as with the two Austro-Prussian conflicts of the 1740s: 1740–2 and 1744–5). Either outcome might have posed major problems for Britain had it been involved, limiting other strategic options. Each outcome was possible as far as contemporaries were concerned.

Moreover, as another critique of the interventionist argument, and in this case specifically the claim that it could—indeed would—have deterred French action (and thus ensured British victory), the British had prior to French entry into the war in 1778 already failed to translate victories in North America (such as the battle of Long Island and subsequent capture of New York in 1776, and the battle of Brandywine and subsequent capture of Philadelphia in 1777) into an acceptable political verdict. Thus, the issue of French strategy was less crucial to British success than might be suggested by the focus, understandable as it is, on the major French role in the Franco-Patriot defeat of the British at Yorktown in 1781. This underlines the need to locate speculation about diplomatic and military options within a context of understanding strategic possibilities. The latter provides a framework for strategic decision-making that is overly easy to underplay.

Goals also need to be kept in mind. Britain was a "satisfied" power after 1763, and as a consequence it was difficult, if not dangerous, to try to strengthen the status quo by alliances with powers that wished to overturn it. There was also no significant domestic constituency for an interventionist strategy—and notably none for any one particular interventionist course of action. Aside from the practicalities of British power, and the nature of British politics, the 'Western Question,' the fate of Western Europe (more particularly the Low Countries, the Rhineland and Italy) had been settled in diplomatic terms in the 1750s. More specifically, an Austrian alliance with Spain and then, far more unexpectedly, one with France resolved issues, whereas France's willingness in 1748 as part of a peace settlement to return recent wartime gains from the Austrian Netherlands and the United Provinces was also highly significant. These alliances, although they challenged established British assumptions, also removed both need and opportunity for British intervention.

This shift in power politics was crucial because in Britain the public support for interventionism on the Continent was fragile, if not weak, unless the Bourbons (the rulers of France and Spain) were the target. Moreover, the domestic coalition of interests and ideas upon which public backing for foreign policy rested was heavily reliant on the consistency offered by the resonance of the anti-Bourbon beat. Thus, British strategy in the war cannot be separated from wider currents of political preference and engagement. A lack of interest in European interventionism was even more pronounced in the British colonies, for the concern of colonists, whether or not Loyalists, focused on the New World.

What British strategy appeared to entail in North America varied greatly during the conflict. The initial British impression was of opposition largely only in Massachusetts, and this assessment suggested that a vigorous defense of imperial interests there would save the situation. This view led to British legislation in 1774 written specifically for this colony, and to a concentration of Britain's forces in North America there. The initial military operationalization of strategy continued after the clashes at Concord and Lexington in 1775, both because the stress on Massachusetts appeared vindicated and because there were not enough troops for action elsewhere. This situation represented a key failure in British preparedness, but was also a product of the small size of the British army.

This policy failed, then, both in Massachusetts and elsewhere. In the former, the military presence was unable to prevent rebellion or to contain it. Indeed, eventually, in March 1776, the British had to evacuate Boston when the harbor was threatened by Patriot cannon. Elsewhere in North America, the lack of troops stemming from the concentration on Boston ensured that British authority was overthrown in the other twelve colonies involved in the revolution. Moreover, in 1775, the Patriots were able to mount an invasion of Canada that achieved initial success, bottling up the British in the city of Québec.

As a result of the events of 1775–6, the second stage of the war, a stage expected and planned neither by most of the Patriots nor by the British government, led to a major British effort to regain control. This policy entailed both a formidable military effort and peacemaking proposals. Here, again, it is necessary to look at the military options in terms of the political situation. The end of the rebellion/revolution could not be achieved by reconquering all the Thirteen Colonies (and driving the Patriots from Canada). Prefiguring in a way the Union's position during the Civil War, the task was simply too great, leaving aside the challenge of maintaining any such verdict. Instead, it was necessary to secure military results that achieved the political outcome of an end to rebellion in the shape of surrender. Such an outcome was likely to require both a negotiated settlement and acquiescence in the return to loyalty, and in subsequently maintaining obedience.

What was unclear was which military results would best secure this outcome. Was the priority the defeat, indeed destruction, of the Continental Army, as it represented the Revolution, not least its unity, and was the prime defense of the Revolution? Or was it the capture of key Patriot centers, notably Philadelphia in 1777? Each goal appeared possible, and in practice there was a mutual dependence between them. The British would not be able to defeat the Patriots unless they could land and support troops, and, for this capability to be maintained, it was necessary to secure port cities. Conversely, these port cities could best be held if Patriot forces were defeated. Otherwise, it would be necessary to maintain a large garrison as, indeed, would be the case in New York.

The equations of troop numbers made these issues apparent, not least through the problems posed by finite British military resources and for supply provision by maintaining large garrison forces. Indeed, the latter point lent further military attention to the political strategy of pacification, as such a strategy would reduce the need for garrisons and produce local Loyalist forces, as well as diminishing the number of Patriots.

In an instance of a longstanding issue in both strategy and operational planning—notably, but not only, in counterinsurgency struggles—the British emphasis possibly should have been on destroying the Continental Army. It was not easy to fix opponents and then destroy them in battle. This, however, was definitely a prospect in 1776–7, and certainly in the immediate aftermath of Long Island. Instead, the stress was on regaining major centers, not least as this policy was seen as a way of demonstrating the return of royal authority, particularly by ensuring that large numbers of Patriots would return under the Crown. Indeed, from the period when the Empire struck back (the summer of 1776), the British gained control of most of the leading cities, either for much of the war (New York from 1776, Savannah from 1778, Charleston from 1780), or, as it turned out, temporarily (Newport from 1776 to 1778, and Philadelphia from 1777 to 1778).

Yet this policy still left important centers, most obviously Boston from March 1776, that were not under British control, as well as much of the interior that included territory within striking distance of the cities, which forced a need for substantial garrisons. This point indicated the fundamental political problem facing the British and something more generally true in all strategic planning: Whatever they won in the field, it would still be necessary to achieve a political settlement, at least in the form of a return to loyalty. The understanding of this issue was an achievement for the British, but it also posed a major problem. Correspondingly, this understanding was likewise both an achievement and problem for the Patriots.

The British government and army were cautious in their treatment of the Patriots despite the fact that they were legally rebels. Raids on rebel-held towns, such as the one by the amphibious force that destroyed Falmouth (now Portland, Maine) on 18 October 1775, created outrage on the part of the Patriots, but they were not typical of the conflict. Similarly, the propaganda use the Patriots made of the scalping of Jane McCrea by Indian scouts working for the British in 1777 created a false impression, although such propaganda was seen as important to the stiffening of resistance. It also reflected normative values on the nature of acceptable violence.

The Declaration of Independence complained that George III "has endeavoured to bring on the inhabitants of our frontiers the merciless Indian savages, whose known rule of warfare is an undistinguished destruction of all ages, sexes, and conditions." In fact, the generally cautious British approach reflected the politics of the war—that is, the restoration of the colonies to royal government would be of limited value if subsequently holding them down required a substantial garrison and if the embers of rebellion remained among a discontented population. In contrast, conflict between Patriots and Loyalists could be far more vicious, and it was so in particular in the South in 1780–1. Local Patriots considered the Loyalists as rebels against the legitimate government, and so justified their inflicting the harsh treatment appropriate for defeated rebels or in accord with the "law of retaliation." One retaliation naturally led to another, particularly in an environment where so much of the military activity was carried out by independently-operating and institutionally-weak militia forces, where kinship loyalties were strong, and where there were established rivalries, notably over land.

There was a contrast between the treatment of civilians (and prisoners) in Scotland in 1746, however, and what took place in the War of Independence, although in each case the British were responding to a rebellion. In Scotland, there was considerable harshness on the part of the regular army. This indicates the extent of variety that subverts any single or simple account of the subject.

The need to secure support helps explain the attention devoted by Patriot leaders throughout the war to politics, as political outcomes were needed to secure the persistence and coherence of the war effort. The British, in turn, could try by political approaches and military efforts to alter these political equations within the Thirteen Colonies. At times, they succeeded in doing so—for example, in the new political prospectus offered in South Carolina after the successful British siege of Charleston in 1780. Indeed, in tidewater South Carolina, the part of the colony most exposed to British amphibious power and most dependent on trade, British authority was swiftly recognized. This success appeared to be a vindication of the British strategy of combining military force with a conciliatory political policy, one offering a new imperial relationship that granted most of the Patriot demands made at the outbreak of the war. It was scarcely surprising that Northern politicians, such as Ezekiel Cornell of Rhode Island, came to doubt the determination of their Southern counterparts.

To treat this conflict, on either side, therefore simply as a military struggle is to underplay the key role of political goals. Indeed, these goals affected not only the moves of armies (a conventional, but overly limited popular understanding of strategy), but even the nature of the forces deployed by both sides. The British use of German "mercenaries" and, far more, of Native Americans and Blacks, provided opportunities for political mobilization on the part of the Patriots hostile to this use even though, in practice, there was little British use of Blacks as soldiers and certainly nothing to match the Union during the Civil War.

The Patriot reliance on France, correspondingly, increased domestic support for war in Britain and greatly compromised sympathy there for the Patriots. They could now be presented as hypocrites, willing to ally with a Catholic autocracy (two, when Spain joined in in 1779), and with Britain's national nemesis (enemies from 1779) as well. These alliances brought the war to a new stage, as there was no inherent clarity as to the allocation of British resources between the conflict with the Bourbons and that with the Patriots. It was relatively easy for the Patriots to abandon the greater American plan of conquering Canada after failure in 1776 was followed by British military efforts in the Thirteen Colonies that had to be countered. This prefigured the challenge posed by Britain in 1814 when British forces attacked the Chesapeake, and, even more, what would have been Britain's strategy had there been intervention in the Civil War.

In contrast, during the War of American Independence, there was no such agreement over strategy in Britain among those committed to the war. Partisan politics came into play, not least the politics of justification, with the Opposition (itself far from united) repeatedly pressing for focus on the Bourbons (France and Spain) and not the Patriots, and the ministry unwilling to follow to the same extent. It neither wished, nor thought it appropriate, to abandon hopes of regaining America.

This debate was not settled until Yorktown—and not so much the surrender of the besieged and defeated British force on 19 October 1781 as, rather, the political consequences felt in Britain. This was specifically the fall of the North ministry the following March, and the fact that it was succeeded not by a similar one that maintained royal views, but rather that the Opposition came to power under Charles, 2nd Marquess of Rockingham. As a result of the central role of politics in strategy, 1782 was a key year of the war.

In turn, in both the short and the long term, Britain won the battle of conciliation by dividing the opposing coalition and offering peace terms separately. Crucially, the alliance between the Patriots and France ceased to be effective. Instead, there was a flexibility that created opportunities for new alignments. In June 1786, William Eden, an MP who was acting as the British envoy in Paris to negotiate a trade treaty (which he succeeded in doing), reported:

> there are strong appearances here of a disposition to believe that Great Britain and France ought to unite in some solid plan of permanent peace: and many of the most considerable people talk with little reserve of the dangers to be apprehended from the revolted colonies, if they should be

> encouraged to gain commercial strength and consistency of government.[27]

That was not an option. But in 1787 when Britain and France came close to conflict in the Dutch Crisis, there was scant prospect of America wishing to help—or being able to help—the French.[28] So also in 1790, when Britain came close to war with France and Spain in the Nootka Sound Crisis. This outcome underlines the conceptual problems of conceiving of strategy in terms of its military operationalization. At the same time, the dynamic character of strategy had been amply displayed by the unexpectedness of the challenge posed by the American Revolution. However much they might seek to see politics and strategy in a bilateral fashion—that of Britain and that of the Patriots—there was a number of other players, and the combined consequences were not that these also needed to be considered, but that they also greatly affected Britain and the Patriots. The most significant of these others were France, Spain, the Dutch, the Loyalists, the Native Americans, and European powers that were not directly involved but whose power politics could affect those otherwise involved—for example, Austria and Prussia.

For France in 1778, there was a stark choice between intervening in North America or fulfilling treaty commitments to Austria in the War of Bavarian Succession. Had the latter choice been taken, France might well not have benefited, as it later would, from the weakening of British power caused by supporting the Patriots in order to secure the loss of the Thirteen Colonies (for France would have been involved in war with Prussia, the dominions of which included territories in the lower Rhineland). Prussia would also have been in a position to attack France's other and more vulnerable allies in Germany. From this perspective, the absence of German unification was a precondition of American independence, for the rivalry between Austria and Prussia and the extent to which—unlike in 1866 when they fought—there was no rapid and decisive result, provided France with an opportunity to fight Britain in 1778. In contrast, France abandoned its commitment to the civil war in Mexico in part due to the rapid Prussian victory over Austria in 1866.

That war between Austria and Prussia would provide France with an opportunity to fight Britain was the feared outcome among British ministries in the 1740s and 1750s, notably in 1741 and 1757. Yet rather than providing an obvious pattern of causation, there is still no clear path to American independence, whether owed to Patriot progressivism and fighting methods, or to French intervention. It is time to turn to the narrative.

## 4. 1775: BEGINNING HOSTILITIES

Every conflict is different and particularly civil wars, for in them the politics are most clearly to the fore. And every rebellion is a civil war however it is defined. This includes anti-imperial struggles not least those that, like the American Revolution, resulted in the establishment of an independent state, even though this was not the original intention. Indeed, even after independence was declared in 1776, it could have been negotiated away had the war ended in a different compromise settlement (although that is not a theme pursued in the standard account of the conflict). Nevertheless, this potential outcome provides one way to approach British strategy and assess its viability.

By 1775, Britain had had much experience of civil wars. Moreover, with the position of England in the British Isles understood at least in part in anti-imperial terms (as it should be from the perspective of Ireland, Scotland, and Wales) there had already been a considerable history of such rebellions. Most recently, the Jacobite Rebellion of 1745–6 had been a major anti-imperial rebellion and one that was more serious than the American Revolution because it saw rebel forces get as close to London as Derby on 4 December 1745, and was accompanied by serious ministerial instability. From that perspective, the American Revolution was significant not so much due to the military challenge posed but rather because of the outcome.

Success makes the American Revolution more important, but in terms of immediacy and gravity the events of 1745 were more serious, and likewise William of Orange's seizure of power in 1688–9 was both more grave and significant than the American Revolution. The events of 1745 also offered a cautionary note for the American Patriots because the Jacobites were initially very successful. They were victorious in the first battle (Prestonpans), captured Edinburgh, and outmanoevred the regular forces in northern England. Yet, despite subsequent success in the second battle (Falkirk), there was eventual defeat and then utter defeat.

In contrast to the Jacobite advance to Derby, the challenge posed by the American Revolution only became truly serious for Britain after France entered the war in 1778 and, more particularly, in the wake of the failure to defeat the French Brest fleet off Ushant in 1778 and of the invasion scare in 1779. There was no equivalent earlier on, or, indeed, in practice, from the Patriots throughout the war. They were unable to produce a challenge to the fleet strength of the British or, in part as a consequence, to mount an invasion of the British Isles; The British ministry, furthermore, was both stable and able to win the parliamentary elections of 1780. The Patriots at sea could drive up the resource cost to the British of defending Atlantic power-projection and commerce, but did little more than this.

Although the British ministry was sorry that the death of Louis XV in 1774 led to the fall of D'Aiguillon, the new administration was clearly pacific and concerned with domestic problems, and the French navy was not ready for war. The British were careful to offend neither France nor Spain and in 1774–7 successfully promoted a peaceful settlement of the likeliest cause of Anglo-Bourbon War—namely, the border conflict between Portuguese Brazil and Spanish South America. This goal led to unsuccessful Portuguese attempts to enlist military assistance from their British ally. The American Patriots were disappointed in their hope that war would break out and Britain be obliged to assist Portugal, and therefore that the Bourbon powers would offer them assistance.

This is an important context within which to assess the early years of the war, and notably the first year (1775) or, indeed, the period that ended with the British counterattacks in 1776 from Canada to Charleston. On the one hand, 1775 saw failure for Britain and, indeed, a serious collapse of authority and power across much of British North America and not just the Thirteen Colonies. By the end of 1775, British forces in the Thirteen Colonies were restricted to Boston where they essentially lacked operational mobility and as a result did not have much strategic value or, indeed, operational significance.

Meanwhile, the Continental Congress had established its authority over the army, choosing George Washington as commander, a position he accepted with humility on 16 June. Washington very much sought an army that was no federation of state forces. His first General Order, that of 4 July, describes the "Troops of the United Provinces of North America, and it is hoped that all distinctions of colonies will be laid aside," a theme he later repeated. The Patriots also were rapidly organizing the production of armaments, establishing arsenals, foundries and gunpowder mills, and making saltpeter.[1] All of this put them in a very different position to the Native Americans who opposed the British.

In addition, the Americans had advanced into Canada where the military target was very different in scale and vulnerable to the situation by the War of 1812, let alone the American Civil War. Montreal had been captured and Quebec besieged, both in 1775. The interior of British Canada had in effect been driven in and, excepting besieged Quebec, the British presence essentially restricted to Nova Scotia and the major naval base at Halifax, as well as to the islands of Newfoundland and Prince Edward Island. There appeared to be a potential parallel to the situation in the Thirteen Colonies, with British power limited essentially to that of a coastal periphery at most. Furthermore, this power was likely to be restricted as ports were seized by the Patriots, and they would not be easy to retake by naval action and amphibious attack. The British were to discover this at Charleston in 1776 and would have encountered the same outcome had they mounted an amphibious operation against Boston.

Conversely, the Patriots had only achieved so much by December 1775, which was understandable but also strategically critical. They had achieved far more in relative terms than the Parliamentary forces in 1642 (the first year in the English Civil War), but the circumstances then were very different as the Royalists were dominant in many parts of the kingdom, and Britain was scarcely knocked out in 1775. Even were Quebec to fall (which it did not do), the Patriots had no way to project their power to take Nova Scotia, and if Quebec held out it would be possible for the British to relieve it only once the ice in the St. Lawrence melted in the spring and warships could sail there (which indeed happened as it had occurred in 1760 when the French besieged the newly-established British garrison).

There was no equivalent in the St. Lawrence in 1776 to the French fleet preventing the relief of besieged Yorktown in 1781 at the battle of the Virginia Capes. The Patriots simply lacked the naval capability. Moreover, if in Massachusetts the British were confined to Boston, by the end of 1775 they still had not been forced out. Their situation there might have prefigured the situation later in the war in New York. In addition, while the Patriots in 1775 had put in a good defense at Bunker Hill and had not collapsed before the British show of force, ultimately the battle saw the British take the Patriot position.

Most seriously, even though operational successes and the dynamic of events had both helped the Patriot cause greatly, there was no end to the strategic dilemma facing the Patriots—namely, how to make events in North America affect the situation in London. Fundamentally, the Revolution had begun as a result not of a campaign for independence, which was not indeed proclaimed until 4 July 1776, but rather as a consequence of a determination to change British policy (this was an easier issue around which to cohere and not a challenge to what was eventually defined as Loyalism). In 1775, what in earlier stages had been a large-scale sequential tax demonstration culminating with the Boston Tea Party, became a more diffuse demand for political change in the sense of a recognition and redress of grievances. Understandably, in light of the geographical and political range of the colonies this demand was not yet focused on a fixed point, which independence was subsequently to offer as a form of necessary unity for the fragile would-be federalism of the Revolution. Instead, there was an expectation of change from the basis of the existing political relationship, an expectation shared in both North America and Britain.

This expectation gave both the Patriots and the British agency. This, indeed, was at once the situation from April 1775 onward, but in practice it was also a continuation of the pre-war situation. Thus, what was war in the sense of fighting was also a case of politics just playing out by other means. In this scenario, there was nothing inevitable about goals or means, and no clarity as to what would be the action-reaction cycle of mutual influence or even causality.

For George III, the way was open toward offering outcomes, or the possibility of outcomes that might have affected Patriot purposes, or unity, or the degree of support and enthusiasm held by Loyalists. This introduced an unknown element as it proved the prime strategic context in

1775, one unknown not so much by George but by Americans—both Patriots and Loyalists. However, George's obduracy prevented him from taking advantage of what was a political opportunity of strategic significance, but one that he persistently misunderstood and mistimed. Thus, in 1776 and 1778, political offers were made that might well have had a major impact if they had appeared in 1775. This, of course, is an argument from hindsight and, separately, one that ignores the values held by George and his supporters, both American and British. There is a need, of course, to take not simply and solely a functional approach to British policy and the crisis, but rather one that accepts the validity of goals (and differing goals at that). This approach challenges the teleology of the war, and, separately, may appear to be rendered redundant by functional and practical issues and capabilities. The latter is an understandable approach, but not one that makes much sense of contemporary assumptions. Indeed, from the point of practicality, rebellion in the face of British naval power and without the support of France might appear to be highly foolish.

In the absence of such a political outcome, military operations took precedence. The advance on Lexington and Concord both presented a key turning point in the conflict and established the nature of the challenge to the British—a challenge of scale, character, and environment, human and physical. The scale was that of the number of Patriots who rose and the geographical extent of opposition. This was further expanded by the Patriot invasion of Canada that year. This demonstrated the danger to Britain of failing to restore the Thirteen Colonies to royal authority, one that might be extended if the Patriots encouraged opposition in the West Indies. The invasion of Canada could also be seen as changing the basis of the struggle as the result of:

> [...] the commencing of an offensive war with the sovereign. Opposition to government had hitherto been conducted on the apparent design and avowed principle only, of supporting and defending certain rights and immunities of the people, which were supposed, or pretended, to be unjustly invaded. Opposition, or even resistance, in such a case [...] is thought by many to be entirely consistent with the principles of the British constitution.[2]

On 26 October, opening a new session of Parliament, George declared it necessary "to put a speedy end to these disorders by the most decisive exertions." This led him to favor campaigns on land rather than the idea of a naval blockade. In contrast, Augustus, 3rd Duke of Grafton, the Lord Privy Seal and a former Prime Minister, used the debate on the Address to express his doubts about coercion, only to lose his post. Meanwhile, the war was going badly in America. Brigadier-General Henry Percy, wrote from Boston in 1774: "We have days here full as hot as Spain, I am at this instant writing to you sweating without clothes. But our climate is horribly inconstant, for we have it sometimes very cold."[3] Temperatures of 90–100 ℉ during the day, with sudden drops to around 60 ℉, are not unusual in a New England summer. Percy, the commander of the relief column, reported to Gage the day after the advance to Lexington and Concord on 19 April 1775. Having met the retreating troops at Lexington, Percy ordered his two cannons to fire on the pursuers, thus encouraging them to caution, and then sought to cover the retreat:

> sending out very strong flanking parties which were absolutely necessary, as there was not a stone wall or house, though before in appearance evacuated, from whence the rebels did not fire upon us. As soon as they saw us begin to retire, they pressed very much upon our rear guard […] we retired for 15 miles under an incessant fire all round us […] losing a good many men in the retreat behaved with their usual intrepidity and spirit.[4]

Wounded on the retreat, Jeremy Lister wrote of "a general firing upon us from all quarters, from behind hedges and walls."[5] Serious difficulties were captured by Captain William Evelyn, part of the relief force:

> They [the British column] were attacked from the woods and houses on each side of the road and an increasing fire kept up on both sides for several hours, they [the Americans] still retiring through the wood whenever our men advanced upon them we [ the relief force] were attacked on all sides from woods, orchards, stone walls, and from every house on the road side […].

Evelyn later added "some other mode must be adopted than gaining every little hill at the expense of a thousand Englishmen." This was a reference to the battle of Bunker Hill outside Boston on 17 June 1775 where 228 had been killed and 826 wounded, 42 percent of the force engaged (compared to 100 and 271 Patriots).[6] The battle arose from the British attempt to gain control of hills from which the harbor could be threatened. The troops who attacked the Patriot defenses at Bunker Hill advanced uphill carrying 70-pound packs in a scorching 90℉ heat. The display of strength failed to intimidate the defenders, and these defenses were only carried after two advances had failed. The Patriots had made good use of the terrain and fought well, including blocking the attempt by British light infantry to outflank the Patriot left. The high British casualty rate lessened the numbers available and discouraged further offensive operations, such that the British lost the strategic, operational, and tactical initiative.

The fighting near Boston is that which is remembered, but across the colonies militia units overcame royal governors and defeated supporting Loyalists. This was especially so at Great Bridge, Virginia, on 9 December in which a force of 861 Patriots defeated 409 men (regulars and allies) under John, 4th Earl of Dunmore, the governor, who advanced toward the attack without knowing the true strength of his opponents. The British column was hit hard by the musket fire of the defenders, and this led to a comparison with Bunker's Hill; Although, on this occasion, the Patriots, against a far smaller British force, held their position and the British were compelled to fall back.[7] This weakened the British position in Virginia and prefigured its abandonment.

The British failure to crush the rebellion in 1775 gave the Patriots time to organize themselves politically and militarily, to extend the rebellion greatly, and to weaken the Loyalists. Those who held contrary opinions were intimidated and Loyalist publications were attacked. The disorientating experience of the agencies of law and authority being taken over by those who were willing to connive, or support, violence affected many who were unhappy about developments. These successes helped give the Patriots strategic depth, lessening the importance of British operations, first in New England and subsequently in the Middle Colonies. Many sought to avoid taking sides.[8]

Meanwhile, the Patriots had invaded Canada. The Lake Champlain axis was open to the Patriots, not least because there was only a scant British presence, and with small and unprepared garrisons Crown Prince and Ticonderoga both fell in May, a marked contrast to the situation the British had faced in 1758. A separate force under Benedict Arnold sailed from Newburyport on 19 September and advanced across modern Maine facing major difficulties from the terrain and lack of supplies,[9] difficulties Washington had not anticipated. This force, however, was secondary to that which advanced along the Lake Champlain axis before capturing Montreal, which was not really defended, and then advancing to besiege Quebec.

The Patriots, however, found the war in Canada very different to that in the Thirteen Colonies. That was an underrated difference in the war before the conflict extended in 1778 to include France and, therefore, to offer a greater contrast with that in the Thirteen Colonies. In Canada, despite efforts to win support,[10] there was a very different public political climate and this was particularly felt by the Patriots due to the limited number of overt Loyalists in Massachusetts, and more generally in New England. Crucially, although many in Québec did not favor the British, there was only limited support for the Patriots (as opposed to the situation farther south).

Yet, the Patriots were far more successful that year in Canada than invading American forces were to be in 1812, 1813, or 1814. In each of these years, the British (which very much meant the Canadians as well) held off these larger forces and inflicted serious blows on them. In contrast, there was no ability to protect the St. Lawrence Valley, still more the frontier in 1775, and no force capable of mounting a mobile defense. The Patriots outside Quebec felt able to close the year by storming the position and needed to do so due to bitter weather, terms of service due to end on 31 December, and the British refusal to sally out and risk defeat in the field. This attempt was defeated,[11] but it was more than the Patriot army outside Boston had been able to mount.

It was unclear at this point how the war would develop. The Patriots had done well, but unlike what occurred for the Americans in 1812 and 1813, they did not benefit from a diversion of British strength arising from a focus on conflict with France in Europe. This meant that the British could choose to counterattack in force.

## 5. 1776: WAR FOR INDEPENDENCE

The change in the politics of the war in 1776 was fundamental and twofold. The most obvious was the Declaration of Independence, and understandably this engages the greatest attention, not least in America. It is an iconic occasion and document, one reiterated through its role in the public myth and in national commemoration. The American Revolution drew on the "Glorious Revolution" in Britain in 1688–9, which had led to the overthrow of Stuart autocracy, there and in the colonies, including in North America where it brought the would-be centralization of the Dominion of New England (1686–9) to an end. However, the established conservative practice and language of looking back for validation and inspiration was superseded with this Declaration. That was due to the combination of the radical intent seen with republicanism and the revolutionary context of the long war that would likely result. Whereas the Glorious Revolution (much like the earlier Dutch Revolt against Philip II of Spain in the late sixteenth century) had seen a turn to another monarch or monarchical figure (William III of Orange in 1689, the Duke of Alençon, and William of Orange in the late sixteenth century), this was not the case with the American Revolution. Instead, it followed the course of republicanism. This, indeed, helped affirm the radicalism of the Revolution for it represented a rejection of the ideological heritage from the seventeenth century. Republicanism had been the reality in England and therefore its American colonies from 1649 to 1660, but the experience of the Interregnum had helped discredit republicanism in the British world. The Declaration was therefore more radical in intention and impact than might be assumed from the perspective of the present.

Yet in the short term, the most important political decision was probably that of George III to dispatch a large expeditionary force, indeed the largest hitherto sent across the Atlantic. A total of 32,000 men were landed on Loyalist Staten Island[1] beginning on 2 July. The British army benefited from the German troops made available through subsidy treaties that survived an Opposition parliamentary assault in March.[2] The most prominent and well-known are "the Hessians," troops from Hesse-Cassel, although there were also troops from Hesse-Hanau. Other German principalities providing troops were Brunswick, Waldeck, Ansbach-Bayreuth, and Anhalt-Zerbst.

To George, this deployment reflected a belief that only force could resolve the matter and that force must do so. For George, a firm response to domestic rebellion was a matter of duty as well as geopolitical necessity. His feeling of duty had religious undertones in terms of his sense of responsibility toward God as well. This was an attitude that would later emerge in his protracted opposition to Catholic Emancipation, an opposition that also had deleterious consequences for British politics and the British empire. Providence was for George a reality and so it is not helpful to see strategy simply as a secular process or to assess it as such.

His attitudes did not ease subsequently. Firmness, not animosity, was the key, and commenting in October on a draft of the royal speech opening a parliamentary session, George writes: "Notes of triumph would not have been proper when the successes are against subjects not a foreign foe." Yet, in the same letter, he presented Patriot privateers as pirates, a group treated harshly as criminals, and shortly before he suggested that Patriot prisoners might beneficially be sent to India (an unhealthy destination). This was a commitment to the empire that revealed a lack of empathy.[3]

The year 1776 saw the most radical shifts in fortune of any year in the war, and it is understandable that it attracts considerable attention from commentators and has been extensively memorialized. This was the year, among other items, of the Declaration of Independence, the battle of Long Island, the fall of New Yok, of Washington's resolute crossing of the Delaware, and his victory at Trenton. And there was much more.

The year began with impasse outside both Boston and Quebec. The Patriots outside Boston suffered from a lack of funds and gunpowder, the British garrison from a shortage of food and firewood, and Patriot privateers hit British supply ships. Fearing that his numbers would fall as enlistments expired, Washington pressed in September and October for attacks on the city, but his officers successfully urged caution, a result that would be repeated in February. The siege was resolved by the movement forward on 5 March of Patriot cannon, seized at Ticonderoga and brought thence in a difficult winter operation. Moved to near Boston, these cannons challenged the safety of British warships and led to British withdrawal on 17 March once the wind became favorable. Many Loyalists left with the troops. The Boston presence was a total failure, one that was not to be reversed.

In contrast, in Quebec, British forces held out until relief came from the navy, the varied capabilities, fortunes, and consequences of which emerged as a key element in 1776. This was also seen that year in British failure at Charleston, but then success at New York. The failure at Charleston was scarcely on the scale of those at Saratoga (1777) and Yorktown (1781), and it is easily forgotten due to a concentration on more prominent battles. Yet Charleston in 1776 was important as the first major clash in the South and erupted when the Revolution was not yet consolidated. In the event, a poorly prepared strike at an island fortress on 28 June failed and with heavier casualties. Sullivan's Island, a sandspit that protected the harbor, had a fort with 16 feet earth walls faced by palmetto logs and protected by well-aimed cannon. That underlined the difficulty of such naval/amphibious attacks, a key factor in the failure of the Union assault on Confederate-held Charleston in 1863. In 1776, in contrast, the British landings on Staten and Long Islands were not contested. They reflected the value of British naval strength that extended to the firepower of the warships present.

One loose basis for contextual reflection is provided by the similarities and differences between the War of Independence (1775–83), the First English Civil War (1642–6) (which was far from the first civil war in England), and the French Revolutionary Wars (1792–1802). Each led to the establishment and securing of a revolution, with republics resulting in 1776, 1649, and 1792, respectively. Each also has instructive military history in which the victory of the revolutionary side has been presented in terms of successful military innovation, as if the latter ensured the former. That is an implicit or explicit basis for much of the discussion of the war, as if innovation explained outcomes. It is, however, a misleading approach, conceptually, methodologically, and empirically.

Nevertheless, even if there was no revolution in weaponry, formations, or tactics, the Continental Army, like both the New Model Army eventually established on the Parliamentary side in the First English Civil War, and the republican army of the French Revolutionary Wars, had to create and struggle toward an organization, process, and rationale that could survive early disappointments. These armies served as the expression of the political thrust of the revolution, as well as providing its force. Comparison between the wars can be both by years of the conflict, as in what happened in the third year of each (for example), diachronically (across the respective chronologies), and overall. There were naturally major differences between the wars, but some elements, such as foreign intervention, reward careful consideration. In the case of the First English Civil War, this was the Scots in 1644 on the Parliamentary side and in the War of Independence that of the French in 1778. In contrast, the French Revolutionaries did not win comparable international support, including from the Americans. Instead, foreign intervention was directed against them.

The year 1776 was similar to 1643 and 1793 in that all the participants in these second years of conflict were afforded opportunities to make plans and preparations that were different in scale and timing to the rush of circumstances in the opening year of these wars, and also had the need to do so. Moreover, these plans and preparations had to take note of the respective capabilities of opponents, and of the developing circumstances of the conflicts, circumstances that were inherently unexpected. There was the need to understand opposing capabilities in new and unexpected circumstances, and to plan operations accordingly.

In 1776, British amphibious capability did not make the destination of an expedition at all clear, not least because there was no central point of the Revolution comparable to that which was to be provided by the Continental Army. Furthermore, it was unclear how far and with what force it would be necessary to respond to developments in Canada. There was a parallel to the issues that Britain had faced on previous occasions when mounting amphibious operations in conflict with Spain and/or France. Capability did not dictate nor enable implementation, and there was often a serious lack of realism. Sir Henry Clinton, sent in command of an expedition against Charleston, complained about his instructions: "It is expected that after I had (with less than 2,000 men) reinstated government in the four Southern provinces, I was to join the Commander in Chief [Howe] early in the Spring" at a great distance.[4] In the event, the attack on Sullivan's Island, not launched until 28 June, was a failure, and a serious strategic mistake.

Tasking and prioritization, notably in amphibious operations, were not issues that were not novel in the case of the American Revolution. In some respects, the American case was harder for Britain as there was no comparison to the issues and vulnerability of imperial articulation posed by the French and Spanish empires. On the other hand, the North American colonies were more exposed to amphibious attack than France or Spain. There were also comparisons in that the amphibious operations did not necessarily match in practice with their theoretical capabilities.

From 1775, ideas for targets were offered for a host of reasons. Thus, George III argued in favor of an expedition to North Carolina as the Scottish settlers there were believed to be favorably inclined.[5] This was an instance of the more general tendency to mix, in a non-systematic fashion, military and political factors, something understandable in a counter-insurgency struggle that was also a civil war. It has been argued that the British exaggerated Southern Loyalism, ensuring that their southern strategy, then and subsequently, and other strategies were inherently flawed irrespective of their execution.[6] This is an interpretation that was to be vindicated by the course of the conflict. Yet, that itself is not a reason to hold that the strategy was misinformed. It did not work out, and contingent circumstances as well as the strength of the Patriot opposition played a major role in this.

It is also important to link specific strategic and operational choices in the American war, as well as the overall British strategy to the more general nature and context of British strategic culture. Without army conscription, with a significant need for manpower for the navy, and with only a modest population, Britain repeatedly had looked to allied manpower and the American war was no exception. It entailed a significant use of German troops as well as a search for Loyalist and Native American support.

After its evacuation in March, Boston was not an attractive destination for an attempted British return, not only because of the tactical problems posed by the site, which, indeed, was not to be the target of subsequent British plans (in this war or that of 1812), but also as it was no longer clear how success there was going to affect the situation elsewhere.

Patriot expectations of British attack helped make New York the key focus of the campaign. In part, this reflected the British ability to act there. Under the command of Sir William Howe, they were able to land unopposed on Staten Island and, on 22 August, at Gravesend Bay, Long Island. Having arrived at Staten Island, Howe, in light of his belief that the Patriots were numerous, strongly entrenched and with plentiful cannon, had decided not to attack New York until his army was strengthened by the arrival of Clinton's men from South Carolina and by more troops from London. Better intelligence would have encouraged a bolder course. Washington's correspondence indicated his acute concern with British moves and the weakness of his army. Colonel James Clinton wrote from Fort Constitution on 13 July: "We want more officers of the artillery here very much [...] we are scarce of gun flints and good arms." Washington commented on 8 August that his army was "weak" and heavily outnumbered, and in another letter added, "I cannot help feeling very anxious apprehensions. The new levies are so incomplete, the old regiments deficient in their complement."[7]

More generally, New York, which Washington saw as the likely target once the British withdrew from Boston, was impossible to hold with the forces Washington possessed, and when facing the power of the Royal Navy. In a typical instance of the problems of lacking the initiative, Washington, who moved from Boston for New York on 4 April, placed his forces all over the large harbor area, each section too small to do anything other than attempt to hinder a landing. Moreover, he could not necessarily concentrate his forces, although he did achieve a significant concentration on Long Island. Washington, however, failed to carry out an effective study of the terrain there.

The British faced difficult circumstances, but there were no new weapons that might make British war-making redundant. One was tried and, had it worked, it would have changed the war, neutralizing British naval power; but the submarine could not yet fulfill its potential: The dependence on human energy for movement, and on staying partially above the surface for oxygen, made it only an intimation of the submarine of the future. Submarines would need stored air, powered movement, and detachable torpedoes in order to become a threat.

However, as an instance of a classic problem with amphibious operations, the operational opportunities of the New York area for the British and their amphibious capability proved difficult to translate into practice once the British forces had moved ashore. This was to be found at the battle of Long Island on 27 August, a battle the British won. This was no Bunker Hill, not least because it was a manoeuvrist battle, and one that thereby repaid command skills as well as combat flexibility. Reflecting a lack of intelligence, the Patriot failure to guard Jamaica Pass on the left of their line was discovered by Sir Henry Clinton and exploited by the British, who outflanked the seriously outnumbered Patriots, while the left of the British army engaged and sought to fix the Patriot front (the deployment also used with success by William III at the Battle of the Boyne in 1690 and by the British again at Brandywine in 1777). William Congreve, a British artillery officer, observed of Long Island:

> I found the enemy numerous and supported by 6-pounders [cannon]. However, by plying them smartly with grapeshot their guns were soon drawn off but the riflemen being covered by trees and large stones had very much the advantage of us, who were upon the open ground [...] [had] not the light infantry of the Guards [...] come up in time I believe we should all have been cut off.[8]

The Patriots on the front mounted a rearguard action, but were captured or dispersed as their main force fell back on positions on Brooklyn Heights. The British, exhausted after the battle, did not force these on 28 March, which may have been a serious mistake. But, the British lacked cavalry, the usual arm for exploiting retreat by opponents, for example at Waterloo. Moreover, mindful of heavy casualties at Bunker Hill, Howe was unwilling to lose troops when, as soon as the winds abated, his brother, Admiral Howe, could bring his fleet up the East River and cut the Americans off. In fact, when the wind abated, a fog rolled in and even as the British fleet was lifting anchor preparatory to sailing Washington used the cover of the fog to row his men across the river to Manhattan. Washington was able to retreat on the night of 29–30 April across the East River to Manhattan because British warships had not moved into these waters, which raises the question of what would have happened had they done so and, indeed, leads to questions about the attitudes and intentions of the British commanders.[9] The 9,000 Patriots withdrew without loss of life, which was very rare in the case of withdrawal across bodies of water.

Once defeated at Long Island, the Patriot position on Manhattan was exposed, but the bold proposal for a landing in the south Bronx, followed by an advance to cut off Washington's escape route from New York, was rejected by the cautious British commanders. In one light, they never made full use of their combined capability. Yet, it was understandable that there was a tendency to land in front or at the flank of Patriot positions rather than behind them. The latter threatened to leave the force isolated and exposed, and not least if the wind shifted, a point that modern commentators often neglect. On 31 August, Washington wrote, "I am much hurried and engaged in arranging and making new dispositions of our forces," but British naval power left Patriot position warfare vulnerable.

The potential impact of amphibious attack was noted by Captain William Leslie of the 17th Foot who describes the landing on 15 September of about 4,000 troops at Kips Bay, near the site of the modern United Nations (the details of the topography have changed with subsequent developments):

> We landed under cover of the shipping, without opposition, although the Rebels [mostly Connecticut militia] might have made a very great defence as they had high grounds, woods, and strong breastworks to cover them, but they scoured off in thousands when the ships began to fire.[10]

Washington commented next day:

> I found the troops that had been posted in the lines retreating with the utmost precipitation and those ordered to support them […] flying in every direction and in the greatest confusion, notwithstanding the exertions of their generals to form them. I used every means in my power to rally and get them into some order but my attempts were fruitless and ineffectual.[11]

That day, at Harlem Heights, the Patriots put up stiffer resistance and were able to mount an effective resistance, but the British on Manhattan retained the initiative. On 18 September, worried at the prospect of a British breakout, Washington wrote of Howe:

> Whither his operations may be directed is uncertain—perhaps an irruption into the Jerseys—possibly he may bend his course towards Philadelphia (for I conceive that 2,000 men with the assistance of their shipping will effectually preserve New York against our whole strength […].

The Patriot abandonment of New York City was followed by the burning down of about a fifth of the city on 22 September, probably as a result of arson and maybe condoned by Washington in order to deny the British shelter,[12] although there is no evidence that Washington (who certainly greeted the news of the fire) in fact ordered it. The uncertainty prefigures that regarding the burning of Moscow after Napoleon seized it in 1812, but the damage in 1776 was less widespread and the consequences very different: Napoleon, in an exposed position, abandoned Moscow whereas Howe retained New York.

With many troops deserting,[13] Washington's army was under great pressure, with a lack of supplies in late October leading him to fear mutiny: "We want both flour and beef […] the fatal consequences attendant on mutiny and plunder must ensure […]. I will do the best I can, and leave the rest to the supreme direction of events."

At White Plains on 28 October, the British exploited Washington's retreat by inflicting a fresh defeat, one in which the Hessians made a major contribution. This provided the basis for further success at Fort

Washington. Yet the Continental Army had displayed continued resilience. It had not collapsed in failure.

More generally, the British anticipated in 1776 that one of their armies would clear Canada and then link up with another that would land in New York, exploiting naval strength and amphibious capability. This would cut off that hotbed of disaffection and sedition—namely, New England—from what was seen in Britain as the more loyal middle and southern colonies. This strategy might appear relatively sound had there been energetic commanders and boldness of execution, but both in Canada and in New York there was a professional caution.[14] The opposition was weak. Washington's army had dissolved in the late summer of 1775, and, having reassembled, dissolved again that winter outside Boston.

In military terms, the successful quelling of the rebellion required rapidity of movement, flexibility of action, and boldness of execution. Indeed, 1776 was a year of British attacks—the Southern expedition that culminated in the unsuccessful strike at Charleston; the relief of Quebec and the subsequent clearing of Canada; and operations in the New York area. The last two were significant achievements, but neither was as conclusive as had been hoped. Defeats were inflicted on the Patriots and territory was gained, but there was no decisive blow, in part because Washington proved successful in retreating, such as after both Long Island and White Plains. In truth, sequential success was never easy to arrange. The Charleston expedition had been designed as a prelude to that against New York, but there was no such sequence.

Politically, the year was bad for the British. Patriot resolve stiffened and independence was declared on 4 July. This was necessary if foreign alliances were to be made. This led Richard Henry Lee to move, on 7 June, that Congress declare independence, seek such alliances, and unite by adopting a Constitution. Hesitation in the middle colonies, including opposition by some prominent politicians such as John Dickinson from Pennsylvania, caused delay. The measure was finally passed on 2 July, although New York still abstained. The text was approved two days later. This measure made it possible for some, for example prominent Lutherans, who argued that they owed loyalty to duly constituted authority, to switch to the revolutionary cause. The Declaration also signaled to actual and potential foreign supporters that there was a considerable degree of resolve and that the struggle would be sustained.

Contributing to this, Congress slowly became better prepared to wage war, a Board of War and Ordnance being instituted on 12 June, while Congress voted to raise an army of 75,000 men. This was an ambitious goal but one apparently made necessary by British moves. Yet "better prepared" is a judgment that must come with many caveats. It is easy to focus on resource shortages but there were also serious institutional deficiencies as well as a political culture that was unaccustomed to the goals, methods, and practices of national mobilization. The degree to which new facilities were attempted was impressive, notably in arms manufacture but also faced many problems and could not meet requirements.[15]

The Patriots also strengthened their position at state level. The militia was used to consolidate the new revolutionary establishment and to harry or intimidate its opponents. In Pennsylvania, where radical Patriots seized power, a new Constitution destroyed the political ascendancy of the Quakers, many of whom were loyal to George III.

Patriot activism also challenged the British attempt to retain a presence in or near ports in order to obtain supplies, a method followed for example at New York, Norfolk, Sullivan's Island, and the Savannah River. This was also a way to retain links with Americans, notably Loyalists and neutrals, and to exchange specie for fresh produce. However, in 1776, these expedients were brought to an end by force and intimidation.[16]

The principal Loyalist initiative in the Thirteen Colonies, an uprising in North Carolina, was defeated by the North Carolina militia at the battle of Moore's Creek Bridge fought near Wilmington on 27 February. The Loyalists had planned to link with British regulars who landed at the coast, which, again, was the crucial area of operations. The battle centered on control over a bridge, and the attacking Loyalists swordsmen were shot down by Patriot musketeers. The Loyalists then broke and fled, but many were captured. This battle proved crucial for the fate of the Revolution in North Carolina, wrecking Loyalist support and morale. Thereafter, there was only limited Loyalist activity there. At the same time, support for the Patriots, including in North Carolina, especially from 1779, was to be compromised by the burdens of supporting the struggle—notably, impressment and conscription.[17]

In Canada, the Patriot army had faced the consequences of their weak military system. Their force was affected by expiring enlistments, poor discipline, a shortage of provisions, powder and money, and a lack of support from the local population, some supporters of the Patriots, more hostile to the so-called *Bostonnais*, and many neutralists yet swayed by the conduct of the combatants.[18] Without hard cash, the Patriots were forced to issue a proclamation declaring that those who would not receive their paper currency as an equivalent were enemies, a measure that lost them Canadian support (of which they had little to begin with). This factor helped underline the importance of the provision of bullion from France and Spain. The British equivalent was the availability of bullion from the Portuguese colony of Brazil. Both reflected the significance of Atlantic trade.

The Patriot army in Canada was also greatly affected by smallpox, lessening the chance of an effective attack on Quebec. Whereas British forces benefited from inoculation and immunity, the Patriots were at a major disadvantage. In contrast, later in the war, Washington's great care to limit smallpox, not least by encouraging from 1777 onward a large-scale inoculation, was important to the effectiveness of his forces, especially in 1780–1. Accusations that the British army deliberately spread smallpox are of limited value.[19]

When the St. Lawrence ice broke in May 1776, a British relieving force reached Quebec. The Patriots were defeated the following month at Trois Rivieres, which broke their will to remain in Canada. It was one of the most important battles in the war, although one that is underrated in the standard discussion of the war, both by Americans and the British.

The Patriots then fell back southward. This ended the Patriot's best chance to conquer Canada. Fresh attempts were to be suggested, not least by Canadian emigres, such as the Massachusetts-born Moses Hazen. However, invasion plans were not followed through for a variety of reasons, including the logistical difficulties of operating in this largely forested region, a lack of French support (which markedly and understandably contrasted with the French attitude in the Caribbean,) and, crucially, more pressing opportunities and problems for the Patriots in the Thirteen Colonies.

Militarily, indeed, the Patriots benefited from being driven from Canada, both in general and with specific reference to the campaigning of 1776–7. Extended lines of communication and supply, and the commitment of manpower required, would have bled the Continental Army dry. Without Canada, the Patriots maintained their advantage of interior lines, and this was important in responding to the British offensives in 1776 and 1777.

British success in Canada and New York might have snowballed. The Patriot attack on the British camp at Trois Rivières on 8 June had certainly suggested a significant difference in fighting quality:

> About 4 in the morning an alarm was given by an outpiquet of the approach of a strong body of the enemy [...] soon after the alarm was given a few shots were heard from one of our armed vessels that was stationed a small way above the village who fired on part of the enemy advancing between the skirts of the wood and the river. In the meantime the troops on shore were ordered to line every avenue from the village to the wood, and take post in the best manner possible [...]. About 5 o'clock strong advanced parties were sent towards the wood, where they discovered the enemy marching down in three columns, who immediately began a heavy fire with small arms, which was instantly returned. In the meantime, a strong reinforcement of our troops with some field pieces arrived, which soon swept the woods, and broke their columns, the remains of which were pursued by us, as far as was prudent. The enemy from that time did nothing regular, but broken and dispersed, fired a few scattered shots, which did little execution.[20]

However, the British failed to exploit the opportunity adequately. George III, indeed, responded to General Guy Carleton's retreat toward Canada from Lake Champlain in late 1776 by suggesting that he was "too cold and not so active as might be wished."[21] Carleton defeated a Patriot squadron at the battle of Valcour Island on 11 October, with Patriot ships sunk or captured. He then occupied the fort of Crown Point lost in May

1775 and now abandoned by the Patriots. However, Carleton failed to attack Ticonderoga or sustain the position on Lake Champlain. His retreat toward Canada meant that the advance southward the following year required more territory to cross.

In the New York campaign, the British initially proved more able in sustaining success, though choices that posed issues of operational priority might well have limited the chance to deliver a stronger blow on Washington. He might have been pursued more closely after the battle of White Plains but that would have left the British with a major Patriot force at their rear at Fort Washington, at the north end of Manhattan. After the battle of White Plains, the British did not cross the Hudson to pursue Washington but returned to Manhattan, capturing Fort Washington on 16 November, with 2,837 men in the garrison surrendering after only 59 had been killed. Colonel Robert Magaw had refused to abandon the fort as he thought he could hold it, but the British assault from three sides with support from warships in the river proved rapidly successful. The "British" here included an important Hessian force that took casualties from Patriot riflemen before overcoming them, in part with a bayonet charge. Washington got away before the collapse of the Patriot defensive formations. His hope that the defenders could hold out until an overnight retreat proved abortive. The fall of the position also involved the loss of 36 pieces of artillery and led the Patriots to abandon Fort Lee three days later. This turn of events at Fort Washington revealed that British forces could handle attacks in strength against defended positions. The result, which was very different to Bunker Hill, did suggest that the lines at Brooklyn likely would have been attacked with success earlier in the year.

The British then crossed the Hudson and advanced across New Jersey, although without inflicting further defeats. Their opponents were no longer "fixed" as they had been at Fort Washington. Nevertheless, many of Washington's men returned home while Loyalists came forward in numbers. Monmouth County, New Jersey had 6,000 adult males of whom 580 provided long-term service to the Patriots and another 1,374 served in the militia, whereas 605 enlisted in Loyalist and other British units and 252 served as Loyalist irregulars.[22] This was clearly not the British versus "the Americans." The porous nature of the allegiance of many[23] provided a clear political point to conflict and benefit to victory. It was indicated anew in Newport, Rhode Island, when the British occupied it on 8 December. Many of those who chose to stay were Loyalists.

As 1776 neared its end, the question of how far the British would be able to exploit their success came to the fore. The British were hopeful that many Patriots would accept the offer of pardon made on 30 November, and their press carried reports of the strength of American Loyalism. A pessimistic tone was set by Sir George Savile, the Opposition MP for Yorkshire who had described Patriot resistance as "justifiable rebellion" in 1775. Now, he wrote to the Opposition leader, Charles, 2nd Marquess of Rockingham:

> We are not only Patriots *out of place*, but Patriots *out of the opinion of the public*. The repeated successes *hollow as I* think them, and the more *ruinous* if they are *real*, have fixed or converted 99 in 100. The cause itself wears away by rapid degrees from a question of right and wrong between *subjects*, to a war between us and a foreign nation, in which Justice is never heard, because love of one's country, which is a more favourite virtue, is on the other side. I see marks of this every where and in all ranks.[24]

Conversely, although Washington had been reinforced by Pennsylvania militia and the Philadelphia Associators, a volunteer force, the inadequate response of the New Jersey militia was discouraging. Furthermore, acute Patriot supply problems were being exacerbated by widespread demoralization which affected the Patriot cause at every level, as the new government appeared unable to stop the British and protect its supporters. Congress itself adjourned from Philadelphia, the capital of the Revolution, to Baltimore, which was far less exposed to any British advance from New Jersey. Sessions were held there from 20 December to 27 February 1777.

As an ugly side in relations, and one that reflected the stress arising from the conflict, many British and German troops perceived Americans as a whole to be rebels, and pillaging and rape were rampant, especially in northern New Jersey. As a result, some Americans who had hitherto been lukewarm toward the Patriots turned against Britain. Already, on 11 September, Edward Rutledge, a Patriot delegate at a peace conference, had told Admiral, Lord Howe, his British counterpart, that Britain would receive greater advantages by an alliance with an independent America than she had hitherto done from the colonies. That was not an approach that left anything for Loyalists, but it was one that depended on Patriot success.

The crisis in New Jersey developed rapidly and it was unclear to what it might lead. Patriots seized or destroyed all the boats on the Delaware River to prevent their opponents pressing on farther toward Philadelphia. However, that desperate step did not appear a decisive stop to combined operations, for it was assumed that the British would press on when the river froze or when rafts or pontoons could be built. Indeed, General Sir Henry Clinton had proposed sending a fleet carrying the necessary number of troops up the river.

Instead, it was Washington near the close of the year who took the initiative to display a combination of tactical flair, operational skill, and an understanding of strategic necessity. This was Washington as martial hero not administrator. He displayed the ability to confront water obstacles, with a difficult night crossing of the icy Delaware River as a prelude to the defeat of the surprised, outnumbered, and outgunned Hessian garrison at Trenton on the morning of 26 December. Most of the Hessian garrison surrendered after a short battle in which the defenders took casualties from Patriot fire and the use of the bayonet. The Hessians lost 22 dead, including all their senior officers, and had 896 men captured. This was an important and unexpected blow for the British, and one that threw them off balance, whereas enthusiasm and political support for the Patriots was sustained. The battle appeared to as a counterpart to the loss of Fort Washington.

At the same time, it was unclear what the result would be. The possibility that Trenton, which was a victory for a surprise attack, would be merely a flash in the pan, was matched by a lack of clarity on the likely consequences for British plans. The year 1776 ended in a far more unpredictable fashion than the previous year.

Given the eventual outcome of the conflict as a whole and the war in the South in particular, it is understandable that there is an emphasis on Patriot tactical flexibility. This factor contributes to a sense of inevitable outcome. Yet, it is also the case that the British varied their tactics, not least by adopting in the middle colonies a more open, less packed, two-deep line that was possible due to the relative unimportance of cavalry. At Long Island, the Hessians first advanced in skirmishing order.

This was the reality later in the South where the British made their forces more mobile. This was the case not only on the flank, as with Banastre Tarleton's infantry advancing to the battle of Waxhaws on 29 May 1780 on horseback, but also with Cornwallis's command as a whole. Eventual failure leads to an underplaying of British flexibility and mobility, as in 1778 with Clinton's successful flanking maneuver at Brandywine and Campbell's rapid capture of Savannah, in 1779 with Prevost's success in outmaneuvering and routing opponents at Briar Creek, in 1780 with the encirclement of Charleston and victory there, at Camden where the British fired accurately as they advanced, and in 1781 with Cornwallis's march across North Carolina.

Meanwhile, the French government was shifting its stance. In the spring of 1776, there was a ministerial debate between advocates of peace led by the Controller-General of Finances, Anne Robert Turgot, who pressed the importance of financial reform and the folly of spending on America, and those who saw an opportunity to defeat Britain. The debate was won by the latter.[25] On 2 May, Louis XVI agreed to provide one million livres in secret aid to the rebels. Turgot was ordered to resign ten days later, in large part due to ministerial hostility. As a key step, the new ministry began strengthening the navy. The British were swiftly made aware of the change thanks to their excellent intelligence network. By November, Stormont was convinced "that much will depend upon the continuance of success in America."[26]

# 6. 1777: THE CAPITAL OF REVOLUTION FALLS

> "They have stood out to sea again, but how far, or where, they are going remains to be known. From their entire command of the water they derive immense advantages, and distress us much by harassing and marching our troops from post to post. I wish we could fix on their destination. In such case, I should hope we would be prepared to receive them."
>
> George Washington[1]

In what was the last year of the war without foreign intervention—the last year of the pre-Bourbon stage and crucial characteristic of 1777—the British enjoyed the initiative. They had both secure naval dominance and a now-safe nearby base in Canada. The British were also clearly established in the middle colonies not only controlling New York but also nearby areas. But the likely result of using the initiative was unclear.

In particular, there was the question of the follow-up to Trenton and of the consequences of the British defeat there on 25 December 1776. It was followed by another at Princeton on 3 January when, in an escalating battle, a larger advancing force pushed back its British opponent. The British benefited from many Patriots having rifles that lacked bayonets, but the Patriots profited both from the fire of the riflemen and also from their cannon, and Washington provided keen battlefield leadership that steadied the Americans. The British were defeated with heavier casualties in what, unlike Trenton, was not a victory by surprise. A British army surgeon reported:

> [T]he 17th and 55th [regiments] were on their march from Princeton [...]. There was a rising ground which commanded the country [...]. The Americans endeavoured also to gain the rising ground and their first column reached the one side

> of it rather before the two regiments got to the other, so that just when the 17th reached the top they received the fire of this column. The 55th (who would not advance in line with the 17th in spite of Colonel Mawhood frequently calling out to Capt […] who commanded them to mind his orders and come up) as soon as they saw such a slaughter among the first rank of the 17th, immediately ran off on their commanding officer saying it was all over with the others. The 17th returned a very well-levelled fire against the provincial column and instantly leaped over some rails […] and charged them with their bayonets […] they ran off […]. Upon the whole rebel army, advancing […] retreated.[2]

These battles, however, did not prevent a possible resumption of the overland British advance on Philadelphia once the winter ended, and this reality was fully grasped by contemporaries. In contrast, there was certainly no likelihood that the Patriots would on their end advance on New York. In the meantime, there was vigorous partisan warfare in New Jersey, with the militia active in combat with British regulars and Loyalists. Washington's force had taken winter quarters at Morristown, New Jersey, in conditions of considerable discomfort. Yet Washington benefited greatly from the partisan warfare and from the absence of a British spring offensive.

The far greater chance of a British advance on Philadelphia than a Patriot one on New York indicated a fundamental operational asymmetry between the two sides that resembled those in strategy and resources. The pressures of taxation were certainly heavy in Britain. In May, Charles Mellish MP wrote from Nottinghamshire to his patron, Henry, 2nd Duke of Newcastle (cousin and supporter of Sir Henry Clinton), "This county is weeping over the tax upon bricks,"[3] the basic building material. Yet, Britain had an institutional system and political practice that could turn resources into revenue, whereas the Patriots found it difficult to match this capability, either in resources or in administrative structure. Arthur Duff, a government MP, wrote to his sister-in-law on 23 January: "The tide is much turned against the Americans, and they seem now to have as few friends out the House [of Commons] as in it."[4]

North complained to his father in August that the summer had been very difficult and that he was "almost worn out with continual fretting,"[5] but, in practice, Parliament was readily managed.[6]

The political situation in America had changed greatly in recent months, and that both underlined and increased the volatility of the struggle. The failure of the meeting on Staten Island on 11 September 1776 between the representatives of both sides (Admiral Lord Howe, John Adams, who said he was no longer a British subject, Benjamin Franklin, and Edward Rutledge), with independence proving a fundamental stumbling block, had triggered the British landing on Manhattan. However, this failure did not mean that future negotiations were impossible, but simply that a major shift in success would be necessary before a productive resumption was likely. This put the focus on the fate of Philadelphia, the capture of which was seen by Howe as likely to change American opinion, hitting the morale and cohesion of the Patriots and strengthening the resolve of the Loyalists.

Responding to Chatham's attack in the House of Lords on government policy in May 1777, George represented the Patriots in terms of the sin of pride and, underlining his preference for consistency over flexibility, linked the maintenance of authority in America to that in Britain:

> [L]ike most of the other productions of that extraordinary brain, it contains nothing but specious words and malevolence, for no one that reads it, if unacquainted with the conduct of the Mother Country and its colonies, must but suppose the Americans poor mild persons who after unheard of and repeated grievances had no choice but slavery or the sword, whilst the truth is that the too great leniency of this country increased their pride and encouraged them to rebel; but thank God the nation does not see the unhappy contest through his mirror; if his sentiments were adopted, I should not esteem my situation in this country as a very dignified one [...].[7]

For in this case policy would move in a parliamentary direction.

In the short-term, the political direction which had moved in the

British direction in late 1776 was shifted with the British abandonment of New Jersey in early 1777. The local Loyalists were hit hard, compromising future chances of winning Loyalist support in the middle colonies. Both sides understood that it was necessary to win civilian backing, in part because there was no real divide between civilians and the military. Instead, such backing was a major resource for the latter. Lord George Germain, Secretary of State for America, indeed wrote to Sir William Howe in May expressing the hope that that year's campaign would end the war:

> I am extremely concerned to find that you do not imagine your force to be as suitable to the operations of the ensuing campaign as you confess it was to those of the last: My concern is however in a great degree diminished by the intelligence which we daily receive of the rebels finding the utmost difficulty in raising an army.

This was a commonplace government attitude. It was based on accurate information but also reflected an overly optimistic assessment of the likely context and consequences.

Germain continued his instructions by envisaging a multilayered military. He anticipated that Howe's success "will enable you to raise from among them such a force as may be sufficient for the interior defense of the province, and leave the army at liberty to proceed to offensive operations."[8] This, however, was to be an outcome that the Patriots proved more successful in pursuing.

Howe in May decided to move on Philadelphia by sea, but delayed in June as he tried to engage Washington in northern New Jersey only to find Washington understandably reluctant to fight Howe's army as a whole and so close to Howe's main base. Moreover, the winter had exhausted the Continental Army.

Howe, in turn, left New York once he heard that Burgoyne, advancing from Canada, had taken Ticonderoga—a move indicating Burgoyne's likely success—that also pleased George. Concerned that an overland advance on Philadelphia would involve the difficulties of a crossing of the Delaware, both resistance and the securing of necessary shipping, Howe then turned to an amphibious campaign, only to be delayed by contrary winds, although these were less stormy than those in the Atlantic in early 1776. Sailing from New York on 23 July, the British did not weather the Virginia Capes until 17 August nor land at Head of Elk (modern Elkton) until 25 August, and they thereby lost the initiative. There was no swiftness comparable to that in 1781 when the Patriots and French moved rapidly to concentrate their forces at Yorktown. Instead, the British delay in 1777 prefigured similar events in 1956 when moving against Egypt in the Suez Crisis.

On 3 September, Howe, advancing from Head of Elk, drove back a Patriot advanced light force at Cooch's Bridge. Washington was convinced that an advance on Philadelphia via Wilmington was imminent, but Howe moved more slowly into Pennsylvania. Howe was mindful of the uncertainty of Patriot response. He also hoped to win Loyalist support in Pennsylvania as well as to acquire supplies from its agrarian riches. The two were linked in the British official's mind. Washington meanwhile was able to deploy in a blocking stance behind Brandywine Creek to protect Philadelphia.

This could have been a parallel to the Patriot defensive position against the British advance from Canada. However, both battlespace and context were very different and Burgoyne had fewer troops. Brandywine could also have been a precursor to the successful use of blocking moves against Confederate advances in 1862 and 1863, resulting in battles at Antietam and Gettysburg. However, in the event, Washington's army was outflanked at Brandywine on 11 September, much like he had been at Long Island the previous year. The British success in reading the possibilities of the Patriot deployment was magnified by the inadequate intelligence, lack of coordinated command practice, absence of standard training, flawed communications, and absence of grip, all of which characterized too many of the Patriot soldiers. Their retreat was in part disorderly but was covered well enough to avoid a rout. Nevertheless, the Patriots suffered about 1,300 casualties compared to about 600 British.[9] This is not a ratio that was characteristic of battles fought to overcome a defensive position.

Defeat at Brandywine was particularly problematic because of the many difficulties already facing the Patriot forces—not least desertion, expiring enlistments, supply problems, and weak garrisons.[10] Howe entered Philadelphia on 26 September. (There was no fighting in cities as there would be when Buenos Aires was successfully defended by local forces against British attack in 1807.)

Later in the campaign, British warships supported troops in capturing Forts Mifflin and Mercer that blocked the advance along the Delaware River to Philadelphia. However, this was only after an attack on the first had been defeated, on 22 October, with heavy casualties due to fire from the fort and its supporting ships.[11] British success led to the scuttling of Continental Navy ships to prevent British seizure.

The capture of Philadelphia was to be an operational rather than a strategic or political success for the British, in part due to the poorness of execution of the total plan, but also as a consequence of its overall deficiencies. This is a topic that has received much attention from scholars, in part because it is regarded as crucial to Britain's overall failure, and the main themes in the analysis are well-established. These are both apparent, but it is also true that they altered as the year passed and factors of timing are important in the criticism. These also relate to the ability of Germain and his colleagues to incorporate information and adapt their ideas in light of it. Prior assumptions were part of the equation of decision-making but there was also a desire to leave relevant decisions to commanders in theatre. This, however, posed serious problems.

Operating in conjunction, as intended by Germain, the two major field British forces (under Howe and John Burgoyne) might have been able to wreck their Patriot opponents, to gain control of the middle colonies, and isolate New England. Instead, with both generals essentially autonomous in a campaign that was far from micro-managed,[12] the forces operated on external lines without providing any form of mutual support, a situation accentuated by the inherent difficulties of operating both offshore and onshore, difficulties ranging from adverse winds to "wilderness terrain."

Similar terrain posed a problem for Clinton in advancing from New York into the Highlands: "The many, and I may say extraordinary difficulties of this march over the mountains, every natural obstruction; and all that art could invent to add to them."[13] Clinton was greatly helped by warships on the Hudson, but for Burgoyne this terrain prevented the movement forward of heavy cannon or of sufficient light guns, and these took away a potential ability to overcome Patriot defenses. As such, the British suffered when they moved away from coastal waters where they could use naval artillery.

For Burgoyne, a "human terrain" of insufficient supplies and an absence of reliable popular support were also major problems, with both Burgoyne and Howe overestimating the likely number of Loyalists. There was to be a similar issue with British intervention in France during the French Revolutionary War in the 1790s.

The views of the local population were a particular issue for Burgoyne, whose force depleted by casualties and leaving troops in posts to protect his communications, nevertheless, continued to move southward. In part, this was because in its dire logistical situation it had to advance or retreat. The first was risky but in accordance with Burgoyne's instructions, while the second was also risky, albeit less so and would entail a failure to contribute to the goals of the campaign.

The advance was difficult even without the serious resistance that the British eventually faced. Had it been at Ticonderoga there would have been a chance to cut the Patriots off and inflict a serious defeat[14] but, instead, the Patriots fought farther south where they were in a far better position. This resistance contributed to a tactical nightmare both for Burgoyne and for the unsuccessful supporting drive under Lieutenant-Colonel Barry into the Mohawk valley on Fort Stanwix (now Rome, New York) in August. Failure there—in part due to inadequate artillery and the advance of a Patriot relief force—led Barry St. Leger to fall back. Seeking supplies, another subsidiary British force aiming for Bennington, Vermont was seriously defeated by a New Hampshire militia on 16 August.

For Burgoyne there were failures on 19 September and 7 October to drive in well-defended Patriot positions that benefited from the use of riflemen, as well as skirmishing between the two battles. With a retreat blocked by the Patriots, the British force (5,895 strong) surrendered at Saratoga (now Schuylerville) on 17 October. A well-trained force could only achieve so much, especially if on difficult terrain, in the face of considerably more numerous opponents and with inadequate reconnaissance. Most of the fighting on the Patriot side was done by men detached from Washington's army who provided battlefield experience, but they were enabled to stand and fight because of the large number of militia who had rallied to their support. Patriot fighting quality was enhanced by the skillful use of appropriate field fortifications.[15] This was a major success prior to French entry into the war and one won, unlike Yorktown in 1781, only by Patriots. Moreover, this was victory without Steuben and training under him and others at Valley Forge. Hugh Elliot, envoy in Berlin, who had served with the Russian army against the Turks, criticized Burgoyne for a lack of grip and his command:

> […] to remain in an entrenched camp from the 20th of September to the 7th of October, without secure magazines, to let the Rebels throw up entrenchments at their leisure in every pass through which he could retreat.

Surrendering the cannon aroused Elliot's particular ire and he suggested that Burgoyne should have "burst his cannon, destroyed his stores, and either sought to fight his way through sword in hand or surrendered."[16]

A defensive success of this type helped stop the British from creating the impression of victory, thereby counteracting the impact of the loss of Philadelphia. Howe's focus on this latter task ensured that he was unable, as Germain wished and as Howe had originally envisaged, to help Burgoyne by advancing early and in strength up the Hudson to meet Burgoyne at Albany—or, at the very least, to reduce pressure on him to the north. The advance that was eventually made northward from New York was not by Howe and came too late to help Burgoyne. This prefigured the delayed preparation of a second naval attempt to relieve Cornwallis at Yorktown in 1781. The 1777 advance north from New York had some specific successes but their timing, range, and scale did not match needs.

Focusing on counterfactuals, it is worth considering what might have happened had the British forces met at Albany, as Clinton hoped as late as October,[17] or, more modestly, if Burgoyne had avoided defeat at Saratoga. Although, the latter entails considering the alternatives of his not advancing so far and, separately, his doing so but avoiding defeat in the series of battles summarized as Saratoga. As Clinton pointed out, the advance from New York was risky as he did not know where Washington was while the British would have to garrison the communications between New York and Albany.[18]

After Saratoga, the northern frontier remained disturbed, not least with conflict between Loyalists and Patriots.[19] Ticonderoga was evacuated from 6 November as the British garrison withdrew to Canadian winter-quarters. However, thereafter, although there was much violence, as well as significant raids, for example by British forces in 1780 and 1781,[20] there were to be no major advances northward by Patriots or southward by British forces until the War of 1812. Nor were the British able to exploit the situation and cooperate effectively with the Native Americans. British forces in Canada were affected by crop failures in 1779–80 and by a lack of sufficient supplies from Britain, and this precluded a concentration in strength. On the other hand, there was yet no French intervention.[21]

Despite Saratoga, there was the need on the Patriots' side for offensive successes to stop the British from mounting renewed attacks, and protection of citizens and supply sources. There was also the need to regain the capital and interrupt the perception of cumulative British achievement. As in 1776, the viability and legitimacy of the Patriot government appeared to be greatly challenged.

Washington mounted a counter-attack on Howe in Philadelphia, which led to a battle at Germantown on 4 October. With a larger force his attacking columns pushed the British hard, but, in the confusion of a thick fog and in the face of a strong resistance that prefigured another fog attack, Inkerman in 1854 failed to defeat them. It was no Trenton. The poorly coordinated Patriot columns were driven back and their casualties were heavier (although Washington preferred to blame the fog for failure).[22]

Not in a position to drive the British from Philadelphia, or to blockade them and repeat Saratoga,[23] the Patriots were obliged to take winter shelter elsewhere. Being within striking distance of Philadelphia would protect Pennsylvania's agrarian resources from British attack as well as offer some security to Congress, now in New York. Washington agreed to winter at Valley Forge from where he pressed Congress to provide assistance in part by emphasizing, and to a degree exaggerating, the plight of the army. At the same time, the leadership and reforms that helped the Patriot army survive the difficult conditions of the winter of 1777–8 counted as a key element in helping lead to eventual success. Defeat at Brandywine lent force to the need to standardize army doctrine and practice, a process linked to the role at Valley Forge of Baron von Steuben.[24]

This result, however, simply highlighted the lack on the British part of strategic execution as their operational success in and near Philadelphia had been countered by Saratoga, while even the operational success was only so effective. Indeed, Clinton, a bitter critic of Howe, wrote to his cousin: "Our Chief [...] has drawn every thing to him [...] and left his humble servant with much too slender a corps for the defence of a very extensive and important command."[25] This experience possibly lay behind George's reflection in 1799 that:

> it is impossible without being on the spot and seeing the face of the country that any well grounded directions can be given, farther than pointing out what is the general object wished, but how to be effected or when must be left to those who are on the spot.[26]

Following the American war particular problems arose due to the length of time it took to receive news,[27] and the difficulty of checking its veracity speedily. This put pressure on the king and his ministers. Eager for news of campaigning,[28] George's personal familiarity with commanders and officers added to his involvement, and he also wanted news of the German contingents.[29] This represented a particular strand of his commitment, something that is easy to overlook. George's war in America was a coalition enterprise and one that brought into renewed focus the German basis of the Hanoverian dynasty. Such a coalition enterprise was scarcely new. It had been seen, for example, in the Williamite conquest of Ireland in 1689–91, which drew on Dutch and Danish troops as well as on local Protestants, and was also seen in campaigning in Scotland and Continental Europe under the Hanoverians.

Joseph Yorke had reported from The Hague in April: "[T]he Continent is certainly strongly infected with American Politicks,"[30] and this was eventually to help the Patriots. Encouraged by Patriot threats that a lack of help might force them to settle with Britain,[31] France moved closer to entering the war, although, as a reason to retain more than one narrative, Britain and France continued friendly discussions on other issues—for example, both seeking to encourage Russia and Turkey to avoid war.[32] Already, expenditure on the French navy had considerably increased and led the American Commissioners in Paris to argue that they would fix the British fleet and thus provide more opportunities for Patriot privateers[33] (although they ignored Vergennes' advice that France was not yet ready for war). Partly in return for tobacco, France sent military supplies to the Patriots, including 23,000 muskets. Other ammunition came from Spain.[34] In reference to this development, David,Viscount Stormont, the reassuring British envoy in Paris, nevertheless noted: "The behaviour of this Court to the rebels is not to be sure consistent with their professions."[35]

In June, the navy was instructed to search any French ships encountered near America. The French stepped up their naval preparations and their efforts to win Spanish support. Meanwhile, Spain provided the Patriots with gunpowder and bullion via Havana.[36] Tension with Britain over French aid to the Patriots—specifically allowing their privateers to use French ports—led Charles, Count of Vergennes, the French Foreign Minister, to press Louis XVI in the summer for French entry into the war. There was also the concern that success in America would leave Britain free to act elsewhere against French interests, for example helping Portugal against Spain.[37] However, David, Viscount Stormont, reported from Paris that Britain was unlikely to face intervention that year, which, he argued, provided an opportunity to win the war.[38]

The British responded by seeking to delay French intervention until they had won in America. The British switched in July 1777 from their earlier position of moderation to threats designed to intimidate. George was confident that if Britain acted "an open firm part," peace with France could be maintained,[39] a process that would be encouraged if the Patriots were beaten. British threats succeeded in distancing France from the Patriot privateers in August–September, but the French caution was designed to preserve peace only until the situation was deemed ripe for war, and did not preclude increased preparations.

The privateers increased British insurance rates, and George III saw them as a threat, writing to John Robinson, Secretary to the Treasury:

> I trust the different vessels that hover round the island will be put on their guard particularly to protect Liverpool, Whitehaven, the Clyde, and even Bristol, for I do suspect that the rebel vessels which have been assembling at Nantes and Bordeaux mean some strike of that kind which would undoubtedly occasion much discontent among the merchants.[40]

Separately, as a sign of anxieties and tensions in the British command, Howe sent a letter of resignation in October complaining that he had received inadequate support. His brother resigned later, not serving between September 1778 and April 1782, and both were to be criticized in Parliament in 1779.[41] The discussion in Parliament of military failure extended to Saratoga and to naval failure in 1778. It was far from limited just to this war, and indeed this would be the case in both World Wars. Opportunities for debate and criticism were far greater in the War of American Independence as there were many senior officers in both Houses of Parliament and it was regarded as normal for them to take part in debate. Those who were linked to the Opposition spoke accordingly.

On 4 December 1777, the news of Saratoga reached Paris. Two days later, the Patriot commissioners were asked to resubmit their proposal for an alliance with France. Saratoga had not only affected French attitudes. It also swallowed up British confidence,[42] and there was already great uneasiness about the struggle prior to full-scale and overt French entry into the conflict. The war had clearly not been won.

# 7. 1778: THE WAR GOES GLOBAL

> "I have no doubt next spring, Spain will join France but if we can keep her quiet till then I trust the British navy will be in a state to cope with both nations; Lord North must feel as I do the noble conduct of the three fifty gun ships that with so much bravery have driven off separately ships of far superior strength; I doubt not whenever it shall please the Almighty to permit an English fleet fairly to engage any other a most comfortable issue will arise; armed as France and Spain now are no peace could either be durable or much less expensive than a state of war [. . .]. I trust in the justness of my cause and the bravery of the nation, and you may depend on my readiness to sheath the sword whenever a permanent tranquility can be obtained which certainly the present moment is not the one for accomplishing."
>
> George III to North, 13 October[1]

On 8 January 1778, a prominent London newspaper, the *London Evening Post*, presented developments between John Bull and his divorcing wife, an American, and with Nic Frog played a role. From 1778, the war went global[2] and became bifocal. It is easy, using the title of the War of American Independence or the American Revolution, to focus on the struggles in North America—notably, for 1778, the battle of Monmouth Court House on 28 June, and the British capture of Savannah on 29 December—and to bind these disparate episodes into a common narrative and analysis of the conflict as a whole, and likewise to treat French entry as an adjunct and a contributing factor. This then becomes a context within which subsequent French operations might be considered as well, such as those involving Spain and the Dutch once they joined in the war in 1779 and 1780, respectively. From such a perspective, Spain and the Dutch can be presented as having joined on the Patriot side, whereas instead they had allied themselves with France, as is demonstrated by both the warfare and politics of the struggle.

The standard American view is a seriously misleading account, for the purposes of France, Spain, and the Dutch were not focused on helping the Patriots. The notification on 13 March 1778 of the Treaty of Commerce between France and the Patriots led to the recall of David, Viscount Stormont, the British envoy in Paris, and on 17 March, Vergennes, the French Foreign Minister, wrote to his French counterpart in London ordering him to leave.[3] Convinced of hostile British intentions, Vergennes did not see how Britain could fight the Bourbons successfully,[4] while Stormont felt obliged to emphasize "steady resolution, and manly fortitude joined to the greatest vigilance" as the necessary resources.[5] As, however, neither power wished to appear an aggressor to its allies, hostilities did not flare up until June when the struggle to control the English Channel began.

The importance to the American Revolution of the entry of other powers hinged in large part on the British reaction, and to a considerable degree this moved operations in the Thirteen Colonies into a secondary sphere. For France, the Caribbean was the prime sphere of operation in the Western Hemisphere, as it also was for Spain. Both powers had been defeated there by the British in the Seven Years' War, and each was eager to reverse this defeat (this did not appear immutable, and, indeed, was not so). The Napoleonic Wars, instead, were decisive to this process, and even then it was unclear what would have happened had Britain been left to fight alone against France onward from 1812.

The Caribbean offered wealth in the shape of plantation goods that were readily accessible and with their economies, governance, and defense dependent on island port capitals, they were particularly vulnerable to naval action. Furthermore, attack was the best form of defense, as rival bases were located in close proximity. Compared to this, the value of operating in America was more limited and the likely cost of doing so greater (rather than acting in the Caribbean). On the other hand, the Caribbean posed serious hazards in the shape of disease and hurricanes, while the density of fortifications was far greater than in America, as was their strength.

The Jacobites, whom France had supported from 1689 to 1759 when at war with Britain, had failed. They lacked strategic depth because they did not control any of the British Isles. In contrast, like Scotland when it had been independent and a French ally from the thirteenth to the sixteenth centuries, the American Patriots had this element of strategic depth, even though it was unclear what this would mean in practice. This provided them with durability and entailed (from the French perspective) a sustained diversion of British resources, both army and navy. Moreover, this was within the context of the major administrative strain of sustaining a global struggle.[6]

In particular, as in the 1730s and the early 1750s, France and Spain had put a major effort into developing their navies. As a result, Britain had lost its relative degree of naval superiority, leading Vergennes to suggest in 1775 that France and Spain when united could beat Britain.[7] That helped ensure that, for all powers, the naval dimension would be foremost in any conflict with Britain. This factor was accentuated by the slowness to mobilize the British navy and by the degree to which Britain was faced by a French–Spanish closeness even greater than in the early stages of the Seven Years' War. France and Spain would try to play to what was now their advantage, and this was even greater because neither power was simultaneously at war with another state, whereas both had been so during the Seven Years' War—France fighting Prussia (as well as resisting British coastal attacks which were not a factor in 1778–83), and Spain fighting Portugal.

In European waters, the desirability of blockading French ports, for which there were arguably too few British ships, clashed with the prudent argument of John, 4th Earl of Sandwich, the First Lord of the Admiralty, that naval strength should be concentrated in home waters. This was not only to deter invasion, but also to permit a serious challenge to the main French fleet (which was based nearby at Brest), and thus to gain a position of naval dominance—a concept understood at the time, not least in political and strategic terms. This goal would be compromised by dispersing much of the fleet among distant stations, where it might support amphibious operations and protect trade, but could not materially affect the struggle for naval dominance. Due to the state of communications technology (a situation that was to be transformed by the telegraph in the nineteenth century, but that was not to change radically until the use of radio in the early-twentieth century), the commanders of those distant stations were difficult to control effectively. These commanders jealously guarded their autonomy and resources, leading to a flexibility in dealing with local challenges, of which only they were well-informed, but then an overall inflexibility that was ill-suited to the demands of reacting to French initiatives.[8] In theory, a matching squadron could be sent from home waters in pursuit of any French or Spanish naval moves, but there was no guarantee that it would arrive in time.[9] The fierce government dispute over strategy[10] was matched by public concern for the level of naval preparedness, not least because there were no victories to ease political tension and to counter suggestions that there was only limited support for the war effort.[11]

In 1778, with supply shortages very much hitting the fleets in European waters,[12] the operational paradigm became that of keeping a close eye on Brest, although there were no invasion plans that year, and the British failed to blockade Toulon or block the Straits of Gibraltar. This left the Toulon fleet free to sail to North America, which posed major dangers for the British and led Germain to complain bitterly and demand the dispatch of ships to North America, only to be opposed by the Admiralty.

Sailing on 11 June, d'Estaing was able to reach American waters, leaving the British vulnerable in three respects. First, British forces were based on ports—New York and Newport—and if these were cut off from maritime supplies they might well be forced to surrender. Indeed, in the winter of 1775–6, the garrison in Boston had been challenged by the successful attacks of Patriot privateers on British supply ships. In a later Parliamentary hearing, General Sir William Howe, the Commander-in-Chief of British land forces in North America, was to claim:

> [T]hat had the French got to Sandy Hook, all the naval force that England could send out, could not have saved the army, who must have been starved, as the victuallers could not in that case have reached the port of New York.[13]

Secondly, army movements were by water and thereby vulnerable to naval interception, a factor conspicuously missing prior to 1778 as the Patriots lacked that capability and moved by land. In 1778, a number of important moves were made—both short distance in the case of the last stage of the retreat from Philadelphia via the New Jersey shore to New

York by General Sir Henry Clinton, Howe's replacement; and the long range, in the case of the projected detachments for St. Lucia, the Floridas, and eventually Georgia. On 19 April 1779, Admiral Lord Howe reflected in Parliament on a vulnerability that was to be further shown at Yorktown in 1781:

> He said, that the army could never have made their retreat good from Philadelphia, if D'Estaing had arrived a few days earlier; that the Delaware would have been blocked up; and that the supply of provisions being cut off, the army under Sir Henry Clinton must either have been starved or be compelled to force their way to New York under every possible disadvantage: or supposing that army might have gained New York without any considerable loss, the force under his command in the Delaware, deprived of their co-operation must have fallen into the enemy's hands.[14]

Thirdly, if a superior French fleet defeated a smaller British one, it would alter permanently not only the balance of naval advantage in American waters, but also the Anglo-French maritime balance, with possible fatal consequences for the defense of home waters.

Proposing in March 1779 a motion of censure on the government for not sending reinforcements to Admiral Lord Howe (brother to Sir William) at New York the previous year, Charles James Fox, the leading Opposition figure in the Commons, claimed that:

> [I]f Lord Howe had been reinforced, or the Streights of Gibraltar watched, in either event the net effect would be similar: that of securing to Lord Howe the full advantage of the force under his command, or giving him a superiority in case the Toulon squadron [the French Mediterranean fleet] was permitted to cross the ocean.[15]

Outnumbered, Howe had prepared in 1778 off New York for one of the frequent occasions in naval history, "the battle that did not occur." He anchored his ships so that they would be able to cannonade the French warships as they were obliged to enter the channel individually. This prefigured the strength of the French position at the mouth of the Chesapeake in the battle of the Virginia Capes in 1781. The unwelcome nature to the French of Howe's position in 1778 was compounded by the shallowness of the bar at Sandy Hook covering the approach to the harbor (a bar on which the French, who lacked adequate pilots and information, might run aground), and the deployment of British troops and cannon. Having, understandably, failed to attack, d'Estaing finally sailed away on 22 July. A week later, he appeared off Newport which an American force was preparing to attack.

However, Howe's fleet in turn approached Rhode Island on 9 August, leading d'Estaing to sail to engage. Having manoeuvred to gain the weather gauge, Howe was prevented from attacking by a storm on 11 August that damaged both fleets. D'Estaing fell back to Newport but on 29 August, in the Battle of Rhode Island, the British garrison in Newport sortieing from the besieged position supported by newly-arrived warships attacked their opponents. The hard-fought battle was followed by the separate withdrawal of the Patriot army and the French fleet. Due to adverse winds, Howe failed to intercept d'Estaing before he reached Boston. The British used their command of the sea to raid New Bedford and Martha's Vineyard, but Howe rejected Clinton's pressure for an amphibious attack on Boston aimed at destroying the French fleet,[16] a measure that would have had major strategic and political consequences. As with d'Estaing at Sandy Hook, the obvious note was of a reluctance to take chances and risk warships and crew, notably in partly unknown inshore waters. Yet, in July 1776, the British had run what were supposed to be strong Patriot batteries at the entrance to the Hudson, thus threatening the western flank of the Patriot troops on Manhattan. Moreover, in 1759, Hawke's willingness in very high winds to pursue the French fleet into shoal-strewn Quiberon Bay led to a striking victory that put paid to the risk of French invasion of Britain.

In the case of France, there was also an expeditionary force to North America that did operate, and eventually in 1781, significantly so, in the Thirteen Colonies. Alliance with France, moreover, brought the Patriots cooperation with a power that was greatly improving its artillery, as well as raising its domestic production of saltpeter, a key constituent of gunpowder. This helped Patriot supplies.[17] However, Congress's idea for a Franco-Patriot invasion of 1778 was as foolish politically as militarily. Washington opposed the scheme for military reasons but also for concern about subsequent French expansionism in the interior, notably into the Ohio Valley and along the Mississippi. This concern served as a reminder of potential tensions, but in practice the French were interested in the Caribbean.

For Spain, in contrast, the comparable force sent to North America took part in what in essence was a separate conflict—the conquest of the far-flung colony of West Florida—culminating in the capture of Pensacola in 1781. This was pursued not for the benefit of the Thirteen Colonies, but for Spain. France lacked this opportunity, in large part due to the cession of Louisiana to Spain in 1763 and because, for reasons of alliance politics, the French had not supported the rebellion in New Orleans against Spanish rule in 1768, whereas they were to back that in the Thirteen Colonies.

Commentators are therefore faced with a choice: On the one hand, that of concentrating on the war in the Thirteen Colonies but, arguably, offering a misleading account of priorities and significance; On the other, trying to address the global dimension adequately. Yet in a story that stretches from the Indian Ocean via the Mediterranean and the English Channel to the Caribbean, this latter option risks rendering the Thirteen Colonies as not so much an afterthought but rather as a bit-player in a wider struggle. Americans understandably are not inclined to see this, and the major significance for later global history of American independence encourages a focus on the war in the Thirteen Colonies.

Yet this is to anticipate the future, both the result of the conflict in 1783 and its later significance, notably after the challenge of the Civil War of 1861–5 had been overcome and the American economy had grown rapidly. Prior to the latter, in practice, it was Britain's ability to survive France and its allies from 1778 to 1815 that was of greater importance for world history. Rather than determining the agenda, the Patriots/Americans operated in the shadow of these assaults by France and its allies. Indeed, the latter helped them win independence (1783), purchase Louisiana from France (1803), and benefit from a less than outstanding war record against Britain in the War of 1812 (1812–15). For example, due to the Anglo-French struggle, the French were unable to protect New Orleans adequately and needed America's purchase money for Louisiana. America, in contrast, was in no position to force them to sell it.

At one extreme, a focus on the American dimension of the warfare in 1778–83 at the expense of non-American spheres is comparable to focusing on the War of 1812 rather than the remainder of the Napoleonic Wars. A variant would be to focus on those aspects of American warfare in 1778–83 in which the French played a key role—in short stressing Yorktown in 1781 but, prior to that, looking at Newport and Savannah. This again would be to lessen the importance of Patriot operations and, in some cases, deny them agency.

At the same time, it can be pointed out that France became willing to commit in 1778 in part due to the signs of Patriot resilience. This approach is very comforting to American perspectives of the war, with the news of Saratoga and Germantown apparently helping prompt French moves and the debate over which was most significant. Reasons can be found for both, Germantown showing resilience and a taking of the initiative after the loss of Philadelphia.

Yet, that view gives the Patriots too much agency, for they were not to the fore in French policymaking. Thus, the influential French Foreign Minister, Charles, Count of Vergennes, sought British cooperation against the partitioning powers in Eastern Europe—notably Russia.[18] There was an analogy to ideas today. Vergennes, who had served at Constantinople, the capital of Turkey (the Ottoman Empire) and was, as a result, particularly concerned about Russia, thought that a weakened Britain would be more likely to follow the French lead against Russia. This provided a very different logic for war with Britain to that offered by other ministers. In contrast, the Ministry of the Marine, under Antoine de Sartine (1774–80) and in particular Charles, Marquis de Castries (1780–7), wanted Britain weakened so that France could pursue colonial expansion, notably in the Indian Ocean and the Caribbean. Sartine had no military experience, but the very anti-British Castries had served in the army from 1739, not least in command of the expeditionary force sent to St. Lucia in 1756.

Separately, the French in 1778 were immediately challenged by the outbreak of war between their ally Austria and Prussia. Nevertheless, in

January, Vergennes had stated that France would not be distracted from America by the Bavarian crisis.[19] The French focused on war with Britain, thwarting British hopes that the Patriots would be left exposed and therefore seek reconciliation.[20]

This conflict got off to a poor start for Britain when the Brest fleet—the major French fleet—was fought off Ushant on 27 July to an indecisive draw. No ships were lost. The British, who lacked the advantage of numbers, did not need to fight the battle but there were public and political expectations that they do so. The French had sought to evade battle and thereby avoid the risk of losing their fleet, but after several days of successfully doing so a change in the wind gave opportunity for battle. The British, who failed to coordinate their attack, lost more men in the exchange of fire.[21] William, 4th Earl Fitzwilliam, a supporter of his uncle Rockingham, reflected that the battle had made Britain no more secure.[22]

This result ensured that the British were unable to defeat the French before Spain entered the war. A dissatisfied George unsuccessfully pressed for a new head of the Admiralty Board in place of John, 4th Earl of Sandwich:

> In a war and more so in the present which is a naval one, it is highly advantageous to have in the Cabinet a person able to plan the most effectual manner of conducting it.[23]

George himself was publicly committed to the navy, visiting the fleet in 1778, paying minute attention to the naval review that year, and following closely the contentious political aftermath of Ushant, a battle that divided the officer corps as blame was allocated.

The Patriot turn to France increased domestic support for war in Britain, stiffening for example the resolve of Edward Gibbon (MP as well as historian), and also hit sympathy for the Patriots, who could now be presented as hypocrites, willing to ally with a Catholic autocracy (two when Spain joined in in 1779), and with Britain's national enemy as well. Although there had been strong sympathy for the Patriot cause in Britain, there was no movement of civil disobedience and many backed the ministry, as the Norwich debate on 28 January indicated with William Windham attacking the war, but George, 4th Viscount Townshend, the

Master-General of the Ordnance, succeeding in opening a subscription very well and noting "clergy, farmers etc. in number with us."[24]

The major outbreak of violence in Britain, the Gordon Riots in London in 1780, obliged the government, directed by the angry George, to use troops to restore order (and with success), but these riots were directed against legislation favorable to Catholics, and not against the war. There were no equivalent demonstrations over the latter.

The Opposition argued not that Britain should simply devote more of its military effort to war with France, which was the government response, but rather that Britain should concentrate on reconciliation with the colonists and prepare for war with the Bourbons. This was Chatham's argument in the Lords in November and December 1777, and in his last parliamentary appearance on 7 April 1778, but the previous month George had rejected the suggestion from North for an approach to Chatham in order to weaken the Opposition: "[N]o advantage to this country nor personal danger can ever make me address myself for assistance either to Lord Chatham or any other branch of the Opposition [...] I would rather lose the Crown I now wear than bear the ignominy of possessing it under their chackles." Chatham's demands helped wreck the negotiation for a reconciliation, but so also did George's attitude.[25] George was determined to thwart negotiations unless Opposition leaders agreed to keep the empire complete, which meant refusing to yield over America. Independence was unacceptable to George who kept North in office despite much talk of his likely removal.[26]

Counterfactual speculation by parliamentary speakers and other commentators played a role, both in discussing the campaigning, notably setbacks such as Saratoga,[27] and also with reference to the probable actions of foreign powers. The possible entry of France and Spain was of great concern well in advance of their actual entry. In February, Charles, 3rd Duke of Richmond, a vocal Opposition peer, declared "he did not believe we should be precipitated into a war with France" as "he relied on the French king and the French cabinet, who he well knew were adverse to war."[28] That war in fact followed swiftly and lent impetus to calls for flexibility in goals, with Charles, 1st Earl Camden, another Opposition peer, pointing out, in February, that "ministers who had all along contended for unconditional submission" were forced to consider "plans of conciliation."[29] Charles Mellish, who was not an Opposition figure, told the Commons that the Patriots were only a minority and that alliance with France would further limit their support there, but added that if the British army in America could not "make any decisive strike" it "should be drawn off."[30]

The ministry argued, however, that once the Patriots had ports they could attack the West Indies, which would increase the risk they posed. George claimed that to give way in America would lead to the loss of other colonies, not least because Ireland and the West Indies would find it useful to follow suit, in particular due to their commercial links with America. George was clearly thinking of America when he wrote of Ireland, "Experience has thoroughly convinced me that this country gains nothing by granting to her dependencys indulgences, for opening the door encourages a desire for more which if not complied with causes discontent and the former benefit is obliterated."[31]

The 1777 campaign, and more particularly defeat at Saratoga, had been followed by a strategic re-evaluation by the British government and changing French policy gave that new content and energy.[32] The American-French treaties led the British government in 1778, newly mindful of vulnerabilities, to order the evacuation of Philadelphia, carried out on 15–18 June, and to send a large expedition, including 5,147 army "effectives"[33] from North America, that captured the Caribbean sugar island of St. Lucia. The evacuation was not necessary militarily as the British had successfully resisted a would-be Patriot blockade both by using specie to purchase supplies and by sending out foraging parties. The Continental Army proved unable to prevent either, although from Valley Forge they mounted successful foraging expeditions—notably into New Jersey, Delaware, and Maryland.[34] The conduct of the British in Philadelphia alienated some of its citizens, but the British position there really collapsed when evacuation undermined the Loyalists.[35]

Howe had been informed in April that his resignation was accepted and on 24 May he sailed for England. His successor, Clinton, formally appointed on 4 February 1778, set off from Philadelphia overland on 15–18 June in a great summer heat, often of over 32oC (90oF), and fought off the Patriot pursuers in a battle at Monmouth Court House on 28 June, an attack that due to poor intelligence the British had failed to anticipate.

Patriot hopes of a second Saratoga,[36] with the British caught before embarkation, were thwarted. This was a confused battle that divided Patriot commanders, Washington disgracing Charles Lee in the aftermath. Lee had failed in the attack on the British rearguard that began the battle, and this clash provided the British with an opportunity to move units back and to drive back the Patriot vanguard. The Patriots then stabilized their position and held off the British before gaining a stronger position by bringing forward their cannon. That the Patriots held the battlefield suggested a newfound fighting quality, but that did not extend to command cohesion, with Washington unable to shape the battle and deploying his units without a clearly articulated plan. Moreover, the Patriots held the battlefield because the British were withdrawing anyway. The overall nature of the battle does not substantiate assertions about a transformative nature of Steuben's training at Valley Forge, and suggests that the winter at Valley Forge, while it had improved the training of the troops, had not had a comparable impact on the officers.[37]

The British were able to withdraw at the close of the battle, and thwarted Washington's wish to resume the fighting the next day. The British instead continued their withdrawal to the coast and sailed thence to New York before the arrival of the French fleet. Washington, nevertheless, was widely seen by the Patriots as a hero and his position was greatly strengthened.[38]

It would be mistaken to present war against France and war in America as necessarily alternatives, most notably on the pattern of earlier British strategic debates about "Blue Water" policies as opposed to Continental ones. Instead, there was a belief in Britain that Bourbon entry linked the two conflicts, and that the Bourbon system had a cohesion, such that the application of British power at appropriate points would have a major impact. West Indies' trade was seen as a crucial source of French government revenue, thanks to the profit derived from the re-export of colonial goods in Europe and to the possibility of raising loans on this trade. Thus, for Britain to seize colonies such as St. Lucia and interrupt trade was regarded as a way of harming France's ability to wage war. This strategy had been employed against Spain, but essentially, as in 1726, to affect its ability to pursue objectives in Europe. A key element from 1778 was an attempt to affect France's ability to pursue its objectives in North America, but that also represented a wish on the part of the British ministry to give coherence to policies that lacked real alignment.

The West Indies were also important to British strategy in North America. It was one of the reasons for the focus on the South from late 1778 as it was the belief that it provided a key source of supplies for the British West Indies, and especially of food, without which the viability of the slave economy, and thus the trade, prosperity, and security of the British colonies was limited.[39] The plantation system had large demands for food due to the number of slaves and because the best land was used for plantation goods (notably sugar) and not for food production.

If, therefore, the compromise that ended the war was to lead to a partition of British North America (as indeed occurred in 1783, with Britain retaining Canada), then it was hoped that Britain might also retain South Carolina and Georgia, if not North Carolina. Moreover, such a retention would accord with the concentration of Loyalists in the region, as well as the potential to win Native American and Black support to the cause of counter-revolutionary kingship; and would also strengthen the case for holding onto East and West Florida, neither of which had rebelled.

This strategy appeared both politically and militarily viable onward from 1778.[40] Patrick Tonyn, an officer who was governor of East Florida from 1774, pressed for such action: "I am certain the four Southern provinces are incapable of making any very formidable resistance, they are not prepared for a scene of war."[41] Loyalist supporters were generally weak if not in the South, and notably so in New England and Virginia. Indeed, Loyalist activity at times represented an insurgency against Patriot dominance, as with the unsuccessful Clow Rebellion in Delaware in mid-April 1778, a reaction to Patriot foraging which was suppressed by militia. More generally, Loyalists were very harshly treated by the Patriots.[42]

So it was with Native Americans who were harried by Patriot punitive expeditions designed to protect the frontier from raids supported by British supplies. General John Sullivan's invasion of Iroquoia in 1779 proved particularly destructive but did not bring victory in battle, and Niagara and Detroit remained in British hands.[43]

Yet, a focus on the South because of limitations elsewhere was not the best basis for optimism. It was understandable that British commanders in America were less sanguine about developments. In 1778, worried that French entry meant the need for a bigger stockpile of supplies, and yet also hopeful of exploiting Patriot vulnerability,[44] Clinton, with reference to the units sent to the West Indies, complained: "All the world are witness how mortifying this command has been to me. I was promised an army complete, and a reinforcement of 12,000 British and 2,000 Germans; instead of which 9,000 are taken from me." The following February, Clinton commented on the possibility that the fall of Georgia to the British might affect South Carolina: "[T]here was a time when this operation must have been attended with every success, but that time is no more. Instead of near 36,000 men [...] I am reduced to little more than 18,000."[45] In short, the opportunities of conflict were in part set by conjuncture—notably the availability of troops. In September 1779, the rank-and-file, present and fit for duty were 16,184 men based in New York, 3,781 in Rhode Island, 3,587 in the South, 1,750 in Halifax and 1,241 in West Florida.[46] Overall numbers might sound considerable, but many troops were committed to garrison duties and others were operating in hostile country.

The war had moved against the British, not least because they now lacked the initiative and thus were reliant on the resources of individual positions. Partly as a result, strategy as a very process was now a vulnerability for the British, as indeed was the operational level of the conflict. Both were to be demonstrated in the case of Yorktown in 1781.

There was a sense, nevertheless, of desperate resolve, and notably so on the part of George III. That November, Joseph Yorke, still envoy in The Hague, "the listening gallery of Europe," and a MP and recently considered as a Secretary of State, wrote to Amherst: "[I]t is plain that no moderation will content them [the French], they must annihilate you or go on quarrelling, for which reason I would not for the future make anything but truces."[47]

The navy played a key role in British plans, a reality that after French entry into the war was not only due to the need to confront the French navy. For example, British warships covered the coastal raids Clinton sought to pursue.[48] On 5 August, although the orders only reached him on 10 October, Clinton was instructed to pursue the strategy outlined in the instructions of 8 March of attacks on New England and a winter expedition to the South,[49] which indeed took Savannah that December. Lord George Germain, the Secretary of State for America, had followed this up that November:

> [T]he rebels will severely feel the effects of a war which will keep their coast in perpetual alarm, and by taking or destroying their ships and stores whilst we prevent their growing into a maritime power, our own commerce may be freed from the insults of their privateers.[50]

Clinton, complaining about the risks of attack by a French and maybe a Spanish fleet, wrote: "The Admiral tells me that the number of ships which he is to have on this coast will not be above a peace establishment and one half of those are detained in the West Indies."[51]

The year 1778 ended with the British seizure of Savannah on 29 December, which suggested new beginnings and what could be achieved with a small force. It was a propitious step and certainly more so than failure against Charleston in 1776. Indeed, Savannah was one of the most successful amphibious operations of the war. It was also very different to the successful use of the navy earlier in the year to withdraw Clinton's army from New Jersey to New York. Clinton had proposed a concerted operation against Georgia with Lieutenant-Colonel Archibald Campbell and a force of about 3,100—regulars and Loyalists—sailing from New York on 27 November, while the Genevan-born Brigadier-General Augustine Prévost was to advance from Saint Augustine, and with local Native Americans in cooperation. The Patriots had responded to the threat by moving Continental troops from Charleston in November, but they were heavily outnumbered, and even had Virginia not refused a request to send 1,000 militia to Charleston, the troops would not have arrived in time. The British reached Tybee Island on 23 December. The Patriots, regulars and militia under Major-General Robert Howe, stood to fight near Savannah, but a rapid British advance that made good use of the terrain led to a Patriot collapse with heavier casualties, including 453 prisoners.

In the equations of British and French power, however, St. Lucia was more significant than Savannah and that focus on the Caribbean put a much stronger demand on naval power, one that necessarily diminished its role in American waters. Indeed, this makes the importance of the navies there in 1780–1 somewhat ironic. In part this was a question of the need to move out of the range of hurricanes, but there was also an interest in using this for the benefit of combined operations. The geography of the South played a role here. For Patriots and Loyalists, there was the interior, an interior of King's Mountain and Cowpens. However, for Britain and France, the South was a series of islands, with Savannah and Charleston in effect island positions joined by maritime links maintained by naval power, a process that was to culminate for both powers in the Yorktown campaign of 1781.

Discussions surrounding the South can lead to a failure to consider the significance of the leading field armies of Britain and the Patriots centered in the middle colonies, a situation that was taken further when the French expeditionary force was based in Newport. In 1778, once Clinton had withdrawn from New Jersey to New York, there was no attempt to move his army to a new field of operations to the north or south. New York had to be protected, from both Patriots and the French, and it operated as the nexus of an established supply system. What might follow was unclear, but there was certainly no collapse of the British presence in the Thirteen Colonies.

Meanwhile, although faced by the attritional if not dissolving pressures of war, pressures highlighted in the House of Commons by North on 14 December,[52] the very continuity of the Revolution—which was strengthened and became more normative by the year—helped to establish it not only domestically but also internationally. That it was the first revolution seeking independence (as opposed to rebellion) by a European settler colony helped fashion it as a radical step, although it was not surprising that the Revolution was not necessarily perceived in that light. This Revolution represented not so much a rejection of the European world, one that could be fitted into the existing pattern of relations with non-Europeans, as rather a new type of European state—the first indeed of the new Western world.

The very determination of the Patriots to have relations with the European states thus created issues. This determination was linked not only to a striving for legitimacy for the new regime, with the Declaration of

Independence asserting a right to statehood among other states, but also to a practical desire to acquire resources. In particular, France and Spain were key sources of arms and funds for the revolutionaries.

The importance of legitimacy in what was an independence struggle helped ensure that the diplomatic recognition of the new state, in turn, became a fundamental issue in relations between Britain and other European states. The British government sought to block any such recognition, and treated the reception of Patriot diplomats as a hostile act prefiguring the response by the Union in the Civil War to the treatment of Confederate representatives, notably by Britain; although this comparison, made at the time, was not one that was welcome to Union leaders. The signature of treaties between Louis XVI of France and the Patriots in 1778 was correctly regarded as a sign of imminent hostilities with Britain. Lacking an equivalent to the ancestral aristocracies of Europe, the Patriots pursued a different diplomatic model to that of Britain. Indeed, the departure from the latter was part of the rejection of the British *ancien régime*. The international model seen as most pertinent in America was that of the United Provinces (Netherlands); and, in fact, republicanism as a diplomatic ethos was well-established in Europe, with the Dutch taking forward the achievement of the Venetians. Indeed, alongside any emphasis on the novelty of the American Revolution, it was scarcely a novelty in being a republic, and the Interregnum of 1649–60 meant that it was not even the first republic in British history. Moreover, compared to the Haitian Revolution that began in 1791, the American revolt was distinctly unradical.

In practice, the basis for American diplomacy was the system by which individual colonies had maintained agents in London. This system provided the necessary experience, and there was an overlap in representation between the colonial and early-republican periods, as with Benjamin Franklin. He proved a considerable success as American envoy in Paris, although Franklin was helped by the popularity there of his cause and of the idea of New-World virtue, which he was held to represent and that he carefully cultivated. His published correspondence covering November 1778–February 1779 indicated the continual disputes between the Patriot agents in Europe and, more especially, in France, and the amount of time that had to be devoted to shipping disputes and related diplomatic issues and legal quarrels. A particular issue was how French ships captured by the English and recaptured by Patriot privateers should be treated.[53] In 1779, Franklin, an ever-busy diplomat, went on to design a script typeface for passports. As the Patriot position was regularized, the volume of Franklin's surviving correspondence increased: In March-June 1779, the first full months of his tenure as sole Patriot envoy in Paris, he wrote on average fifty letters a month. As a reminder of the extent to which diplomacy attracted individuals of talent and was a key source of intellectual and cultural activity, Franklin also acted as a man of the Enlightenment, delivering a paper on the *Aurora Borealis* to the *Académie des Sciences*, becoming involved in an attempt by Jean-Paul Marat to challenge conventional views on the nature of science, staying in touch with the British intellectual and scientific world, establishing a type-foundry and press, and writing an essay, *The Morals of Chess*, which asserted that "we learn by chess the habit of not being discouraged by present bad appearances in the state of our affairs, the habit of hoping for a favourable change, and that of persevering in the search of resources"—a fitting description of his embassy.[54]

Patriot relations with the French government were often difficult, as French assistance was rarely as unreserved as required, while there was justified concern about France's pursuit of its own national interests, not least in terms of territorial goals in the West Indies. There were the customary tensions of any alliance, especially one that linked two powers with such dissimilar objectives; Yet Spain and the Patriots were more dissimilar due to Spanish concern about the example of revolutions for their own colonies. There were also, at least for Franklin, the problems of introducing a new revolutionary state into the world of *ancien régime* diplomacy, and of acting as military and financial agent for the Patriots.[55]

The rival British diplomatic system proved weak in its response to the American Revolution. In part, this situation was a matter of the limitations in Britain's international position and the deficiencies of its foreign policy. Yet, replying in June 1779 to criticisms of the government for the absence of allies, Alexander Wedderburn, the Attorney General, refuted the idea:

> [A]s if it were in their power to oblige foreign courts to enter into alliances with Great Britain [...] no state would enter

> into an alliance with another unless it stood in need of some assistance, which the other had it in its power to afford [...] the necessity was solely on our side, and therefore it was not at all to be wondered at, that other courts were not much inclined to enter into alliance with us.[56]

Nevertheless, there were also weaknesses in British diplomacy, weaknesses seen in a failure to manage the tempo of Britain's increasing isolation. This isolation gathered pace in 1780.

# 8. 1779: A YEAR OF IMPASSE

> "The face of affairs becomes every day more agreeable to our wishes. The dissensions among the rebels and the great depreciation of their paper [currency], promises the happiest effects. If Great Britain will persevere, America must soon be conquered."
>
> Major Robert Rogers, Loyalist, writing from New York to General Lord Amherst, Commander-in-Chief of the British Forces[1]

As so often happens, another year brought thwarted hopes, indeed making 1779 "the forgotten year of the war."[2] Germain wrote to Clinton: "It is most earnestly to be wished that you may be able to bring Mr. Washington to a general and decisive action at the opening of the campaign."[3] This would have left the remainder of the campaign open for exploitation. Such a prospect appeared possible because the British forces would have already been present in close proximity at the start of the campaign (unlike in 1776), and were not sent to a more distant field of combat (as in 1777). Instead, there was no such "action," which ensures that the year can be seen in part as a failure to exploit success at Savannah, when in practice it was an inability to force the desired outcome in the middle colonies.[4] The latter goal would have been rendered far more difficult had troops been diverted to Savannah, and there would also have been a need to deploy more warships to protect army bases and to convoy troops. Clinton argued that a shortage of troops made it very difficult to exploit the success in Savannah, noting "there was a time when this operation must have been attended with every success, but that time is no more."[5] Earlier in the year, he had thought there was an opportunity, if reinforcements were on hand, to capture Charleston.[6]

The key event in 1779 was the failure of the Franco-Spanish invasion attempt in Britain. This was a formidable force, but its preparation was thwarted by poor coordination, delay—notably the French having to wait in Brest for the Spanish arrival—and the disease that spread as a consequence of this delay.[7] There was no precursor, however, to Horatio, Lord Nelson's victory at Trafalgar in 1805 over the main Franco-Spanish fleet. If in 1779, as in 1805, the French and Spanish fleets also faced major problems in coordination, the British were unable in 1779 to defeat them either separately or together. This compounded the failure in 1778 to defeat the Brest fleet off Ushant. There was no equivalent to the Glorious First of June in 1794, the first naval battle of the next Anglo-French conflict, a battle in which the French fleet suffered heavily, with Admiral Howe as the British commander.

The ministry had sought through negotiations to keep Spain neutral, but the Spaniards were less concerned with British views than with what France was willing to offer in return for Spain's entry into the war. When France promised to fight until Spain obtained Gibraltar, the Spaniards signed the Convention of Aranjuez in April 1779, recalled their envoy from London the following month, and began preparations for a Franco-Spanish invasion of Britain. France's success in bringing Spain into the war increased the necessary European focus of British naval attention as well as the army's need to defend Britain and Gibraltar. This helped the Patriots, French, and Spaniards in their offensive plans in the Americas.[8] Spain's position suggested to other European governments that the general situation was moving against Britain.[9]

However, in 1779, the Spanish fleet did not reach the rendezvous point off Corunna until 22 July nor pass Ushant until 11 August. By 14 August, the joint fleet, of 66 ships of the line, was within sight of the English coast. The response in Britain was "prodigious confusion [...] we have no force to oppose such a number."[10] In the event, as the British diplomat Sir Robert Murray Keith was to comment of the Bourbons, "surely never was such a prodigious force so completely misapplied."[11] The Bourbon fleet off Plymouth was hit by a storm on 18 August and was subsequently unable to engage the smaller British fleet. On 3 September, the expedition was abandoned.

A different verdict in 1779, as in 1778, would have transformed the conflict elsewhere; just as would have been the case in 1805, or, indeed, 1812 when American hopes against Britain in part rested on an anticipation of Napoleon defeating Russia. The landing of a Franco-Spanish invasion force might not have knocked Britain out of the conflict, but it would have transformed the war. The British, even if successful, would have been obliged to focus thereafter more land and sea forces on the defense of southern England, which would have greatly reduced the numbers available for operations elsewhere. On 6 January 1781, the French were able to land a force on Jersey, but being outnumbered it was defeated with heavier casualties as the result of a vigorous defense. Earlier, on 1 May 1779, the French had tried to land on Jersey, but the rapid arrival of the defenders at the planned landing site led the French to abandon the scheme. The major failure in the expedition sent against Algiers in 1775 had revealed serious deficiencies in Spanish amphibious warfare.[12]

Previous French invasion attempts against England had failed, defeated in battle at sea in 1692 and 1759 and by storm in 1744, and storms had also put paid to a Spanish attempt in 1719, with only a subsidiary force attacking Scotland. Yet, the success of the Dutch invasion of England in 1688, as well as the French ability to invade Ireland in 1798 (and to land troops there on behalf of James II in 1688) and to threaten a landing in Scotland in 1708, indicated the vulnerability of the British Isles. Even if the Royal Navy was strong, it could be kept from position by southerly winds, as had happened in 1688 and as was feared in 1745–6. Moreover, there was no assurance of British naval success if there was a battle, as had been shown by the British failure to defeat the French off Ushant in 1778. Indeed, this battle was a precursor to the invasion attempt of 1779, and thus showed how failure potentially could snowball. The degree to which Brest offered the French an invasion port was important, for westerly winds enabled warships from there to move down the Channel.

The invasion attempt saw a British military voluntarism that focused national resolve and led to confident claims of naval prowess.[13] It also took artistic form. Benjamin West, an American Loyalist, the Historical Painter to the king, responded to the sense of crisis by depicting crucial victories from the past in *The Battle of the Boyne* and *The Destruction of the French Fleet at La Hogue* (events that had occurred in 1690 and 1692, respectively).

The sense of relevance as well as interest helped explain the major impact of Edward Gibbon's *Decline and Fall of the Roman Empire* (1776–88). A politician as well as an historian, Gibbon was a MP from 1774 to 1780 and 1781 to 1784, and a member of the Board of Trade from 1779 to 1782. In 1779, at the request of Thomas, 3rd Viscount Weymouth, one of the Secretaries of State, Gibbon wrote the *Mémoire Justificatif* against the hostile conduct of France and Spain in the war.

Hypotheticals, "what-ifs?", and counterfactualism might all appear of limited value, not least because it can be difficult enough to explain what actually happened. Yet, the latter in part depends on this very counterfactualism because contemporaries had to anticipate a range of possibilities and these affected their planning and their assessment of what occurred. The impact of hypotheticals on planning was particularly seen in the decisions of where to station warships, a matter of choice and one in which the possible decisions of a number of states influenced the situation.

The state with the least significance in this respect was the American proto-state of the Patriots which, alongside its privateering, was unable to produce a navy of consequence as far as fleet actions were concerned. This was a situation that also pertained to the Americans in the War of 1812 and for the Confederacy in the Civil War. As a consequence, this naval element might be underplayed for the Wars of Independence and 1812 in American accounts with the exception of references to heroic frigates. These were able to offer protection of commerce but could not challenge British fleet action. However, George Johnstone, a naval officer and former governor of West Florida who was an MP who earlier had supported conciliation and pragmatism in America, told the Commons on 24 February 1779, that were the British to abandon North America,

> [it] would leave the Americans at liberty to let loose all their privateers against our islands [...] for America was so situated, that what with the raw materials she had herself, and the assistance she could draw from France, in canvas and cordage, she could soon raise a navy, that in conjunction with that of France, would beat us out of the seas.[14]

The geopolitics of the war were transformed in 1778, both by its much, much greater scale, and by the transition from a continental versus an oceanic power in North America to the same alongside a struggle between oceanic powers, indeed the foremost such powers in the world—the British were the greatest naval power and the French second. A result of this was a change in the geography of the struggle in North America, for the interaction of these two elements became significant or, as a reminder of hypotheticals, potentially significant. This began in 1778 when the British garrison in New York unexpectedly faced the arrival off Sandy Hook of a French fleet, which ultimately decided not to attack. Indeed, there was to be no such unsupported attack of a fleet on a British position in North America during the war. Instead, French warships cooperated with French and Patriot land forces, an aspect of naval history that can be underrated but pushed to the fore the failure to stop French squadrons setting out.[15]

This capability emphasized the importance of ports because in offering anchorages and replenishment it was at these that locations that the French were most able and willing to use their strength. This provided an offensive option, seen at Savannah in 1779, Newport in 1780, and Yorktown in 1781, and in hopes of an attack on New York in 1782. It was not (as Germantown in 1778 and Monmouth Court House in 1779 had shown) that Patriot forces lacked the ability to attack, but rather that their usual stance was defensive. French entry helped alter this. William Eden, one of the commissioners in the unsuccessful negotiations with the Patriots, observed:

> Fleets employed to cover a coast, are not only precarious in their exertions, which depend much on winds, but are miserably confined as to all the effects of naval war. Those effects are only felt when our fleets can keep the sea, in order to protect our commerce, and annoy that of our enemies, as well as to defend our distant possessions, and to cover descents and continual incursions. Such objects, however, cannot be pursued, nor can we in wisdom hazard anything, whenever the state of our internal defence is such as to require the presence of our fleets for the protection of our dock-yards, of our ports, and even of our metropolis.[16]

Within North America, the war changed in a different geographical direction, one powered by the interaction of political factors with the wider geopolitics of the conflict, although in part this was due to the failure of Germain's operational plan. On 23 January, he had instructed Clinton that if he could not beat Washington in battle:

> [I]t is imagined that with an army of about 12,000 men in the field under your immediate command you may force him to seek for safety in the Highlands of New York or the Jerseys, and leave the inhabitants of the open country at liberty to follow what the Commissioners represent to be their inclinations, and renounce the authority of the Congress and return to their allegiance to His Majesty which would obviate the chief objection to the re-establishment of civil government in New York, as a majority of the counties in the province could then send members to the Assembly and the ancient constitution could be restored in its due form.

The plan was to fix and weaken Washington while strengthening the British through Loyalist activity:

> [T]he operations proposed to be carried on in other parts would be greatly facilitated by your obliging General Washington to keep the whole of his regular troops together to oppose your army; and on the other hand those operations could not fail to prevent his receiving succours from the countries attacked. It is therefore intended that the two corps of about 4,000 each assisted by a naval force should be employed upon the sea coasts of the revolted provinces, the one to act on the side of New England and New Hampshire, and the other in the Chesapeake Bay and by entering the rivers and inlets wherever it was found practicable, seize or destroy their shipping and stores and deprive them of every means of fitting out privateers or of carrying on foreign commerce.
>
> A considerable diversion will also be directed to be made on the side of Canada by a succession of parties of Indians

> supported by detachments of the troops there alarming and harassing the frontiers and making incursions into the settlements [...] it surely is not too much to expect that your force will be so much increased by new levies [...] enable you to strengthen the corps you appoint to attack Virginia and Maryland so as to give protection to the Loyal inhabitants of Jersey or the lower counties on the Delaware in any attempts they may be disposed to make in the absence of the rebel army to deliver themselves from the tyranny and oppression of the rebel committees and to form a force sufficient to withstand any efforts of the Congress to continue them under its authority.[17]

Geopolitical factors encouraged a focus of forces elsewhere, notably in the Caribbean, while the former, in the shape of Loyalist strength in the South, encouraged the development by the British of what became a southern strategy in which there was an attempt to develop a Loyalist dynamic. This entailed establishing control of areas within which a Loyalist civil government could develop. Savannah was captured in December 1778 in a victory for both amphibious power and the successful boldness not displayed against Charleston in 1776. It was given greater strategic depth by the strength of Loyalism in Georgia, where Augusta was captured by Campbell in January 1779, and by British control of East Florida, which was a colony centered on nearby Saint Augustine.

The arrival of the British at Savannah led to an upsurge of Loyalist activity. Campell wrote on 19 January: "Shoals flock to the Royal Standard daily; and I have got the country in arms against the Congress [...]. I have taken a stripe and star from the rebel flag of America."[18] However, Loyalist moves were contained by the militia at Kettle Creek on 14 February: The casualty figures—twenty Loyalists and seven Patriots killed—are a reminder that "battles" were often small-scale. In addition, the Georgia militia defeated a force of Creeks on the Ogeechee. Augusta was abandoned on 14 February.

In turn, the British, under Brigadier-General Augustine Prévost, who had joined Campbell "with 900 rag tag and bobtails [...] too old and unactive for this service,"[19] invaded South Carolina in May and marched on Charleston. Prévost argued that British success in the South "might reduce them [the rebellious colonies] to reason, much sooner than anything that can be effected to the northward" in part because the troops in the South were better fed.[20] Summoning the town, he was offered its occupation by John Rutledge, governor of South Carolina, in return for a guarantee of the neutrality of the harbor and the rest of the state for the remainder of the war. These proposals scarcely imply a bellicose spirit on the part of the Patriots, and suggest that negotiation by the British from a position of strength was not a policy without hope.

Prevost foolishly insisted on unconditional surrender and then had to withdraw on the approach of a larger relief force under Benjamin Lincoln, who had replaced Robert Howe. The British rearguard at Stone Ferry, a position that included Loyalist troops, was attacked on 20 June but initial success was followed by eventual failure.

In September, in turn, Lincoln advanced to besiege Savannah in conjunction with a French amphibious force. After a four-day bombardment by 33 cannon and nine mortars had failed to obtain surrender, and mindful of the limited amount of time the French fleet could stay on the coast,[21] a storming attack was launched on the morning of 9 October. Thanks to a deserter, the British were forewarned (a crucial contrast with the successful British attack the previous December), the attacking columns did not coordinate their operations, and despite the bravery of the South Carolina Continentals and the French they were repulsed with heavy losses from defensive fire, which had been enhanced by naval cannon mounted on the walls. The French re-embarked on 20 October.[22] This failure rendered ideas of Lincoln advancing to attack St. Augustine implausible.

The absence of major engagements in the middle colonies in 1779 and 1780 did not indicate a disinclination to fight, although while growing in experience as a planner Washington felt handicapped by a lack of numbers and supplies.[23] Furthermore, his force had to respond to Clinton's ability to take the initiative, as on 2 June when, benefiting from the use of warships on the Hudson, British forces took King's Ferry, threatening West Point. British amphibious raids inflicted serious damage, but a "very bold and daring" night attack led to the capture of the British position at Stony Point on the Hudson on the night of 15–16 July.

In the face of a British advance, however, Washington ordered Stony Point's works destroyed and the position abandoned. The British reoccupied it.[24] The lack of major achievements helps explain Clinton's euphoric response later in the year to the Franco-Patriot failure at Savannah: "I think this is the greatest event that has happened this whole war."[25]

The manpower situation in both armies was a testimony to the strains from which they were suffering. The British had lost one army at Saratoga, and now had other pressing commitments. In turn, the Patriots were finding it increasingly difficult to sustain a major army and Washington had become more cautious. Indeed, this stance was to be seen as Fabian.

As a result, both sides sought new support: The British looked to the Loyalists, especially in the South, as a major military and political resource (as they had not done in the first stage of the war); while the Patriots sought to persuade the French to intervene in America, rather than fighting the British in the West Indies. The war therefore became a curious interplay of cautious moves and bold aspirations, as increasingly exhausted participants moved around the vast area in contention and played for stakes that had been made higher as a consequence of the new factor of the intervention of French naval power, and in an atmosphere that the changing arithmetic of naval strength helped to make volatile for both sides. This can be seen in the prevalence of rumors about the intentions of others. There was now an incessant need to assess how best to respond to French moves. For example, in late 1779, Admiral Marriot Arbuthnot, in command of the warships in New York, had to consider how to respond if d'Estaing attacked New York, Newport, or Halifax, a threat that led to defensive precautions on land as well as the recall of troop transports.[26] Preparing to defend New York in October, he positioned his ships at Sandy Hook as Howe had done the previous year, arguing that, unlike Newport, New York was crucial. If it fell, so also would "all the ships stores, provisions and magazines of all sorts." However, Arbuthnot wrote to Clinton that if Halifax fell it would be necessary to retain Newport, "because New York is not a place for large ships." But if Halifax was retained it would not be worth using up troops to hold New York. Arbuthnot added:

> The ships of the line cannot winter in the port of New York, much less can they come upon the coast near it, being of all others the most dangerous for large ships [...] the line of battle ships will be as soon with you from Halifax and in better order than they could be from any other port on this continent.[27]

Regarded by Clinton as of no likely value for land operations,[28] Rhode Island was abandoned in October and the French were able to use it as a base. This, however, freed 5,000 British troops and a number of warships at a time when both were in short supply (not least due to ill-health[29]) and when coastal operations in New England were a decreasing priority: They had neither strategic nor operational impact.

With his characteristic optimism, George offered an account of the war in America that was misleading. In June, he wrote to North:

> The different papers from America show very clearly that had not Spain now thrown off the mask that we should have soon found the colonies sue for pardon to the mother country; I do not despair that with the activity Clinton is inclined to adopt, and the Indians in the rear, that the provinces will even now submit.[30]

George added soon after:

> The enclosed papers [...] confirm me in an opinion long entertained that America unless this summer supported by a Bourbon fleet must sue for peace, and that it would ever have been unwise to have done more than what is now adopted, the enabling the Commander in Chief to put provinces at peace, but that propositions must come from them to us, no farther ones be sent from hence; they ever tend only to increase the demands. I can never agree to healing over an uncured wound, it must be probed to the bottom, if it then proves sound, no one will be more ready to forget offences, but no one sees more forcibly the necessity of preventing the like mischief by America's feeling, she has not been a gainer

> by the contest; yet after that I would show that the parent's heart is still affectionate to the penitent child.[31]

Signs of providential support were welcome,[32] but confidence in divine protection and earthly success enabled George to avoid the difficult issue of reasonable terms. This belief helped keep the war going. He was unwilling to change ministers or measures.[33] In part, the extent to which the change in measures was pressed by Opposition politicians helped keep George determined not to alter course, but it was not just the Opposition, for North was also interested in different policies. Instead, it was George who was obdurate, not least over bringing Opposition figures into the ministry. He wrote to North in June:

> What I said yesterday was the dictates of frequent and severe self-examination. I never can depart from it. Before I will ever hear of any man's readiness to come into office I will expect to see it signed under his hand that he is resolved to keep the Empire entire and that no troops shall be consequently withdrawn from thence [North America], nor independence ever allowed.

This was also George's stance in 1780.[34] His attitude might seem an impressive display of pertinacity and resolve[35] (indeed an anticipation of Churchillian determination) were it not based on a seriously flawed assessment of the military and political situation in North America. George understood the distinction between battle and war and appreciated that victory in the former would not ensure success in the latter. But he underestimated the difficulty of getting the Patriots to accept that they might have lost sufficiently badly so as to ensure their participation in negotiations.

George also as of yet failed to appreciate the depths of the strategic dilemma posed to Britain by Bourbon entry. His politics ensured that the war could not be reconceptualized as a struggle with the Bourbons, the course urged by the Opposition and one that would have freed the British from the strategic incubus of conflict in North America, and more particularly offensive conflict. Instead, George was still determined to defeat the Patriots, and did not see this as a matter shunted into a lesser significance by French policy. Indeed, as so often happens, there was a parallelism between George and the Patriot politicians. Both put the American war front and center and saw it in terms of a significance that others doubted (and correctly so.

Military success in 1779, either in America or elsewhere, might have lessened British isolation by deterring other states from supporting, at least to some degree, France and Spain, or alternatively of encouraging France to emulate Spain in essentially ignoring the war in the Thirteen Colonies. However, there were no moves that offered this potential other than the advance on Charleston. As a result of considering this context, that failure emerges as more significant.

A need for British caution emerged in the aftermath of French entry into the war. The withdrawal from Philadelphia the previous year was not going to be reversed. In May, Lieutenant-General William Skinner, the Chief Engineer, recommended "that all garrisons of large forts should be as near to the shore as possible, that they may be relieved by our fleets," while Clinton pressed in November for the reinforcement of Halifax.[36] Yet, that approach was to go wrong in 1781 at Yorktown.

Comparative dimensions can be instructive, as it helps to undermine uncritical ideas of Patriot uniqueness and of the specific value of particular terrains, techniques, formations, and weapons. In 1779, for example, an advance from Bombay/Mumbai by East India Company forces on the Maratha capital was poorly conducted. The more rapidly moving Marathas were able to surround the British force and press it hard, obliging it on 12 January to sign a convention at Wadgaon under which the British retreated. This was scarcely a case of a need for republican virtue or riflemen to defeat the British. Such was the case in southern India as well, where outnumbered British forces were destroyed by Mysore's army in 1780 and 1782. Yet failure elsewhere did not make the lack of success in North America less consequential. What this failure did accomplish was to draw attention to the multiple pressures around the world from which the British were suffering and that affected their options in particular spheres.

Meanwhile, the British hoped for success from new moves. In the instructions on 23 January 1779 sent to Clinton, Germain wrote:

> It is intended that two corps of about 4,000 each assisted by a naval force should also be employed upon the sea coasts of the revolted provinces, the one to act on the side of New England and New Hampshire, and the other in the Chesapeake Bay and by entering the rivers and inlets wherever it was found practicable, seize or destroy their shipping and shores and deprive them of every means of fitting out privateers or carrying on foreign commerce.[37]

In fact, as so often occurred that year, there were insufficient troops,[38] not least because of Loyalist casualties.[39] However, a successful attack on the Chesapeake in May inflicted extensive damage, including on the shipyard at Gosport.[40] Washington responded by pressing for the removal of stores from coasts and navigable rivers, a comment on American vulnerability to British combined operations, but also the presence of a countervailing hinterland. In July, there were similar British attacks on the Connecticut coast at Norwalk, New Haven, and Fairfield, raids that the Patriots could not thwart and that threatened their morale.

At the same time, looking back to earlier British (and therefore also British colonial) operations against French and Spanish colonies—a longstanding practice, and in part to a popular understanding of tactics based on the Royal Navy's experience—the Patriots not only had a navy that was useful for privateering,[41] but also developed a capacity for amphibious assaults, beginning with a raid on New Providence Island in March 1776. Whaleboats became one means to conduct such operations.[42]

The Patriots launched a major combined operation in 1779. In June, a British force from Nova Scotia established a post at Castine, on Penobscot Bay, on the coast of what was then Massachusetts and is now Maine. This post was designed to deny the Patriots both a naval base from which they might threaten Halifax, Nova Scotia, the key British naval base in Canada, and timber supplies from the area. The General Court of Massachusetts, acting unilaterally without Congressional assent or assistance, decided on a swift response, and a force of 1,000 militia under Brigadier-General Solomon Lovell, supported by a fleet of 19 warships and 25 support ships under Commodore Dudley Saltonstall, reached the bay on 24 July. Patriot attempts next day to force the entrance of Castine Harbor and to land nearby failed. The Patriots landed on the 28 July, but although they outnumbered the British force, whose fort, moreover, was very weak, they did not press their advantage and instead began slow siege operations. Meanwhile, Lovell and Saltonstall sought to shift the burden of the attack on each other, a process more generally seen on both sides.

However, a British squadron of ten warships under Captain Sir George Collier arrived from New York on 14 August, and rather than fighting the Patriot force fled with the loss of its ships, mostly scuttled.[43] Castine was held by the British for the remainder of the war. The Patriot debacle, which effectively knocked Massachusetts out of the war financially, and for which Saltonstall was court-martialed and summarily dismissed from the service, indicated that the Patriots lacked the combined capability enjoyed by the more experienced British. But also, if they gained it, temporary control of the sea at least to the extent of allowing force projection did not have to bring decisive results. Another Patriot advance also met with serious problems—namely, the attempt in July-September to end the Iroquois threat to New York and Pennsylvania. This inflicted serious damage but was hit hard by grave supply deficiencies. The difficulty of fixing opponents was a major problem.[44]

More generally, the Patriots were affected by continuing resource shortages. New York had not been attacked and the campaign ended with the Continental Army again having to accept difficult winter quarters.[45]

In 1779, the last year of major campaigning near New York, the war in America stabilized to a degree. A *modus vivendi*, or at least clear areas of respective strength, was developing, with the Patriots in New England and Philadelphia, the British in Canada and New York, and the South a new area of opportunity and maneuver. Yet, stabilization was more an opportunity for Patriot stabilization than for British recovery. In October, Cadwallader Colden, a Loyalist who had been imprisoned in 1776–8, complained from New York about:

> a strange fatality attending all our military operations [...] why something more has not been done this summer [...] an inglorious campaign has given great spirits to the rebels, and

> depressed the friends to government, both within and without the lines [...] what sufferings thousands still undergo rather than take part in rebellion.[46]

That year, Lord George Herbert remarked, "Eighteen years ago the World at our feet, but alas! now we die at the feet of the World." In the House of Commons, in the 8 December debate on the Army Estimates, Sir Charles Bunbury, an MP for Suffolk and Opposition supporter, not only said that Britain could not afford the war for long, but also castigated the army in the last campaign:

> [that] showed itself incapable of any one offensive operation, and even of maintaining and defending the small part of America which we had for some late years held, for the army had evacuated Rhodes Island.

Arguing that it was as probable as Britain conquering Turkey, Bunbury said there was no chance of conquering America, a view shared in the House by Charles James Fox[47] and already advanced there on 26 November by Sir George Yonge.[48]

As a reminder of the nature of war, the diary entry for William Reidhead, the storekeeper to the British garrison at Castine, for 7 August recorded:

> This morning they began a very smart cannonading and the third shot killed a corporal of the 74th who was assisting to serve out provisions in the store whose head was knocked about in a dismal manner and all his brains knocked about my face and shirt and a piece of his skull almost knocked me down.[49]

# 9. 1780: THE SOUTHERN STRATEGY DEVELOPS

> "I was obliged to conceal myself in a cave dug in the branch of a creek under a hollow poplar."
>
> Loyalist Alexander Chesney after the defeat at King's Mountain[1]
>
> "The misfortune is we have more to defend than we have ships ready to employ."
>
> George III[2]

Despite the anxieties expressed in 1778, French entry had not obliged the British to abandon New York. Nor had it led to another Patriot attack on Canada, one supported by French amphibious action, nor to the permanent postponing of British operations in the South. Instead, hit hard by scurvy, the 6,000 strong French expeditionary force that arrived in Newport on 11 July 1780 achieved nothing decisive in that year beyond establishing themselves—notably by repairing and strengthening the defenses so as not to fear British attack.[3]

At the same time, the French force sent to India was to achieve even less, in part due to the greater impact of disease. These forces were to a degree designed to keep the British busy so that France could pursue goals elsewhere—notably in the Caribbean—but this would be too instrumental an account of French policy. The French government also sought the establishment of a postwar order in which allied states looked to it for alliance and cooperated with its aims. This goal encompassed Spain, the Netherlands, America, and Mysore, and the probable future roles of each were uncertain and likely to be settled by circumstances, although hopes that the Franco-Spanish alliance would collapse rapidly[4] were fanciful.

Yet, although by 1780 France and Spain combined had a quantitative superiority in naval tonnage over Britain of about 25 percent, the British still dominated the Atlantic waters of the eastern seaboard of North

America. They were helped by their base in Halifax, and now also New York. Moreover, if the British impact in the interior was limited, they revealed at Charleston and around the Chesapeake in 1780 an ability to use their amphibious forces to considerable effect, taking the initiative, harrying their opponents (as at Castine in 1779), and disrupting the Patriot economy. Developments in Charleston in 1780 help suggestions of a transformation in relative fortunes. It had seen off British attacks in 1776 and 1779. The one in 1780 was stronger and more sustained, but despite this being the result of a greater effort the overall impression was of a change in fortune toward Britain.

On 26 December 1779, Clinton and Arbuthnot (who Clinton found highly "impracticable"[5]) sailed from Sandy Hook off New York for South Carolina with 7,600 troops, with Clinton seeing the capture of South Carolina as a way to protect Georgia.[6] The voyage illustrated the drawbacks for such operations because, on 28 December, a terrible storm struck the fleet off Cape Hatteras. Much of it was dispersed by storm and current, one transport ending up off Cornwall, while most of the horses and much of the supplies, especially ordnance stores and entrenching tools, were lost. John Hayes, an army physician, suffered a "full forty days beating the boisterous ocean."[7] As a result, the fleet did not anchor off North Edisto Inlet, 30 miles south of Charleston, the original destination. Instead it went to Savannah, now a British base, for recuperation and repair, sailing again on 10 February.

This delay shows the questionable nature of claims that Britain could have made a better effort to move forces between America and the West Indies to achieve seasonally propitious annual campaigns in both. In practice, such movements entailed risk, not least in terms of sticking to any predictable timing. Nevertheless, the forces used in the Charleston campaign could have been allocated to the Caribbean where those that survived disease might have deterred or counterattacked French and Spanish moves, including the Spanish advance in West Florida. There, Fort Charlotte, the position guarding Mobile, was successfully taken in a Spanish siege that began on 2 March, with the walls breached on the 13$^{th}$ and the garrison surrendering the next day. The British attempt to send a relief force from Pensacola had failed. This is not a success that tends to attract American attention.

The navy played a major role in the attack on Charleston. The disruption of the siege train in the storm, as well as the lack of draught horses,[8] meant that cannon and artillerymen had to be supplied by the fleet, which was a normal procedure. Furthermore, in a display of presence, strength, and firepower, Arbuthnot and seven warships forced their way past American fortifications on the north side of the harbor, a Hessian quartermaster recorded: "We could see nothing of the ships except the flashes of their guns because of the smoke. The majesty of this sight can hardly be described."[9] The capture of Charleston entailed the seizure of most of what was left of the Continental (American) navy which had been anchored there and employed only in static defense. Nearly 6,000 seamen, regulars, and militia were captured, many subsequently confined on disease-hit prison ships or escaping, while some were enlisted into the British army, being sent to garrison Jamaica.[10]

Moreover, and significantly so, this success was not simply a military development. The willingness to accept the consequences politically was instructive. Indeed, it poses a question mark against the bombastic claims of liberty or death made by some Patriots. In the face of blockade and bombardment, Charleston rapidly surrendered on 12 May, leading Clinton to predict the rapid conquest of "both Carolinas,"[11] just as the capture of Havana in 1762 led to the surrender of Cuba.

As so often happens, this dramatic display at Charleston of the potential of combined operations owed much to the tactical and operational choices made by the defenders, as well as their willpower. Pressed hard by the civilian authorities against evacuation, the unimpressive Patriot commander (or rather one who failed to rise to the occasion) Major-General Benjamin Lincoln was unwilling until too late—and then unable—to withdraw from Charleston. As with Washington at New York in 1776, the retention of this was necessary for political and logistical reasons, but Lincoln was at a serious disadvantage: He was surrounded and constantly hammered by a British force supported by naval firepower and supplies. The failure to defend outlying forts was serious, not least by affecting the time context within which the dynamic of a combined attack, or indeed any siege, could be lost. The British had discovered this at Cartagena in 1741 when failing against Spanish defenses, and nearly done so at Havana in 1762. This failure enabled the British to concentrate their army and navy against Charleston. Moreover, the defense was irresolute, unimaginative, and on the whole lacking the determined fighting spirit that the Patriots displayed on so many occasions during the war.[12]

On 5 June 1780, over 200 of its more prominent citizens congratulated the British commanders on the restoration of the political connection with the crown. A loyal address came from Georgetown the following month, while several of the leading politicians of the state returned to Charleston to accept British rule, a vindication of the British policy of combining force with a conciliatory stance thereby developing the Loyalist potential.[13]

Clinton, however, failed to apply conciliation effectively—refusing foolishly, in his pressure for support, to accept neutral sentiments, instead requiring clear support. This was a way to anchor the new order by obliging people to commit to it. His requirement of the militia that they be prepared to serve outside South Carolina was very unpopular.[14] Furthermore, the activities of British foragers were unwelcome. Clinton proved similarly hesitant to turn to the restoration of civil government in New York. At the same time, British agency was limited by the extent of Patriot support and the neutralist watchfulness of others, which for example proved to be at issue in and around Augusta, as well as more generally. It proved very difficult for the British to devise an effective strategy for political warfare, or to implement a policy of conciliation.[15]

Meanwhile, Washington, who lacked the resources for an offensive campaign,[16] was unable to shake British control of New York and his troops were increasingly demoralized. The war in the middle colonies appeared to have drifted into an impasse, and this was seen in problems with enlistments in the Continental Army. Resources, supplies, and logistics all continued to be major problems with Lieutenant-Colonel Henry Dearborn, warning from West Point that they encouraged desertions.[17] Nathanael Greene, exhausted and convinced of Congressional hostility, resigned as Quartermaster General.[18] Logistical problems limited the possibility of sending troops to the South.[19]

Instead, Washington planned a joint attack on New York as soon as the French arrived, but the French were delayed by Atlantic weather and British naval action, and Clinton returned to New York from the South, which closed what Washington had seen as a particular opportunity.

Subsequently, a lack of French support that owed much to British naval activity, thwarted Washington's revived plan. By contrast, the Revolution remained strong in New England. In 1780, a new Constitution drawn up as the result of a Constitutional Convention held in 1779–80 was adopted in Massachusetts, finally replacing the Colonial Charter of 1691. Ratified by a franchise unrestricted by property requirements, this included a Declaration of Rights and is still used today.

Clinton had a plan for crushing Washington in the middle colonies by advancing on his position in New Jersey and forcing battle on the outnumbered Patriots. Clinton planned to land two armies on the Jersey shore (each larger than Washington's) and to send them through the two passes of the Watchung Mountains. If Washington waited (and he did not have enough horses to move all of his artillery), he would have been overwhelmed at Morristown. If he attacked either invading force, Washington would have been outnumbered and on the offensive, conditions generally fatal for the Patriots during the Revolutionary War.

Had Clinton achieved that objective, he would have moved against the French when they landed that year in Rhode Island. Unlike the Patriots, the French would not have been able to withdraw into the interior. Instead, their situation would have been dependent on maritime evacuation, as with the British force under Sir John Moore that had intervened in favor of the Spanish revolution against French occupation in 1808. With Washington's army gone, Clinton would probably also have captured West Point thanks to the treachery of Benedict Arnold, and thus would have gained naval access to the entire Hudson Valley, a better option than that offered by any southward advance on the Lake Champlain axis. But he told nobody in New York about this plan, and before he returned from Charleston, the Loyalists, who were convinced that the generally indecisive Clinton was incapable of bold action, had persuaded General Wilhelm von Knyphausen, the more energetic commander of the Hessian auxiliary forces, to land in New Jersey with a smaller force than Clinton had envisaged. By the time Clinton returned, there was no chance for surprise, and he pulled back to New York after the indecisive engagement at Springfield on 23 June, discouraged by Washington retiring "to his fastnesses in the Highlands."[20] This was the last major engagement north of Virginia and it was a significant morale-boosting encounter for the Patriots: A fighting withdrawal by them in the face of large British forces, was followed by the establishment of a stronger defensive position and the arrival of more troops—notably, the New Jersey militia. A British retreat led to the abandonment of the new position in New Jersey[21] while the arrival of French troops led Clinton to fear for the safety of New York and, indeed, Canada. He pressed for troops and criticized their dispatch to the Caribbean.[22]

That year, the British strategy in the South was largely successful. At Camden on 16 August in an encounter battle, Horatio Gates's army, the main Patriot field force in the South, was smashed, with the loss of about 800 dead and wounded, as well as 1,000 taken prisoner, and the capture of their supplies. In contrast, the British had only 300 casualties. Cornwallis had not sought to win by maneuver but rather to focus on the fighting quality of his troops, who were less numerous (1,900 to 3,100) but many were poorly trained. He reported of the battle:

> [A] very heavy and well supported fire on both sides: our line continued to advance in good order, and with the cool intrepidity of experienced British soldiers keeping up a constant fire or making use of bayonets as opportunities existed.[23]

John Hayes wrote of the Patriots: "[B]efore they knew where they were, our troops were with their bayonets at their breasts—a close action."[24] On the Patriot side, Colonel Otho Williams blamed militia "cowardice."[25]

Displaying considerable energy, Gates fled far and rapidly, ending any viability for his wish to replace Washington. Other commanders fought with greater determination. Gates was replaced by Nathanael Greene who took command of the Southern Department on 3 December. Washington had confidence in Greene, and the latter's appointment increased Washington's influence in the South and his knowledge of actual and likely developments there.

Cornwallis, whom Clinton had left in command in the South, faced the familiar problems of insufficient troops and precarious supplies, was uncertain of local support, and found the Loyalist militia lacking in subordination, loyalty, and morale.[26] British detachments faced resistance.

Cornwallis came to the conclusion that he should conquer North Carolina in order to cover South Carolina and Georgia, but he was delayed by sick troops, the enervating summer heat and humidity, and partisan attacks on his supply lines. On 23 August, he noted: "Our sickness is great and truly alarming. The officers are particularly affected [...] incapable of doing [...] duty."[27]

It proved difficult to sustain success, as seen in particular by Patrick Ferguson's total defeat at King's Mountain on 7 October. This battle in which the Patriots attacked rapidly and benefited from tree cover, underlined the Patriot ability to align an understanding of the terrain with particular fighting techniques, "in their favourite manner [...] an irregular but destructive fire from behind trees and other cover."[28] British interest in "a portable *chevaux de frise*," an obstacle behind which infantry could defend themselves, was not brought to fruition, but, anyway, lacked the flexibility of Patriot methods.[29] Clinton initially refused to believe the report of the defeat as he claimed that Cornwallis would not leave a detached force unsupported.[30]

King's Mountain and the heavy defeat of the impulsive Banastre Tarleton at Cowpens on 17 January 1781 did not involve the main field armies in the South. Nevertheless, they crushed the impression of Britain successfully gaining the initiative and thereby tarnished the Southern strategy. Clinton later argued that King's Mountain was "the first link in a chain of events that followed each other in regular succession until they at last ended in the total loss of America."[31] Cowpens saw a major loss of British light troops.[32]

Moreover, the Patriot use of partisan bands in the South led to a civil war in which neither side was in control, but British commanders were left frustrated and unable to gain significant advantage from success in battle.[33] It had been hoped that Loyalist militias would tamp down any violence and root out Patriots, thus restoring local security and royal government. However, the Loyalist militia in western North Carolina was defeated at Ramsour's Mill on 20 June 1780 by Patriot militia. More generally, many of the Loyalists felt too intimidated to supply food to the army, and many neutrals moved toward the Patriots, at least in terms of not actively supporting the British and Loyalists. Meanwhile, the British encouraged Native American allies to divert the Patriots,[34] but without great effect.

Furthermore, each colony/state had a political organization and military and economic resources of its own, and a British victory in one part of America had only a limited effect elsewhere. The fall of Charleston did not make that of Boston much more likely and indeed Clinton's plan to follow the attack on Charleston by retaining Rhode Island was shelved due to a lack of naval support as well as fear of Patriot pressure on New York. In addition, a degree of "pacification" that may have been possible in 1776 was less feasible after several more years of politicization and bitter conflict.

On the other hand, hyper-inflation had wrecked the Patriot economy, and the war indeed reduced median household wealth by more than 45 percent. Contributing to a sense of crisis but also reflecting it, the resources that existed were mismanaged. The limited credit-worthiness of Congress, and the repeated reluctance of the states to subordinate their priorities and resources to Congress, meant that the army had to live from hand to mouth. Nathanael Greene wrote from Charlotte that December:

> Without tools we can do nothing and none are to be got in this country, not even a common felling axe. You will inquire of the Governor what steps have been taken by the Assembly to furnish the artificers and wagons required by me of the State, and press their immediate compliance. For without artificers we cannot aid the transportation.[35]

Much of the supplying of the Continental Army relied on the issue of largely worthless certificates. In January 1781, short of pay, food, and clothes, and seeking discharge, both the Pennsylvania line and three New Jersey regiments were to mutiny. The Pennsylvania mutiny was to be ended only by concession, including the discharge of five-sixths of the men. This episode is a reminder of the precarious nature of the Revolution militarily, and the extent to which the situation did not improve as the Revolution continued. Indeed, Greene was to complain bitterly in 1782 and 1783 about the lack of support from the authorities in Georgia and South Carolina.

This provides an instructive perspective on the war: Both sides faced serious difficulties and had major drawbacks. Militarily, this meant both that there was everything to play for, and that managing limitations was as important as grasping opportunities. Politically, these drawbacks also ensured not only that there remained everything to play for, but also that, whichever side was better able to respond to its weaknesses and persist, was likely to win the struggle of will.

Alongside the pressures on the Patriots in North America, there were the very different and wide-ranging ones for the British. General excise duties in Britain were raised in 1779, 1781, and 1782, the duties on beer, spirits, wine, and salt in 1780 and those on tobacco and soap in 1782. Charles Jenkinson, the well-informed Secretary at War, wrote to Amherst, to say that he did not see how the strength of the army could be maintained, but added:

> I am convinced that any plan of compulsion […] is not only contrary to the nature of the government of this country, but would create riots and disturbances which might require more men for the purpose of preserving the peace, than would be obtained by the plan itself […] besides, that, men who are procured in this way almost constantly desert, or at best make very indifferent soldiers.[36]

There were certainly pressures in British politics and society, including the expression of radical sentiments that helped ensure that the war in America was frequently not at the forefront of Parliamentary discussion. In 1780, the Westminster Association pressed for universal manhood suffrage, annual elections, the secret ballot, and equal associations. In Suffolk, as an instance of a more widespread process, politicians became more sensitive to electors' concerns regarding economical reform, religious toleration, and opposition to the war.[37]

Yet, the 1780 general election, the results of which were followed in America, was still a triumph for the government. George was highly attentive to electoral matters. George also was not interested in a coalition with the Opposition, "for I have never seen any part of opposition inclined to make the smallest concessions, and no power on Earth shall ever reduce me to deliver myself up into the hands of any of them."[38]

Furthermore, thanks to rapid economic growth, taxation's share of national income rose but was still only 11.7 percent in 1780, not much above the 11.5 percent in 1760 during the previous war.[39] Income tax was not introduced until 1798 when the following war proved far more difficult. Indeed, almost half the cost of the war of 1775–83 was covered by borrowing. The new Parliament clearly backed the ministry and this helped ensure that the domestic situation quietened down. Lord Mount Stuart, the envoy in Turin, commented: "[A]s long as our credit can maintain itself we need not fear an enemy."[40]

Meanwhile, the war had broadened out with the inclusion of the Dutch. Disputes over their trade with Britain's enemies, notably France, and over the reception of Patriot privateers had embittered relations. The Dutch had been neutral in the Seven Years' War, and relations thereafter had not been close, although British ministers had continued to assume that they could and should be. The British believed that, under the defensive treaty of 1678, they were entitled to Dutch help against the Bourbons whereas the Dutch were angered by British treatment of their merchantmen.

The cause of neutral trade was taken up by Catherine II who saw it as a possible source of influence for Russia. Having rejected a British approach in the winter of 1779–80, Catherine issued a Declaration of Neutral Rights in March 1780 that was designed to protect neutral shipping from widely-disliked British maritime pretensions. Sweden and Denmark joined the Armed Neutrality that July and the British, aware of negotiations for Dutch accession, declared war on the Dutch on 20 December 1780, hoping to end their supply of naval stores to France before they could accede and thus acquire a Russian guarantee. The British ministry anticipated that this Fourth Anglo-Dutch War might somehow lead to the revival of the pro-British Orangist Party (as Dutch defeat in 1672 and 1747 had led to a revival of Orangist power), but these naïve hopes were to be disappointed. Furthermore, British diplomats, such as Robert Liston in Berlin, found a general lack of understanding of the possible consequences of France rising at the expense of Britain.[41]

The British navy was under pressure but being improved by good administration and by new construction. The army, however, was suffering, Jenkinson reporting in October "the condition of the army with respect to numbers has grown greatly worse." The number of effectives was well below establishment numbers, and drafts of new soldiers were inadequate with Clinton lacking nearly 5,000 men.[42]

At the same time, the war was becoming more unpredictable due to the international context, although the prediction of Matthäus von Vieregg, the Bavarian Foreign Minister, that the war in North America would spread to Europe as had happened earlier[43] proved inaccurate. Secret negotiations with France in the summer and December of 1780 were hampered by the British refusal to discuss the position of the Patriots with a third party and by the French determination to obtain American independence, while Gibraltar proved the stumbling block in Anglo-Spanish negotiations that lasted from November 1779 until March 1781, and which led Clinton to hope for Spain leaving the war.[44] Austrian and Russian attempts to mediate were unsuccessful, for the British wanted to treat directly with the Patriots with no role for another power,[45] the position they were also to adopt in the War of 1812. There was also no success for British offers in early 1781 of support for the opening of the trade of the River Scheldt and of Minorca to Austria and Russia, respectively, in order to win their alliance and, in each case, have a reason to oppose the French alliance. For the British an "essential condition" of peace "must be withdrawing all assistance from the Rebels." George was unwilling to surrender those "great and essential rights and interests, which by every principle of honour and every tie of duty His Majesty is bound to maintain."[46]

This diplomatic impasse was to be cleared only by military defeat for Britain. In the meanwhile, there was a continuance of speculation about geopolitical change, for example of Russia replacing America as a source for British imports.[47]

The close of 1780 saw the central themes of the 1781 campaign in America already clear: The need for Franco-Patriot cooperation if a major blow was to be struck against the British; Cornwallis's problems in the South;[48] the rising importance of the Chesapeake with a British attack into Virginia in October in order to hit Patriot supplies and help divert opposition from Cornwallis;[49] and the crucial role of naval power. British planners kept a keen eye on Bourbon naval moves.[50] At the same time, British and Patriot forces remained more numerous in the New York area than in the South.

Charleston was a location from which the British could move warships and troops north to New York or south to the Caribbean and, in this wider context, offered far more than simply a major advantage in the Southern Strategy. In 1780, yet again, the British failed to turn their position in the Middle Colonies into a decisive advantage. Meanwhile, as 1781 was to show at Yorktown, the war in the South was now a matter of hemispheric strategy, and not simply that of the war in America. The very contrasting results of the campaigns of 1780 and 1781 indicate, however, that these circumstances and problems rendered nothing inevitable. This was the case at the strategic, operational, and tactical levels.

# 10. 1781: DEFEAT FOR BRITAIN

> "Washington has all to fear—I all to hope."
>
> Clinton with news of disaffection in Continental Army, 28 January 1781[1]
>
> "The moment is very critical but his good sense, valour and the bravery of the troops under his command make me hope that he will extricate himself well, and if Sir Henry Clinton can arrive in time perhaps this moment may put an end to the rebellion."
>
> George, 23 November 1781[2] [In fact, Cornwallis had already surrendered at Yorktown on 19 October. News took time to cross the Atlantic.]

Until early 1781, the odds of winning the war on the ground, at least in so far as battle was concerned, were still not too bad for Britain where there was a sense of war for survival, Viscount Stormont writing as a Secretary of State in March:

> On our part it is a war of defence and self-preservation. The purpose of the ambitious policy of France is to give a fatal blow to the greatness and prosperity of this country, by a vast dismemberment of the British Empire.[3]

In America, there were initiatives by the British. An expedition under Benedict Arnold left New York on 20 December 1780 and, having been disrupted by a winter storm, reached Hampton Roads on 30 December. This was in part in pursuit of Cornwallis' request for a diversion on the Chesapeake.[4] Moving up the James River, the British landed at Westover on 4 January 1781, entering Richmond next day. Having destroyed much of the town and nearby supply bases, the British left on the 6

January 1781, retiring, and largely unopposed, to Portsmouth where they established a base from which they inflicted serious damage on the local economy (notably destroying tobacco).[5] The vulnerability of the Chesapeake to British combined operations had been amply demonstrated. On 6 January, Frederich Wilhelm Steuben informed Thomas Jefferson, the governor of Virginia, that he had "not heard of a single gun being fired at them either on their march from Westover or during their stay at Richmond."[6] However, in a classic instance of a common problem with such operations, Arnold, whose command style led to complaints,[7] felt that he needed reinforcements if he was to hold Portsmouth against a likely attack. Instead, he was superseded when Cornwallis arrived on 20 May.

Conversely, the Continental Army was hit by mutinous disaffection as a result of its poor conditions; disloyalty not being the issue.[8] Mounted from Charleston, another British operation took the port of Wilmington, North Carolina, without resistance on 28 January 1781. This was the major port for North Carolina and its capture was intended both to help naval operations and to influence opinion in the state.

The Southern Strategy had not stirred any significant consequences for the British in the middle colonies, but nor had it undermined their position. After the fact, it was unclear that the British could have won in North America, and the Patriots' Fabian strategy appeared increasingly valid.[9] Clinton initially favored an advance on the Hudson Highlands. Subsequently, arguing that in the absence of reinforcements, success in re-establishing control would depend on Loyalist support, Clinton favored not a campaign in Virginia where he thought it lacking, but in Pennsylvania. He proposed an attack on Philadelphia to hit Patriot logistics and finances and take advantage of disaffection in the Pennsylvania regiments of the Continental Army[10] and accordingly pressed Cornwallis to send troops to his assistance.[11] This was part of Clinton's stance that Cornwallis did not need so many troops and that New York was a more significant and less vulnerable base for operations.[12]

Cornwallis discovered the detrimental impact of the loss of public support in his campaign in North Carolina, a formerly heavily Loyalist colony, when he advanced north in 1781. Few came forward to support him and he did not feel he could remain there with advantage or safety. Moreover, Cornwallis's march thereafter into Virginia meant that the

British position in the South was not consolidated with all the discouragement that it might have brought to the Patriots. Cornwallis, however, had been discouraged by the weakness of the Loyalists that had not compensated for his limited numbers, as they were further hit by casualties.[13]

In the meanwhile, the British position in South Carolina was put under great pressure. Lieutenant-Colonel Nisbet Balfour, Commandant at Charleston, reported to Clinton on 6 May that despite a victory by Lord Rawdon over Greene and a larger number at Hobkirk's Hill on 25 April, which overcame a particular crisis,[14] the situation was very difficult: "[The enemy's parties are everywhere, the communication by land with Savannah no longer exists […] the defection of this province so universal that I know of no mode short of depopulation to retain it."[15]

Cornwallis enjoyed an operational mobility as a consequence of his advances but it did not equate to a strategic mobility nor bring a strategic success. Nor was there any equivalent to the impact of Sherman's advances across the South in 1864 and 1865, which is instructive for considering both. Sherman faced no significant opposition, in part because Confederate troops had moved elsewhere in 1864 and he also advanced in far greater numbers than Cornwallis. Indeed, the latter's advance had more of the character of a raid.

Even so, Cornwallis' advance disconcerted the Patriots and was made more threatening by the earlier British victories at Camden (16 August 1780) and, far less easily, Guilford Court House (15 March 1781), a battle in which there were high casualty rates to prevent the collapse of the Patriot position. The extent to which battle was dependent on deployment was captured as the Patriot lines were placed too far apart to enable the defense in depth to permit falling back in an orderly fashion thanks to mutual support. The Patriot force was about twice as large as their British assailants. The North Carolina militia in the front line brought down many of the attackers with two volleys, but most fled the British bayonet charge as expected. The engagement with the stronger American second line was more confused, but it was slowly pushed back, before the third line that had more experienced troops and repelled the advancing British. To block their attack, Cornwallis ordered two cannon to fire grapeshot into the mélée, which led both sides to disengage with casualties. As the British reformed and resumed the attack, the

Patriots retreated, but the British were too exhausted to mount a pursuit and could not afford their losses. This helped make the battle a tactical defeat for the Patriots, but an operational and strategic one for the British.

Nevertheless, the towns lacked defenses that might delay a British advance or prevent a capture. There was no equivalent to the defenses in the Floridas, at St. Augustine and Pensacola, nor to those the British were improving at Charleston.[16]

Concerned to maintain an advantage and demonstrate British superiority to the Loyalists,[17] Cornwallis nevertheless failed to destroy his retreating opponent Greene, in part because the latter benefited from a superior grasp (thanks to better intelligence) of the terrain, notably the rivers. Moreover, the Patriots were better able to understand the possibilities of "small war."[18]

Cornwallis responded when he reduced his supply train and gained greater mobility. He moved north into Virginia to help secure the Carolinas, a policy of which Clinton disapproved.[19] In turn, in a reminder of the abiding role of choice, Greene did not follow but instead marched south from Ramsey's Mill, North Carolina, on 6 April. Intended in part to draw Cornwallis from Virginia and the threat he would pose there to the middle colonies and of action in concert with Clinton, this step was not matched by Cornwallis and this helped ensure two different struggles—in Viriginia and in South Carolina.

Arriving in Virginia, Cornwallis was uncertain "what measures I shall pursue."[20] In the event, he was to surrender mobility and potential when he established himself at Yorktown on the Chesapeake in August. This offered protection, not least for supplies as well as an apparently secure base for covering landing from any squadron or for embarkation, and was in part a response to naval pressure for a local base.[21] But any such position provided a target for attack and was vulnerable if naval support were lost. This situation was accentuated by Cornwallis' failure of energy in the enervating humidity of the Chesapeake. He surrendered to circumstances as he was also to a degree to do in his first (unsuccessful) advance on Seringapatam, the Mysore capital, in 1791.

Yet, at this point, the war in America was far from over. It was apparent that neither the Southern Strategy nor the advance into Virginia had brought the anticipated gains. Attacks could only achieve so much. On the Canadian frontier, two British attempts to recapture Ticonderoga failed.[22]

However, in the South, the British had shown that they could gain and hold important positions and defeat Patriot forces, while the economic burden of the struggle was becoming more punishing for the Patriots, whose armies were weak and whose hopes were highly vulnerable to French changes in policy. Lieutenant-Colonel William Martin wrote from New York on 26 July:

> [T]his city and district are seriously menaced with a general attack, whenever a French fleet shall arrive on the coast, superior to ours, without which we have little to fear, notwithstanding the French and Rebels are gathering round us, and it is said they have a numerous artillery.[23]

He followed up by welcoming the strength offered by the arrival of German reinforcements, which he thought had led Washington to fall back.[24]

Indeed, a different balance of naval power and advantage would have led to a successful British withdrawal from Yorktown in September or October 1781, repeating that from New Jersey after Monmouth Court House in 1778 and reprising the ability to send an expedition by sea into the Chesapeake in early 1781; But a withdrawal would not have resulted in victory. Instead, having fought their way to impasse in the middle colonies and the South, the British would have had to evacuate Virginia.

Flawed naval command decisions made this outcome impossible, and led to a far more serious setback, a failure that reflected Clinton's argument the previous year of one overall naval commander for the Caribbean and North America.[25] De Grasse had been able to leave Brest for Martinique with 20 ships of the line in March 1781, and that August, with loans from Havana's wealthy (and thus access to Spanish New World liquidity), he sailed from Saint Domingue for the Chesapeake. The previous winter, a British force was sent to the Chesapeake. Leaving Sandy Hook on 20 December 1780, it had been characteristically disrupted by a winter storm, reaching Hampton Roads on 30 December and establishing a base at Portsmouth. This was challenged in January 1781 by three French warships that escaped the blockade of Newport, and, more seriously, two months later when the entire French squadron was able to sail because the British blockaders had been badly disrupted by a storm. Fortunately for the British at Portsmouth, the French were engaged by Arbuthnot off the Virginia Capes on 16 March. He was outmanuevered and several of his ships badly battered, but the French did not press their advantage to gain control of the Chesapeake. This meant that the American forces in the area could not act effectively against the British.

British commanders were well aware of the dependence of Chesapeake operations on naval command, Clinton informing Cornwallis on 29 May of:

> a circumstance which I am ever aware of in carrying on operations in the Chesapeake, which is, that they can be no longer secure than whilst we are superior at sea [...] nor have I any reason to suspect we shall not [remain so].

Clinton had pressed Arbuthnot to consider this, "having repeatedly told him, that should the enemy possess it even for 48 hours your lordship's operations there may be exposed to most imminent danger." Although more concerned about the situation at Newport, Arbuthnot promised to guard the Chesapeake.[26] Clinton was concerned about an attack on New York, but:

> I am however under no great apprehensions: as Sir George Rodney seems to have the same suspicions of de Grasse's intention that we have and will of course follow him hither. For I think our situation cannot become very critical, unless the enemy by having the command of the Sound should possess themselves of Long Island, which can never be the case, whilst we are superior at sea.[27]

Clinton pressed Rodney to send sufficient ships to counter de Grasse's expected arrival. Meanwhile, the continual British presence in the

Chesapeake was increasingly discussed in terms of its acting as a naval base, Clinton writing to Cornwallis:

> I am just returned from having a conference with Rear Admiral Graves [...] we are both clearly of opinion that it is absolutely necessary we should hold a station in the Chesapeake for ships of the line, as well as frigates.[28]

This would entail control of the Williamsburg peninsula, but Cornwallis was more skeptical:

> [D]esultory expeditions in the Chesapeake may be undertaken from New York with as much ease and more safety, whenever there is reason to suppose, that our naval force is likely to be superior for two or three months.[29]

The quest for a naval base ensured that the British forces in Virginia were to surrender the initiative. Moreover, although Yorktown offered an anchorage suitable for ships of the line, it was a poor defensive position against land attack.

The navy, however, wanted a Chesapeake base. Graves, who had replaced Arbuthnot, did not think that New York or Gardiner's Island at the eastern end of Long Island, from which Newport had been watched, were suitable winter anchorages. As Newport had been lost, the Chesapeake appeared the only alternative to distant Halifax, and Clinton, who did not want the naval base far from New York, informed Cornwallis that he did not think there was any chance of the French "having a naval superiority in these seas for any length of time, much less for so long a one as two or three months."[30]

The naval situation was unsettled. De Grasse did not sail directly to America but went first to the West Indies where Tobago was forced to surrender on 2 June. De Barras, the commander of the Newport squadron, did not relish the idea of serving under de Grasse and was dissuaded with great difficulty from sailing to attack the British in Newfoundland. In addition, de Grasse might have been recalled, or Rodney might have defeated or preempted him. As it happened, splitting his fleet the indecisive and ailing Rodney sailed for Britain, escorting prizes back to England. De Grasse, with his entire fleet, got to the Chesapeake before Graves, who did not appreciate the seriousness of the situation in part due to his failure to accept intelligence information.[31] Like Clinton, who anticipated attack on New York, unaware that the Chesapeake was becoming the key sphere, Graves lacked de Grasse's strategic and operational insights. More seriously, the global commitments of Britain opened opportunities to the French and Spaniards, and thereby the Patriots—notably the supply of Gibraltar and the need to protect against invasion—although hopes of Spanish cooperation with the Patriots in North America[32] proved unfounded. The French were receiving reports that British economy and society were under grave pressure.[33]

The Patriots and the French were able to concentrate forces against Cornwallis, the French moving from Newport with a speed and stealth that allowed them to arrive at their objective at an ideally opportune moment while avoiding British detection. The bulk of the force moved overland but de Barras was able to bring the French artillery by sea.[34]

The temporary and localized superiority the French enjoyed in the Chesapeake that autumn had crucial results. Although this superiority was neither the consequence, nor the cause, of any climatic battle in which one fleet destroyed the other, and there was no decisive shift in naval advantage against Britain, there was nevertheless a strategic impact in that Cornwallis could not be relieved. The British attempt to force the entrance to the Chesapeake in the battle of the Virginia Capes on 5 September was a failure. The British were outnumbered 24 to 19 in ships of the line. Neither side lost any ships, but the British, who had concentrated their naval strength as they should have done, failed to show the fighting spirit they had displayed when forcing their way into victory at Quiberon Bay in 1759.

Instead, there was more than a little similarity with Byng's humiliating failure to relieve the British garrison on Minorca in 1756. A parallel to the Virginia Capes was the role in securing Greek independence of the Anglo-French-Russian victory over a Turkish-Egyptian fleet at Cape Navarino in 1827, and also the significance of the British naval victories over the French in the French Revolutionary and Napoleonic wars to Britain's ability to sustain the resistance of Sicily, Portugal, and Spain to French schemes. In part, failure in 1781 stemmed from Rodney's decision to sail warships back to British waters rather than move more north into American waters. Yet, it is difficult to feel that even Nelson would have been deterred from forcing the entrance to the Chesapeake. Indeed, in 1797 George affirmed:

> [H]is confidence in naval skill and British valour to supply want of numbers. I am too true an Englishman to have ever adopted the more modern and ignoble mode of expecting equal numbers on all occasions.

Graves, in contrast, after the Virginia Capes did not feel able to engage de Grasse again and, instead, decided to sail to New York for repairs first, but before doing so delayed a week. Clinton promised Cornwallis naval relief, but the repairs took longer than anticipated. New York did not have a naval dockyard, there was a shortage of naval stores and food, and a number of accidents further delayed matters. As de Grasse had been strengthened by the Newport squadron, but Graves only by three ships of the line from England, the French superiority increased and Graves was worried about the danger of attacking a superior force. This was understandable as the risky plan advocated by Clinton and Hood endangered both the largest British naval force in the Western Hemisphere and the continued viability of the New York garrison. Graves did not sail until 19 October, but on that day Cornwallis surrendered. Clinton blamed the disaster totally on the lack of sufficient warships.[35]

Cornwallis, besieged from 28 September by larger Patriot and French forces, in total about 16,000 men, and under heavy artillery fire in his very exposed position at Yorktown, was obliged to surrender on 19 October. The siege operations had been well-handled by the assailants who had shown good understanding of the terrain and been able to push forward their positions and expose the British to heavier fire.[36] In particular, there was a successful combination of the digging of siegecraft with well-chosen advances.

Cornwallis had just over 6,000 rank and file, but only 3,273 remained fit for duty when he decided to surrender. Two days earlier, Johann Conrad Döhla, a member of the Ansbach-Bayreuth forces in Cornwallis's army, recorded:

> At daybreak, the enemy bombardment resumed, more terribly strong than ever before. They fired from all positions without let-up. Our command, which was in the Hornwork, could hardly tolerate the enemy bombs, howitzers and cannon-balls any longer. There was nothing to be seen but bombs and cannonballs raining down on our entire line.

The extent to which the result of Yorktown may be differently explained can be seen by comparing two French maps of the siege. The *Carte de La Partie de La Virginie où L'Armée Combinée de France et des Etats-Unis de l'Amérique a fait prisonnière l'Armée Anglaise* put much emphasis on the battle of the Virginia Capes, whereas the map by Georges-Louis Le Rouge closely focused on the action immediately surrounding Yorktown.

Like surrender at Saratoga in 1777, Yorktown did not end the war. Indeed, after the Patriot defeat at Hobkirk's Hill, at Eutaw Springs on 8 September, the last major battle in the Carolinas, the Patriot pursuit of a hitherto defeated British force collapsed in disorder as the hungry troops looted the British camp, especially eager for food. This threw Greene's advance into disarray, allowing the British to rally and drive the Patriots from the field.[37] British fighting quality remained strong, although the balance of support in South Carolina as well as the heavy British casualties at Eutaw Springs helped restrict the British increasingly to Charleston and its surroundings.[38] Greene faced formidable difficulties with other commanders when ensuring that sufficient supplies were provided by the civilian authorities. He was able to weaken the British position considerably but faced an able opponent in Lord Francis Rawdon. Greene was moved to despair at the bitterness with which Loyalists and Patriots clashed in the South and disapproved of the killing of prisoners.[39]

The war was not to be settled, however, in South Carolina. Instead, Cornwallis's surrender brought the war's strategic conundrum to the fore. Lieutenant-General James Robertson, the governor of New York and a veteran of success at Louisbourg (1758), Martinique (1762), and Long Island (1776), wrote that there were nearly 13,000 men in the garrison, which compared with the just over 7,000 men, including about 840 sailors, surrendered at Yorktown. He added:

> [W]e can arm four thousand very well disposed militia, this force I should think able to beat any Washington can collect, as he has now only 4,000 French. But an army confined to a defensive in posts is not only useless but ruinous, an army without the hope of getting back America should not stay in it—a reinforcement of at least of 4,000 well conducted might revive the hopes of our friends and turn the tide of opinion, and people's actions are governed by their belief about what government is to take place—the assistance or resistance we are to meet with depends on this opinion, and that on the measures His Majesty may be pleased to direct. If the war is to be carried on, even an assurance of this will prevent the growth of the rebel army, which the most sanguine hopes cannot collect—nor bring against the place till the middle of May—an army cannot lie on the ground—or horses find pasture sooner—our succours in place of arriving in August should be by the first of May.[40]

Arguments that more might have been achieved by the British, that the war was not lost, that the center of gravity of British forces was in New York, and that the Patriot-French strike at Yorktown was going for easier fruit and was a diversion from the main task, are all correct. However, these arguments ignore the degree to which strategy and the related choices ought to be seen in political terms. Defeat at Yorktown meant failure in a war that was lasting much longer than might have been anticipated at the time of Saratoga. The hypotheticals of success no longer appeared credible. The Southern politico-military strategy had failed, as had attritional conflict between two tired combatants. A new departure appeared inevitable to many.

That, however, was not viable politically, either in Britain or in America. In 1814, British troops were to land in the Chesapeake, rout the Americans at nearby Bladensburg, and burn the public buildings in Washington, the city named after the victor at Yorktown. Yet not only were they to fail to sustain their presence, but the step brought no political advantage.

In 1782, the question of the relative strength of the combatants remained significant, and the French government was informed that the

North ministry encouraged George to persist by telling him that France had internal and financial problems.[41] Nevertheless, such arguments increasingly appeared redundant because the conflict was now ebbing away, even if the war did not end until 1783. Yorktown proved a decisive battle won with few casualties.

The Yorktown campaign indicated the key element of the international dimension and particularly of the naval war. Clinton reflected of the surrender, "there is perhaps but one cause to impute it to the want of sufficient naval force to cover our operations."[42] The ability of a Franco-Spanish fleet to cruise in the Channel approaches in 1779 without the outnumbered British risking battle was a situation that encouraged the movement of British warships to home waters, including in 1781. In America, the Patriots were dependent not only on French troops, and crucially artillery when on land, but also on the ability of the French navy to prevent the relief of the British force at Yorktown. Conversely, Washington's plan to capture New York in 1782 could not be implemented, not least due to a lack of French support.

These contrasts underline the danger of thinking of this war, and, indeed, of insurgency warfare in general, in teleological terms; in this case, of framing the inevitable defeat of an *ncient régime* army by a revolutionary new force. In practice, the French military, which played a major role in British failure, scarcely conformed to this model, while, indeed, the Continental Army owed its tactics and structure to the general Western model, and more particularly to the British example. Washington did not wish to rely on militia, but instead wanted a regular army that could provide America with legitimacy. Washington also stressed drill and discipline and was a believer in position warfare.

Partly as a result, guerrilla warfare tended to occur only when Patriot regular forces were very weak, as in the South in 1780–1. Then Nathanael Greene, the commander in the South, who was fulsome in his complaints about supplies,[43] found it in his "power to carry on nothing but a kind of fugitive war," while Daniel Morgan was ordered to "spirit up the people" in upper South Carolina and hinder British moves.[44] Moreover, the use of partisan bands appeared an obvious response to the defeat of Patriot regular forces at the battle of Camden, the uncontrollable vastness of the South, and the need to counter Loyalist activity.

The result was a civil war in which neither side was in control, and one that left British commanders frustrated. Furthermore, on both sides, this civil war involved atrocities.

Guerrilla warfare should not be taken as typical of the Patriot war effort,[45] although that approach proved very popular in American public myth, with its emphasis on citizen soldiers attuned to the natural environment—and notably in Hollywood, as in the film *The Patriot* (2000). This account also proved significant in later American discussion of insurgency and counterinsurgency warfare, particularly during the Vietnam War and over the last fifteen years.[46] In practice, American warfare was a hybrid type, an adaptation of European warfare to North American circumstances, not least to wars of conquest against Native Americans.[47] British warfare in North America was similarly a hybrid type, although that did not mean that the solutions were identical to those of the American Patriots. Tactical solutions, in any case, had to bow to strategic realities.

As a reminder of the absence of any inevitability, in southern India, Haidar Ali destroyed a British force at Perambakam on 10 September and breached the defenses of Arcot the following month. Yet in 1781, in turn, Haidar Ali was to be defeated at Porto Novo, Sholinghur, and Polilur.

Yorktown turned the strategic inadequacies of the British in North America and the operational failure of Cornwallis into a much greater defeat for British policy. So it was with pressure elsewhere. On 21 July, a Franco-Spanish fleet of 58 ships of the line and 75 transports carrying 8,000 troops left Cadiz. They could have made a crucial difference to the war in the Western Hemisphere, but on 19 August, this fleet reached Minorca where, after the arrival of reinforcements in October, the British position at Fort St. Philip was besieged.

This was the same year as a Franco-Spanish fleet and force captured Pensacola, bringing to a close the ably-executed Spanish reconquest of West Florida after a successful assault on 8 May.[48] The Spanish campaign was aided by the unwillingness of the Creek, who were being wooed by the Spaniards, to help the British.[49] Underlining the significance of the wider equation of force, the besiegers had been sent plentiful reinforcements from Havana because of the fear of a British relief force from Jamaica.[50] John Campbell, the disgruntled commander of Pensacola, blamed a lack of naval support and attributed this to the role of choice in the defense of empire suggesting that Pensacola "was considered no object of national concern, and left as a gewgaw to a muse and divert the ambition of Spain, and prevent it from attending to objects of greater moment and importance."[51] Cornwallis certainly had argued that he could not spare troops for Pensacola.[52] Gibraltar held out, as did New York, but the British imperial system was tottering.

# 11. AFTERMATHS

The political dimension was front and center when explaining why defeat at Yorktown in 1781 was so significant. Yorktown still left the British in control of New York, Charleston, and Savannah, and on 9–12 April 1782, the crushing victory at the Saintes over the French fleet in the West Indies, was over the fleet from which warships were sent to North American waters. Pre-eminently, the Saintes ruled out the chance of an attack on Jamaica, although local commanders continued to feel vulnerable.[1] The Spanish capture of Nassau, the capital of the Bahamas, without resistance on 6 May was scant consolation for Spain, and a Loyalist force sailing from St. Augustine recaptured it anyway on 17 April 1783.[2] The Saintes, which led to the somewhat implausible comparison of Admiral Rodney to Alexander the Great,[3] also lessened the chance of success for any Patriot attack on New York or Charleston, although in early 1783 the French and Spaniards were able to assemble a major fleet in Cadiz. Moreover, the major potential presented by Franco-Spanish co-operation was seriously lessened by the diversion of forces made necessary by major rebellions in Spanish America.[4]

However, a key element, prefiguring to a degree the impact, in and from Vietnam, of the French defeat at Dien Bien Phu in 1954 and the shock of the Tet Offensive in 1968 for the Americans, was that Yorktown produced a crisis of confidence in the ministry of Lord North in Britain. Government supporters were increasingly uncertain and adrift, Lieutenant-General George, 4th Viscount Townshend, the Master-General of the Ordnance, observing on 28 November: “Things grow very bad indeed; what turn they will take I cannot guess, nor how the Minister [North] can raise the supplies.” Townshend expected a French attack on Jamaica and noted ministerial division in Parliament, adding that “the situation of things grows intolerable.”[5] Two days later, Philip Champion de Crespigny MP reported strong opposition in both Houses of Parliament to the continuation of the war in America.[6]

The Cabinet decided on 8 December that there was no point in sending more troops to North America. George III accepted this but was not prepared to acknowledge that victory was therefore not feasible and that peace could be obtained only by accepting independence. In January 1782, he wrote to North:

> I shall never lose an opportunity of declaring that no Consideration shall ever make me in the smallest degree an instrument in a measure that would annihilate the rank in which this British Empire stands among the European states, and would render my situation in this country unsustainable.[7]

Nevertheless, a loss of political will by MPs was the key element, putting pressure on North who urged George to accept political realities.[8] Many independent MPs shifted their support. On 27 February, the government failed to defeat an Opposition motion in the Commons to abandon offensive operations in America. This was a dramatic challenge to royal power and policy. Responding, George wished to attempt to detach the Americans from France by agreements with the individual American states, but only provided the states remained separate from each other.[9] This was unviable. On 20 March, North lost a Commons' motion relating to the further prosecution of the war in America. On 20 March, North announced his resignation.

The collapse of the wartime ministry with the resignation of North was made more significant because it was not succeeded by a similar one following royal views, as would, for example, have been a ministry under Lord Thurlow, the Lord Chancellor, a close ally of George III. Instead, the Opposition, under Charles, 2nd Marquess of Rockingham, came to power, obliging George to accept unwelcome domestic measures as well as their American policy.

As a consequence, the strategy for fighting on in North America outlined after Yorktown by Lord George Germain, the Secretary of State, was redundant. It is instructive, however, to note his plan for mounting amphibious expeditions along the coast, a policy also backed in the press,[10] regaining Rhode Island if possible, and exploiting Loyalist support in the lower counties of the Delaware. Germain argued that, by retaining New York, Charleston, and Savannah, British trade would be secured and bases maintained from which counter-operations directed against France and Spain could be mounted in the Caribbean.[11] Thus, the French attempt to keep the Patriots in the war, triumphant at Yorktown, ironically increased pressure on France and Spain. The latter appeared a more serious threat, John, Lord Mount Stuart, envoy to Turin, supporting peace with the Americans but not with France and Spain "as long as they have 80 ships of the line to oppose us."[12] Other ideas included evacuating New York and, instead, securing South Carolina and Georgia.[13]

As a result of the governmental revolution that was not matched in France, Spain, or Patriot America, 1782 was a key year of the war, even though it was a year in which the Patriots had singularly little success—Washington, in particular, getting nowhere with his plan to capture New York, despite its garrison being insufficient to man its defenses properly. This situation reflected the extent to which Yorktown led to a new stalemate in the fighting rather than a close, a stalemate that interacted with serious continuing tensions on the Patriot side—political, fiscal and economic.[14] Indeed, desertion grew in scale and there was mutinous talk, both among Washington's men and in Greene's force. Each continued to be badly affected by supply problems. These had not been improved by Yorktown. Indeed, supplies and credit remained urgent problems. Greene had to guarantee the debts of contractors who supplied his army with clothing. The resulting debt left Greene with major problems until his death in 1786.

Moreover, this Patriot failure was more generally significant as it marked the decline in the Franco-Patriot alliance. This decline reflected both the problems of pursuing very different military priorities and, far more significantly, a war-weariness on the part of the French government. This war- weariness arose not only from the heavy cost of the conflict, but also from the priorities of European power politics, specifically the concern of Charles, Count of Vergennes and influential Foreign Minister, that Russian expansion posed a threat to the European system. Indeed, Vergennes, earlier a long-serving envoy in Constantinople (Istanbul), sought cooperation with Britain, albeit a Britain that he intended no longer to be the dominant colonial power and that would be willing to heed the French lead.[15] This situation looked toward the centrality of European considerations in French policy during the Napoleonic years (those of Napoleon I)—notably in 1803 and 1812—and subsequently to Napoleon III's willingness to subordinate New World ambitions to European concerns, especially in 1866–7 when he abandoned his Mexican commitment in order to address Prussian power. Although in 1791 the British came close to war with Russia in the Ochakov Crisis, their attitude was very different in the early 1780s. In February 1782, Stormont, the Foreign Secretary, asking about the possibility of war between Russia and Turkey over Crimea, added: "As this is a business in which we have no direct concern, we should let it take its own course, and not show the least solicitude about it."[16] His successor, Fox, added three months later:

> [T]he whole system of Europe is at present so uncertain, and this country at this moment so totally unconnected with that system, that it is impossible to judge whether such an event is to be wished or feared, or, if it should take place, what conduct it would be expedient for us to hold.[17]

This gave Britain a flexibility France lacked.

Furthermore, while on 12 April, the 30-strong French fleet lost five ships of the line, two more were captured on 19 April in the battle of Mona Passage. The French and Spaniards abandoned plans to invade Jamaica that had led to the contentious dispatch of 1,300 troops from Charleston.[18]

Thus, militarily, the war was going Britain's way. New warships were being launched. Public finances were robust, even if the national debt rose from £131 million in 1775 to £232 million in 1783 and taxation from £10.5 million in 1770 to £11.8 million in 1780. Fears of rebellion in Ireland and of disaffection in Britain were largely assuaged, in part because of conciliation in Ireland comparable to that which had been unsuccessfully attempted in America with the Carlisle Commission.

In addition, in 1782, the Bourbons were increasingly unable to attempt another invasion of Britain such as that which had failed in 1779. Moreover, Gibraltar had been held against a long siege, and the British position in both India and Canada was more resilient than had been feared. Britain, furthermore, was to fight on for longer in the French Revolutionary and Napoleonic Wars.

Yet, despite the reluctance of George, who considered abdicating, the politics in 1782 was now of peace and a settlement that were not focused on a return of America to its loyalty. Indeed, alongside successes there were failures. Albeit without the humiliation when it had last fallen in 1756, Minorca surrendered in February as a consequence of Britain's loss of control of the western Mediterranean, the superior artillery of the Spanish invasion force, and sickness and food shortages amongst the garrison.[19] The British position in southern India was also under pressure, with a French fleet and French troops inhibiting action against Haidar Ali of Mysore. In a parallel with Cornwallis's position, the British commander, Eyre Coote, reported:

> I wish most anxiously for intelligence of the Admiral and the Fleet being again upon the Coast, as I should hope thereby to have it in my power to move to the southward, as a supply of provisions might then be sent me by sea without which I could not in the present position of Haidar and the French undertake such an operation to its full extent, at least with the degree of security so necessary to the preservation of our real interests.[20]

In March 1782, Frederick the Great (II) of Prussia observed: "Britain wishes to fight with all the world. She is a marine Hercules who seeks to surpass with her tasks all that legend ascribes to the Greek Hercules."[21]

The new government that came to power in 1782 was pledged to settle with the revolutionaries by yielding independence, as Thomas Grenville sent to Paris in May was instructed.[22] Grenville told Vergennes that, except for American independence, the terms should repeat those of the Peace of Paris of 1763, adding that "the independence of America would be a point gained more essential to the interest of France [...] than any acquisition we had made by the last peace had been to us." Vergennes replied that Louis XVI could not consider American independence as a concession to France, and that he sought a "more just and durable" treaty than the Peace of Paris.[23] Charles James Fox, the new Foreign Secretary, and Grenville, however, argued that France would be more accommodating once separated from America. The attempt to negotiate peace was not developing well as it "begun upon fake notions, continued upon vague ideas, and therefore dissipated without either ministry being much the wiser."[24]

George meanwhile was angry about government policy, about the "inutility of so openly avowing American independency which is an article in all Mr. Fox's letters to the ministers abroad," and himself arguing that France had no intention "of making peace upon such terms as the country can accept," and that he could only back peace "if it can be obtained without forfeiting the honour and essential rights of my kingdom."[25] On 1 July, George observed that victory at the Saintes had "so far roused the nation that the peace which would have been acquiesced in three months ago would now be matter of complaint."[26]

Rockingham died on 1 July 1782 and was replaced by a supporter of William Pitt the Elder, William, 2nd Earl of Shelburne, who hoped—as he had urged during the war[27]—to establish a close relationship with independent America, thus ensuring that the wartime Franco-American alliance did not survive the peace. He saw America as a country of economic possibilities for Britain and a valuable alternative to European markets closed by tariffs. Fox resigned on 4 July and was replaced by Thomas, 2nd Lord Grantham who had served in Madrid, which helped bring Spain into any settlement.[28] By late 1782, the priority was the disruption through negotiations, if not destruction, of the coalition of powers fighting Britain and, hopefully, better relations with an independent America. Paradoxically, this British strategy was to be successful, which simply underlines the conceptual problems of conceiving of strategy in terms of its military operationalization, and thus of geopolitics only in terms of such strategies. The British used bilateral negotiations to open up divisions among their opponents. Savannah was evacuated in July and Charleston in December.

Preliminaries of an Anglo-American peace were signed in Paris in November 1782. The Patriots' willingness to settle without their allies was instrumental to the destruction of this coalition, and that event was important for post-war geopolitics and politics. It opened the way to an Atlantic world defined by an Anglo-American partnership, however uneasy, and with France very much a lesser player. In turn, eager for peace and postwar cooperation, the British had not sought to exploit the possibilities of dividing Patriot sympathies to create new alignments, notably the willingness of the Vermont Republic to pursue the chance of a separate peace.

Grenville had warned Fox in May 1782 that Spain wanted Florida and Gibraltar, while France sought the Newfoundland fisheries, Caribbean gains, and "very extensive surrenders of commerce and territory in the East Indies."[29] Vergennes told Grenville the following month that far from the Peace of Paris serving as the basis for a new treaty, it "should be annulled except in certain specified articles."[30] Vergennes exaggerated to the new British envoy, Alleyne Fitzherbert, of "what he called the present triumphant condition of France" and the "depressed and humiliated state of Great Britain."[31]

Shelburne, however, rejected the idea of France having more in India than the trading stations she had been left in 1763 with the argument that "it was not to be expected that the King would cede two continents."[32] The British position was helped by Bourbon defeats and difficulties, by the Anglo-American preliminaries, and by the French fear that Shelburne would fall if he could not present Parliament with acceptable terms. George backed Shelburne, supported him in seeking cooperation with France, and was ready in the face of Cabinet opposition to abandon his and Shelburne's policy of relinquishing Gibraltar to Spain in return for better terms in the West Indies. Opening Parliament on 5 December, George said he hoped for "reconciliation" and "union" with independent America.[33] That month, Vergennes persuaded the Spanish envoy to drop the demand for Gibraltar, which had become the principal obstacle to peace. As a result, Anglo-Bourbon peace preliminaries were signed in Paris on 20 January 1783.

However, political division gathered pace in Britain, albeit over ministerial composition not policy toward America. In March 1783, at a time when serious disaffection in the Continental Army led, in the Newburgh Conspiracy, to talk of action against Congress to secure payments to troops—and feelings toward a conspiracy[34] in which Gates might have been a Cromwell figure—in Britain "the most dreadful of all calamities, a civil war" was feared.[35] This was implausible, but Shelburne had resigned on 24 February after, on 17 and 21 February, losing parliamentary debates on the peace terms that was castigated as "degrading and disgusting," especially the lack of any guarantees for the Loyalists and for debts to British creditors, Lord John Cavendish, MP for York, also claiming that the cessions made to Britain's enemies were "greater than they were entitled to, either from the actual situation of their respective possessions, or from their comparative strength," and stating that the Bourbons were exhausted.[36]

Although George's determination to defend his prerogative of choosing his own ministers was widely accepted, that did not help George move toward the policies of ministers. This led Shelburne to complain to the French envoy that hitherto ministers had not made George understand the position of the country and that redressing the issue was not easy.[37] George himself had pressed Shelburne to harden peace terms in light of victory at the Saintes.[38] Yet he acted a conscientious part in supporting his ministers in negotiations. Indeed, opening Parliament on 5 December, George said that he hoped for "reconciliation" and "union" with independent America.[39] As it happened, the defeats that brought down Shelburne were largely blows against the "universally disliked" Shelburne[40] and not against the peace. A major reason for Shelburne's fall was that the other two competing groups of politicians, the largest parties in the Commons by far, led by Fox and North, were aiming to secure office and were prepared to do so regardless of any claim by George to choose his ministers. Grantham complained, "I can only as a public man wish that our civil revolutions may not destroy all confidence from abroad in our councils."[41] The Fox-North ministry, a government of former opponents that replaced Shelburne, in fact accepted the peace preliminaries. Indeed, the power to ratify a treaty was an aspect of the royal prerogative, and the disputed question of whether parliamentary approval was required for any agreement to cede territory was avoided by resolving that American independence had been acknowledged by an Act passed the previous session enabling George to settle with the Americans notwithstanding any existing laws. More vividly, Catherine II declared that rather than accept such a loss, she would have shot herself.[42]

The course of events brought out a central aspect of insurgency conflicts: As the revolutionaries were not in a position to invade Britain, the war could only come to an end when the British decided to cease making an effort, and this decision was very much a political one, as strategy often is. In addition, the Patriots did not support or help to initiate similar "revolutions" in other countries, which made it easier to accept a close to the war that left an independent America.

On 3 September 1783, the peace with the Bourbons and with America was signed at Versailles. France won minor territorial gains, including Tobago and coastal Senegal, and consent to the fortification of Dunkirk, which had been denied under the treaties of 1713, 1749, and 1763. Spain obtained Minorca and the Floridas,[43] but the Spanish governor did not arrive at St. Augustine until June 1784.

However, to fuel the paranoia of many Americans, Patriots and others, the potential remained for the North American coalition that Britain had seemed to be seeking during the war—namely, that with both the Native Americans and the Blacks; although the British call to the slaves to arms (understandably) was focused on military benefit, not social change, and the British scarcely pursued a full-fledged strategy to win over slave support.[44] Many Native Americans supported the British during the war, and pressed hard on the frontier of European settlements, especially in New York and Pennsylvania in 1778, and New York in 1780 and 1781. Their ability to do so in part reflected the Patriot failure in 1776 to sustain their position in Canada, and thus to repeat the British success in 1760 in lessening Native options by overcoming the French.

Expeditions by the Patriots against the Native Americans were often unsuccessful, but despite the fighting quality of the Natives, the cumulative pressure of sustained conflict damaged their societies and disrupted their economies, and indeed proved devastating for many—notably, but not only, the Iroquois in 1779 whose homes and cornfields were burnt in order to force them onto the defensive. The willingness of the Patriots to engage in savage anti-societal violence, for example the slaughter of captives, including children, as with the Gnadenhutten massacre of Wyandot in Pennsylvania in 1782, as well as in the destruction of crops, inflicted enormous damage on Native societies.[45] The war also proved disruptive for Native societies that were not devastated, for instance among the Creek,[46] and for their relations with British traders who had acted as intermediaries.[47] The Chickasaw lost their reservation in Carolina.

The Native Americans were to be those who suffered most from the new geopolitics of North America. The Patriots had strengthened their claim to Trans-Appalachia thanks in part to the actions of George Rogers Clark, a Virginian who had settled in Kentucky and persuaded the governor of Virginia to support his attempt to overcome the French settlements in the Illinois country that had come under British rule as a result of the Seven Years' War. Advancing down the Ohio River in 1778, Clark occupied Kaskaskia, Cahokia, and Vincennes. Two years later, he provided support to Spanish-ruled St. Louis when threatened by British attack. Such activity limited the sway of the British forces based in Detroit. Vincennes was recaptured on 17 December by a detachment from there, but on 25 February 1779 the British garrison was forced to surrender, although Clark's attempts to press on to take Detroit had to be abandoned due to a lack of men and supplies.

Opposition by both Native Americans and Blacks continued after the war, contributing to the bellicose character of many Americans. Calling themselves the King of England's soldiers, some Blacks fought on from the swamps by the River Savannah after the British had evacuated Charleston and Savannah. In May 1786, a combined force of militia and Catawba (Native Americans) defeated them, but, a year later, a governor's message mentioned serious depredations of armed Blacks "too numerous to be quelled by patrols" in southern South Carolina.[48] However, the domestic situation in the aftermath was to be very different to that with the end of the Civil War in 1865. Separately, the geopolitics of the post-war were in part a consequence of the operational history of war.

Made without mention of, or the consent of, the Native American population, the cession of Trans-Appalachia—or the Old Northwest, the area between the Great Lakes and the Ohio River—by Britain in 1783, was followed by American claims, warfare, and settlement in the region. These, in turn, looked toward the background of the resumption of conflict between Britain and America in 1812, because American politicians argued that Britain was behind continued Native American resistance. In particular, Canada in British hands, a verdict the Americans had threatened with invasion in 1775 (only to be totally defeated the following year) was regarded as both the unfinished business of independence and the challenge to America's settlement of the interior and her ability to defeat the Native Americans. Franklin unsuccessfully argued during the peace negotiations that it would benefit Britain to give Canada to the United States. That Canada proved the destination of many Loyalists, for example those from North Carolina, exacerbated the situation. Thus, to many Americans, Canada in British hands underlined past failure and present threat, and that at a time in which British economic and fiscal dominance of the Thirteen Colonies remained apparent and was more problematic due to the contrast with the newfound constitutional situation.

A similar analysis was presented for the southern borderlands. Independence was seen as providing good title to lands occupied by Native Americans. Their continued opposition was linked by Americans to real or potential encouragement by European powers, notably Spain, the colonial power in Louisiana, and, more seriously, Florida. As well as acknowledging West Florida as Spanish, Britain ceded east Florida to Spain as part of the peace. In the mid-1780s, the Creek were not opposed to expansion by Georgia but also had treaties with Spain. There was also concern about relations between the Native Americans and British commercial interests in the Spanish colonies, notably in Pensacola, the capital of west Florida.

As in other instances, the success of the Revolution also owed much to the aftermath. In particular, there was no significant British interest in revanche, even when war resumed in 1812–1815. Moreover, Loyalist émigrés accepted their new situation, and in particular sought to develop British Canada. In marked contrast with the often brutal and sometimes murderous situation during the conflict, the Loyalists who remained in America were treated reasonably well in the last stages of the war and after it ended, in part in 1782 in order to lessen the chances of support for the remaining British garrisons.[49] The reintegration of the Loyalists, however, did not extend to Black Loyalists. They went to Britain, Bermuda, Nova Scotia, and the new colony of Sierra Leone which was established for their shelter. The War of 1812 was to some a continuation of the American Revolution. But it was a conflict between two states, which was different between the earlier war. Yet, to its supporters in America, this was a conflict designed to bring the Revolution to fruition. It was both in conquering Canada and by wrecking Native American opposition to American expansion, an opposition seen as resting on British support from Canada. The Revolution was incomplete so long as Britain could be seen as a menace.[50] This manifests strategic asymmetry, as the British held no similar attitude. The Revolution ended in 1815 with the failure of the scheme to unite British North America under the republic.

# 12. HERITAGES, LESSONS, RETROSPECTIVES

> "When representatives of the British government previously sought to go door-to-door in America, it did not end well for them." Thus complained in October 2024 the Donald Trump campaign team against Labor Party members travelling to America to volunteer for Kamala Harris in the presidential campaign, indeed a sign of the continued resonance of the American Revolution. Susie Wiles, Trump's campaign manager, drew another parallel: "In two weeks, Americans will once again reject the oppression of big government that we rejected in 1776."
>
> This was a reprise of the reference by Sarah Palin when speaking in Boston:
>
> You're sounding the warning bell just like what happened in that midnight run and just like with that original Tea Party back in 1773. I want to tell him [President Obama], "Nah, you know, we'll keep clinging to our Constitution and our guns and religion and you can keep the change."

Visiting Liberty Hall in Philadelphia, repeatedly a moving sight even for a Brit, I was greatly struck to hear George III referred to by a guide as a tyrant. This description is wrong but very much reflects the standard American response to the Declaration of Independence and its role in American public history.[1]

In criticizing George, the Americans drew, and continue to draw, not only on the sense that monarchy (in contrast to an elected president) is an anachronism, but also on British opposition to, and criticism of, George, notably the contemporary (and misleading) Whig myth about his subverting the British constitution.[2] Moreover, the history of countries under republican governments, such as Classical Athens, republican Rome, and the Netherlands in the early-modern period, was scrutinized in order to provide constitutional guidance and political ammunition for use against Britain and the monarchy.

The hostile portrayal of George endures to this day, as seen in the musical *Hamilton*, and is reiterated in popular academic works. Thus, in 1982, Robert Middlekauff found virtue essentially to be an American prerogative in his *The Glorious Cause: The American Revolution 1763–1789*. He and others argued that such a presentation was necessary "to the process of unbecoming British."[3]

The situation was made more complex in the Gilded Era and then in the twentieth century by a marked degree of Anglophilia among part of the American élite. This Anglophilia was political, social, and cultural. The Anglo-American alliance created in 1941 became the key plank of foreign policy for both powers.[4] Moreover, in what can be seen as a reaction within the United States in the 1920s—and notably by the Republican governments of the period—against "Bolshevism," progressivism, and immigration, there was an emphasis on an early America that was under the British Crown. This situation was given visual form in the 1920s in John D. Rockefeller's sponsorship of Colonial Williamsburg. In the 1950s, this combination emerged once again in the Eisenhower Cold War years.

"Culture wars," however, then changed the situation in the United States. The rise of a new historical consciousness reflected a more radical stance from the 1960s onward. In part, this radical stance involved a foreshortening and misunderstanding of American history, with emphasis on the period onward from the Civil War that provided a backdrop to an engagement with civil rights and other contemporary issues. As a result, earlier American history, and certainly the colonial period and that of the early republic, dropped from sight. A similar situation characterized the teaching of American history in Britain, which came to focus on the New Deal (when I was I high school this was the period I studied) and, later, civil rights. When I was on the staff at the University of Durham from 1980 to 1995, there were (unusually) two (not one) Americanists. One specialized on the nineteenth century, the other on the twentieth, but the colonial period did not attract attention at all.

A contrast between the treatment of the conflict in America and Britain is instructive for the significance of origin accounts given that it is important for America but not Britain. Moreover, the continued importance of the founding Constitution for America today understandably further directs attention to the politics of the period. The American Revolution is also far less contentious than the Civil War or, indeed, the foundation of the original colonies; although the accommodating attitude of the Founding Fathers, especially Washington and Jefferson, to slavery has attracted greater attention over the last quarter-century. The consequences can be seen in memorial sites, notably at Philadelphia and Monticello, both in what is written on displays and what is shown to visitors.

The heritage, nevertheless, is largely a positive one, and so also for the conflict itself. A sense of superior American morality, but also of the challenges it faced, was captured by Thomas Sully's painting *The Capture of Major Andre* (1812), which depicts the three young militiamen who captured the British agent André in September 1780, refusing a bribe and thus thwarting Benedict Arnold's plan to betray West Point. This refusal, and the contrast with the (unsuccessful) treason of Arnold, was a symbol of the moral strength of ordinary American citizens, a theme in some battlefield commemorations, notably at Bunker Hill.[5] This strength was seen as the basis for the republic but also of the need for vigilance against the British threat and its alleged American counterpart, which was identified in the Federalists by their Democratic-Republican rivals.

This sense of superior American morality remains culturally important to the present, being seen for example in the film *The Patriot* (2000). Superior morality was in part expressed through the idea that Patriot soldiers were of higher moral caliber and more dedicated than "German mercenaries" and British automated dregs, which is an account that bears little relationship to the truth of a relatively paternalistic British army.[6]

At the same time, the social context has attracted attention. In so far as the colonial and early republic periods now receive public (and even educational) attention, it is in large part in terms that would have made sense from the 1960s. Thus, signs of social radicalism have attracted more attention. From this perspective, the British and the Loyalists might appear anachronistic and reactionary, opponents not only of the new America fought for from 1775, but also, more relevantly, of its fruition being contested in the 1960s. The War of Independence becomes the

American Revolution, and therefore offers a different "lesson" for today. This presentist approach underrates the complexities of the conflict.

Reconsidering the War of Independence in terms of later values certainly leads to a major misunderstanding of empire. This was especially so from the 1960s when the war was compared with the Vietnam War, a comparison, notably of British forces in 1775–83 with American forces in the later war, that was seriously misleading as well as conveniently arresting for its progenitors. In particular, this approach underrated the extent to which the War of Independence was very much a civil war, especially, but not only, in the southern colonies.

Very different contexts continue to be offered when presenting the War of Independence. The Tea Party movement of the 2000s and 2010s drew on a key moment that was part of the foundation account. The drama of the Boston Tea Party, however, is a very poor model for politics within a modern civil society, let alone the rule of law-and-order. Moreover, the events of 1773 scarcely describe modern America, not least given the role of colonial Boston as a slaving port.[7] Furthermore, the treatment of Loyalists in Boston was to be extremely harsh, but so earlier with those of different religious views. Indeed, in 1732, Thomas Sherlock, an influential Church of England bishop, argued that it was ironic that those Puritans who had claimed religious freedom in England left for North America where they had turned persecutors of those who wanted freedom there.[8]

Relations with Native Americans and Blacks put the War of Independence in an instructive context. Ironically possibly (although looking ahead to tensions in Australia and Canada), the British were more mindful of the interests of the former than were the exponents of the new state, and this helped alienate colonial opinion. Indeed, for the Native Americans, the war was more traumatic than it was for the colonial population, whether Loyalist or Patriot. There was a major attempt to clear territory for land speculation and many Native Americans were killed.[9]

The British recruitment of a few Black soldiers was also controversial, notably in Virginia where freedom was certainly not color blind. Moreover, numbers of Black slaves escaped their masters and fled to the British during both the War of Independence and the War of 1812. This flight offered and continues to offer a complication that was/is not really wanted by commentators, and it was/is generally ignored. In *The Hornet's Nest: A Novel of the Revolutionary War* (2003), former President Jimmy Carter observes:

> The revolution in the southern states was initiated by wealthy and influential political leaders along the coast, but the responsibilities for combat were shifting to those backwoodsmen, some of whom would never yield even when their plight seemed hopeless.

Heroism under pressure summarizes the tone of Bunker Hill, and indeed discussion of much of the war, whereas Trenton and Valley Forge provide images of resolution; Saratoga is proclaimed as a triumph of American fighting methods; and for Yorktown Lafayette is treated as an honorary American. Failures are elided or overlooked. That the supposedly decadent Brits won at Long Island or Brandywine, the clearing of Canada or Camden, Fort Washington or Charleston, is attributed to possession of greater resources. The idea of inherent American military superiority, one burnished by Andrew Jackson's spectacular victory over the British at New Orleans in 1815, and by the Americans supposedly "saving" the Western Allies in both world wars, is then projected back onto the War of Independence. The idea of the Patriots as an effective "people under arms" confirms this account and is very much applied to the Continental Army, even though in reality it could entail struggle between two such forces as at King's Mountain in 1780: The Loyalists were also "people under arms."

There is no rival British account because the British simply lack the interest to provide one, even though this was a key episode in British imperial history. In addition, the subsequent political crisis in Britain in 1782–4 suggested that the political system had failed. A lack of interest, however, is unsurprising as the subsequent war with France that began in 1793 was more urgent and sustained, not only compared with the American Revolution but also with the war with France in 1778–83.

Far from this lack of interest being a matter of the British being embarrassed or at least uneasy about the American Revolution, the successes of that war against the Bourbons—notably the defense of

Gibraltar and victory at the Saintes in 1782—also now attract scant attention. In contrast, both were treated very differently at the time and widely celebrated,[10] including in the pantomime of "Harlequin Junior, or the Magic Cestus," seen in Leeds and York in 1784, that showcased the repulse of the attack on Gibraltar. This was also celebrated in John Singleton Copley's large and dramatic painting *The Defeat of the Floating Batteries at Gibraltar*, commissioned by the City of London in 1783 and originally hung in the Common Council Chamber. Restored, it can now be seen in the Guildhall Gallery.

The Loyalist diaspora is one site of British imperial memory about the American Revolution. Linked to their experience, the Loyalists helped to take the empire in a more conservative direction. However, because Loyalism as an identity was greatly transformed by the challenging conditions of migration and exile, no single monolithic Loyalist tradition could be passed on to subsequent generations, even in Canada.[11] The Loyalists would have more invested in the successful defense of Canada during the War of 1812 than in their more diffuse and unsuccessful struggle in the American Revolution. More generally, there was a broader period of adjustment in the Anglo-American relationship with links and assumptions reknitted or adapting.[12]

Writing from Paris in 1786, William Eden, who was negotiating a trade treaty and seeking to develop closer Anglo-French links, noted a sense of a geopolitical transformation of menace:

> [M]any of the most considerable and efficient people talk with little reserve of the dangers to be apprehended from the revolted colonies, if they should be encouraged to gain commercial strength and consistency of government.[13]

Napoleon in 1816 was to follow suit, in the aftermath of the Anglo-American War of 1812 telling Lieutenant-Colonel Mark Wilks, governor of St. Helena, where he was being held prisoner:

> [Y]our [British] coal gives you an advantage we cannot possess in France. But the high price of all articles of prime necessity is a great disadvantage in the export of your

> manufactures [...] your manufacturers are emigrating fast to America [...]. In a century or perhaps half a century more, it will give a new character to the affairs of the world. It has thriven upon our follies.[14]

But earlier, in the late 1780s, any general geopolitical reading from the American Revolution to a wider crisis for European powers in the Americas—still less in the world as a whole, as a result of developments there—appeared questionable. This might seem merely to be a matter of timing, and it was certainly the case that the situation looked very different by 1824. Far from being a different world, 1824 was nearly as close to the end of the period covered in this book (1783) as 1775 was from the start of that period when the latter is seen in terms of the outbreak of Anglo-French war in America in 1754. Yet again, however, there is a need for caution, for the successful revolutions from 1791 in Saint-Domingue, Brazil, and the mainland Spanish colonies were not matched in Cuba, the remaining British, or, indeed, the other French islands in the Caribbean, as well as the Dutch and Danish ones.

Alongside this emphasis on specificity comes the aftermath of the American Revolution. Far from propounding a universal creed for change that it then sought to implement, the new American state did not prefigure or face the challenges of its French Revolutionary counterpart in the 1790s as a result of doing so (other than failing in Canada). There was no earlier counterpart to the Monroe Doctrine of 1823, nor was America in a position to give force to one. A renewed attack on Canada was not launched until 1812, and such an attack was certainly not the policy of the Federalists who dominated the new state until the 1800 presidential election brought Thomas Jefferson to power. Thus, the pieces apparently shattered by the American Revolution had in many respects been less damaged than might have been anticipated. This was true both of European control in the new world, and of Britain's overseas power.

In 1783–7, British geopolitical anxieties were greatly eased by the success of the 1783 peace settlement in splitting the opposing alliance. This meant that American expansionism, had it resumed against Canada or began in the Caribbean, would not be a great threat, but also permitted the emphasis on relations with France that was further assisted by British peace with Mysore in 1784.

Once independent, moreover, the Americans did not match the Europeans in developing a large fleet. Indeed, the initial absence of a federal revenue base helped ensure that there was no navy, for, once independence was won, the Continental Navy, itself weak, was disbanded (its last ship was sold in 1785). The lack of the necessary infrastructure of bureaucracy and naval dockyards was a key problem and contrasted with the situation in Europe.[15] The situation was not to change until a combination of Federalist government and the Quasi War with France led to the buildup of a navy from 1794, and even more in 1797.[16]

The American war led to new constitutional arrangements with Ireland and was followed by major attempts to reorganize the government of British India, unsuccessful pressure for parliamentary reform, and William Pitt the Younger's wide-ranging policies for fiscal regeneration and commercial strength. Yet, there were far greater changes in Britain and the British world as a consequence of the French Revolution and Napoleonic Wars.

Legacies and lessons overlapped, with morality front and center on the American side. However, general military historians prefer to emphasize the French rather than the American Revolution, and so also with contemporaries. The American Revolution could be used as a way to comment on the French one, as in Charlotte Smith's novel *The Old Manor House* (1793),[17] and in America the two revolutions were contrasted to the favor of the Americans—notably by the Federalists. The French Revolution was rejected for its atheism, its social radicalism, and the violence of the Terror. In contrast, for the British, the standard contrast with the French Revolution was not the American one but, rather, the "Glorious Revolution" of 1688–9. Contexts and comparisons therefore provided the basis for assumptions and assessments, and they continue to explain how these might be very different.

This point is also true for military matters. The war was transitional in the sense of prefiguring aspects of the "modern," revolutionary warfare beginning in 1792 although being waged in large part in traditional ways. This was particularly so in looking toward the Latin American wars of independence. Indeed, rather than regarding the American War of Independence as an outlier of European developments, a partial precursor to the French Revolutionary Wars, it is more appropriate to think of the war as the first struggle between European settler populations in the new world and their governments, both "mother country" governments and, subsequently, new world ones—most famously witnessed in the American Civil War. This provides a way to grasp a crucial significance of the War of Independence. It might have little to offer Napoleon, but was more significant for Simon Bolivar and Jefferson Davis.

# 13. CONCLUSIONS

> "Wonders wonders wonders and wonders—dedicated to the wonderfull wonderfull wonderer."

A caricature of 1782 showed Britannia and America, George III, and several British ministers, with some of these appearing as couples shaking hands. John Wilkes is shaking hands with the king, Charles James Fox with Shelburne and Britannia, with a bare-breasted Native American woman representing America, who is wearing a feathered headdress and holding a staff, topped with a liberty cap. "Come, come, shake hands, and let's be friends," to which America replies, "With all my heart, I've gained my end."[1]

As far as British policy, let alone colonial attitudes, in 1754–63 was concerned, the focus had been on conquest and not on pacification. The latter, indeed, was very much subservient to the former, although different policies were pursued for the purpose of pacification. These included an eighteenth-century equivalent of ethnic cleansing in the expulsion of the Acadians from Nova Scotia, as well as the very different post-conquest accommodation of the French Catholics of Québec. Ironically, the latter was a process that helped alienate opinion in New England. Indeed, as with the Boston Tea Party, this was an instance of the problems of empire as a process of reconciling different interests, problems that increased as empire expanded and the process of reconciliation became more active. There was to be a parallel in the eventual move of America, once independent, to a comparable civil war in 1861.

In the War of Independence, pacification was the British strategy, and the question was how best to secure it. The purpose of the war was clear: It was the return of the Patriots to their loyalty, and the method chosen was different to that in response to the Jacobite rebellions in Scotland and northern England in 1715–16 and 1745–6. In the latter cases, as later in the face of the unsuccessful Irish rebellion in 1798, the remedy had been more clearly military and there was a higher degree of violence, notably in the treatment of the defeated.

Yet, in making that argument, it is necessary to note post-war policies for stability through reorganization, most obviously in the introduction of new governmental systems for the Scottish Highlands and Ireland, particularly the 1801 Act of Union that united Ireland and Britain constitutionally and especially their Parliaments, as well as political backing for Catholic Emancipation.

This point raises the question of whether comparable methods for the American colonies might have been devised and successfully implemented, creating new governmental and geopolitical relationships. The most prominent instances of pacification through conciliation were the instructions to the Howe brothers (the British commanding general and admiral) in 1776 to negotiate as well as fight, and, even more clearly, the dispatch of the Carlisle Commission in 1778, while opposition politicians sought to "save America" by advancing their own ideas (although William Pitt the Elder, now Earl of Chatham, refused to countenance American independence).[2]

The stress on conciliation from 1776 to 1778 and its failure suggests that no outcome other than independence was possible, although timing was an important issue. What was offered to the Patriots by the Carlisle Commission in 1778 might have averted revolution in America in 1775, or opposition earlier. Paradoxically, such an outcome might have led to a search for independence in the early nineteenth century when Britain moved against first the slave trade and then slavery, the abolition of which would probably have been treated as a crushing blow to American interests and rights. (This outcome would have proved a very interesting basis for American public history.)

In the case of America in 1775–83, there was not the sequencing seen in Scotland and Ireland. Instead, there was a willingness to consider not only pacification alongside conflict but also any new governmental system as an aspect of this pacification. Indeed, in one sense, pacification began at the outset with the misconceived and mishandled attempt to seize arms in Massachusetts in 1775. Yet, the coercive character of this step and the authoritarian nature of British policy in New England after the Boston Tea Party in 1773 ensured that the pacification then sought was scarcely conciliatory. Separately, the restoration of colonial government in the South that followed the beginning of the Southern Strategy in late 1778 was a concrete step indicating, during the war, what the British were seeking to achieve to end the conflict. There was a military edge to this policy as it was hoped that it would lead to the raising of additional forces of Loyalists, as well as lessening support for the Patriots.

Alongside that, and more insistently, were the practices of British commanders. Although the Patriots were traitors, they were treated with great leniency, and suggestions of harsher treatment were generally ignored by the British. In part, there were military reasons, notably concern about the position of British prisoners, of which there were particularly large numbers after the surrender of an invading force at Saratoga in 1777. But the political dimension was also significant. Despite the urging of some junior commanders, there was no equivalent, certainly no consistent equivalent, to the "hard hand of war" seen in the Civil War from 1863.

This emphasis on pacification provides an essential continuity to British strategy. Yet, there were of course differences in emphasis—including by circumstance, commander, contingency, colony, policy, and timeline. An attempt at evaluation faces the classic problem that history occurs forward, 1775 preceding 1776, but is analyzed from posterity, with 1775 understood in the light of 1776. This approach is understandable but unhelpful because it is teleological and because the course of the war was affected by discontinuities that transformed its parameters.

The usual one given is the internationalization of the war with France's entry in 1778, but, prior to that, the Declaration of American Independence in 1776 transformed the situation. Whether or not geopolitics is seen in terms of structural fundamentals or, more credibly, of shorter-term spatial factors, independence was a key moment. It affected geopolitics both within North America and as far as the wider significance of developments there were concerned. Independence was both a political act that helped create a nation and an act that ensured that the conflict would prove a lengthy war. The war in turn, by late 1777, showed foreign powers that the Patriots would fight, could fight, could fight well, and could fight with success and persistence.

Alongside the transformation of independence, came military unpredictabilities, such as the unsuccessful American invasion of Canada in 1775–6, and the British failures at Saratoga (1777) and Yorktown (1781), each of which led to the surrender of an army. These events were not secondary to the military operationalization of strategy but, instead, helped direct it. The wider political dimension was also affected by events. Thus, the British Southern Strategy, the focus, both military and political, from 1778 on regaining the support of the South, arose to a degree from the need for a new solution after failures or disappointments elsewhere, but, in large part, from the impact of French entry. This entry ended the relatively unusual situation in which Britain was at war solely in North America, and therefore able to concentrate attention and resources on it: That had been the case in 1755, but it ended in 1756 when war with France was declared.

Britain was essentially pushed in 1778 into a bifurcated effort, with a struggle for pacification continuing in the Thirteen Colonies (albeit being complicated by the French presence there, fatally so in 1781), while a straightforward military conflict began elsewhere. Again, this apparently clear distinction can be qualified by noting that Britain had political options to consider that affected its war with France, for example meeting Spanish wishes. The general impression is of progressive moves toward such a bifurcated effort, but, in practice, the political dimension again came first; and was made more complex by the need to consider not only Britain, France and the Americans, but the goals and moves of various powers, including unpredictable responses to the actions of others. Thus, aside from Britain's relations with the states with which it eventually went to war (France, Spain from 1779, and the Dutch from 1780), there were those with neutral powers, both friendly and unfriendly, the last headed by the League of Armed Neutrality organized by Catherine II (the Great) of Russia, who was personally hostile to George III.

To a degree, these relations with neutral powers were linked to the military operationalization of strategy, not least with the possibility for Britain that alliances in Europe would yield troops for North America. This was successful in the case of several of the German states, most particularly Hesse-Cassel. This was long-established as a principality that provided troops to Britain as part of a subsidy treaty. This system worked well during the war, but Britain wished to extend it to yield troops from a major ally. That, however, was not to happen. There was no repetition of earlier alliances with Austria, Prussia, Russia, and Savoy Piedmont.

Overlapping this, the European crisis of 1778, which led to the War of the Bavarian Succession of 1778–9 between Prussia and France's ally, Austria, created opportunities for Britain (notably of France becoming involved in the war and/or of Britain gaining German allies), and indeed it was seen in this light. There has since also been scholarly discussion on the lines that a more interventionist European policy from the early 1760s would have provided Britain with allies and have distracted France from taking part in the American war, with key consequences for British options there,[3] a claim it must be remembered was made at the time by Charles James Fox, as in Parliament on 24 February 1779.[4]

This argument clashes, however, with a fundamental aspect of British strategy in the 1770s. Britain was acting as a satisfied power, keen obviously to retain and safeguard its position, but not seeking to gain fresh territory in Europe. Representing a satisfied power, British ministers were not interested in seeking to strengthen the *status quo* by alliances with powers that wished to overturn it and were accordingly wary of becoming involved in European power politics. Here the American war fitted into a pattern that had begun with George III's rejection of the Prussian alliance in 1761–2 and had continued with a subsequent refusal to accept Russian requirements for an alliance (requirements that included support in conflict with Turkey), as well as with the rejection of French approaches for joint action against the First Partition of Poland of 1772.

Thus, there was to be no recurrence of the situation during the Seven Years' War (1756–63), namely war in alliance with a continental power (in that case, Prussia). This was a situation that, however unintentional, had proved particularly potent, or, at least, had been shaped thus in political and rhetorical terms by William Pitt the Elder, with his presentation of British policy in terms of conquering Canada in Europe: forcing France to commit itself heavily in Europe, and thus making it easier for Britain to win in North America. That Pitt, now Earl of Chatham, was a significant figure in the debate over America made his argument still relevant.

In the War of American Independence, there would be no alliance with Prussia (nor anyone else) to distract France, and thus no commitment of the British army to the continent, as had occurred in 1758, lessening the numbers of British troops available for operations in North America. Even more, subsidized German troops, such as those deployed in 1757 in an unsuccessful attempt to defend the Electorate of Hanover against French attack, would not be used in the War of American Independence for "German," or European, power-political purposes. Some subsidized troops would be retained in Europe—Hanoverians for example being sent to serve in the Gibraltar garrison, but most, notably the Hessians, could be and were sent to America where at peak strength they comprised nearly forty percent of the British army. Britain's fundamental strategy therefore rested on a cohesion that had military consequences—namely, passivity in Europe combined with the preservation of the status quo in America.

This strategy was not dictated by geopolitical imperatives. Instead it rested on policy choices, ones that were shared by George and his ministers. Consideration of alternatives is instructive as it highlights not the apparent determinism of the standard use of geopolitics and some of the discussion of strategy, but rather the extent of choice and the intelligence of the policy chosen. The thesis that post-1763 Britain should have supported Russian demands on Turkey[5] (with which Russia was at war from 1768 to 1774, or, subsequently, Poland, which Russia helped despoil in the partition of 1772) discounts the problems that would have been created by such an alliance.

This thesis also exaggerates what the British state could afford to do, and that at a time when it was struggling because of the Seven Years' War, with the burden of unprecedented debt, and facing serious political problems in Britain and North America over attempts to raise taxation. Indeed, given the problems posed by the latter, it is curious to note scholarly claims that the government should have embraced policies that would have entailed considerable expense. This prefigures the situation in 1814–15, in that fiscal and political pressures then made any continuance of the War of 1812 with America unwelcome. This was not due to the problems posed by conflict in North America, and at the end of that war the British were considering attacks on Savannah and Charleston. Instead, the costs of war with France and its allies from 1793 had left the state financially exhausted.

Secondly, even had Britain allied with Austria, Prussia, or Russia after 1763, there is little reason to believe that it would have enjoyed much influence with its ally or allies, or even been consulted by them, or, more particularly, have won support in the American crisis. This conclusion was suggested by Britain's experience while allied with Austria in 1731–3 and 1741–55, and with Prussia in 1756–63, and is taken further by the personalities involved, a feature generally underplayed in geopolitical discussion. It was not a case of alliance with Prussia or Russia, but with Frederick the Great and Catherine the Great, and each of them both despised George III and had poor relations with him. This issue looks toward the potential problems of British cooperation with the quixotic Napoleon III of France over the Mexican and American civil wars in the 1860s.

Moreover, as the three major Eastern European powers were at, or close to, war amongst themselves in 1768–74, 1778–9, and 1782–3, the caution of George and his British ministers was vindicated. Not only were these conflicts in which Britain had only limited interest, but it was also unlikely that these powers would have been able or willing to provide appropriate support to Britain in her confrontations with the Bourbons. Even had they done so, the transferability of resources was limited, not least because these powers lacked fleets able to influence the struggle at sea.

Moreover, more auxiliaries backing Britain in North America in 1775–83 might have made little more difference than a greater number of French troops supporting Emperor Maximilian in Mexico in the 1860s. In each case, there was a powerful opposition able to sustain resistance. Linked to this but also separate, the "output" of success in conflict between regular forces was unlikely to lead to the "outcome" of a victorious end to the war with the end of the revolution.

What about the arguably far more significant "what if?" of Austrian or Prussian pressure on France, or the possibility of this pressure, deterring the latter from helping the Americans from 1778, and thus justifying interventionist British diplomacy? It is pertinent to ask, however, whether such an alliance would not have led instead to a highly damaging British commitment to one side or the other, both in the Austro-Prussian War of the Bavarian Succession and in other possible confrontations. The Seven Years' War, in which Britain had allied with Prussia, was scarcely encouraging in this respect, as it was initially far from clear that Britain's involvement in the conflict on the continent then would work out as favorably as actually happened. It is only in hindsight that the strategy appears successful. The relationship between crises in Europe in 1863–4, over Poland and Schleswig-Holstein, and the more limited ability of Britain and France (had they wished) to take an assertive role in the American Civil War is instructive in this context.

In addition, had Britain allied with Austria or Prussia in the War of the Bavarian Succession, then George III's German territory, the Electorate of Hanover, would presumably have been exposed to attack by its opponent. Hanover was vulnerable, as was repeatedly demonstrated—for example, with threats of attack by Russia (1717), Austria (1726–7), Prussia (1729, 1737, 1753), and France (1734, 1741). Had Hanover been overrun (as had happened with the French in 1757 and was to happen with Prussia in 1803 and France in 1806) then its recovery might have greatly jeopardized the military, diplomatic, and political options of the British government. The French ability to change Hanoverian policy in 1741 by means of a threatened invasion had greatly troubled the British government.

Furthermore, the War of the Bavarian Succession was restricted to two campaigning seasons, but could have been longer, like the Seven Years' War, or could have speedily resumed, as with the two Austro-Prussian conflicts of the 1740s: 1740–2 and 1745–6. Either result would have posed problems for Britain had it been involved. Unpredictability entailed risk and cost.

Moreover, as another critique of the interventionist counterfactual, and, in this case, specifically the argument that it could have deterred French action, and thus ensured British victory, the British had, prior to French entry into the war, already failed to translate victories in North America, such as the clearing of Canada, the battle of Long Island and the capture of New York, all in 1776, or the battle of Brandywine and the capture of Philadelphia, both in 1777, into an acceptable political verdict. Thus, the "What if no French entry into the war?" is of less moment than might be suggested by a focus on the major French role in the Franco-American defeat of the British at Yorktown in 1781. This point underlines the need to locate speculation about diplomatic options—and counterfactualism as a whole—in a context of understanding strategic possibilities. However, as also with the American Civil War and other nineteenth-century crises, the latter in turn were affected by these options.

The extent to which contemporaries thought through these points clearly varied. Understandably, the British ministry was most aware of counterfactuals relating to its choices as they were centrally involved in the decisions made. Although operational military factors came to the fore from the spring of 1775, nevertheless the strategic dimension, both military and political, was always present, at the very least implicitly. The awareness of these factors by others, British, American and European, understandably varied greatly, as did the degree to which speculation might influence choices. Yet, these elements were clearly significant, with the Patriots seeking French support and (eventual) British acceptance, and, therefore, committed to trying to understand the interplaying contexts and conjunctures of Anglo-French relations.

Imperial overreach can be seen with Britain in 1775–83 and as a consequence in part of the earlier successes of 1756–63 as well as the development of the North American colonies. Such overreach can be presented as lying in part in a failure to create and sustain effective alliances, international and within the empire; but while this thesis sounds obvious, it lacks ready measurement. It may be easier to assess overreach in terms of financial problems, or a lack of adequate military resources, but both are true for most combatants in history. Moreover, far from being opposites, as so often assumed, reach and overreach were part of the same process, while the very success of Britain as an imperial power for so long suggested that overreach was not a terribly helpful concept.

Any understanding of the possibilities for British alliance diplomacy had to address the extent to which there was also in 1775–83 no significant domestic constituency for an interventionist diplomacy; and notably none for any particular interventionist course of action, for interventionism could mean very different policies. Aside from the practicalities of British power, and the nature of British politics, the Western Question, the fate of Western Europe, more particularly the Low Countries, the Rhineland and Italy, had been settled diplomatically in the 1750s, by the Austrian alliances with Spain (1752) and then France (1756), removing both need and opportunity for British intervention. This shift in power politics was crucial, for British public support for interventionism on the Continent was fragile, if not weak, unless the Bourbons (the rulers of France and Spain) were the target, a situation also seen more generally in British foreign policy. Indeed, the domestic coalition of interests and ideas upon which public backing for foreign policy rested in the eighteenth century was heavily reliant on the consistency offered by the resonance of the anti-Bourbon beat. Thus, British military strategy in the War of American Independence cannot be separated from wider currents of political preference and engagement. Looked at differently, the North American Question, both before and after the outbreak of the war, was not separate from concerns that were domestic as much as foreign, and "European" as much as "Atlantic."

What British strategy appeared to entail in North America, however, varied greatly. The mistaken initial British impression was of opposition largely only in Massachusetts, and this impression, which drew on a longstanding (and in part justified) belief that New England was different to the other colonies, suggested that a vigorous defense of imperial interests there would save the situation. This view led to British legislation in 1774 specific to this colony and to a concentration of Britain's forces in North America there. The initial military operationalization of strategy continued after the clashes at Concord and Lexington on 19 April 1775, both because the stress on Massachusetts appeared vindicated and because there were not enough troops for action elsewhere.

British policy failed both in Massachusetts and elsewhere. In the former, the military presence was unable to prevent rebellion or to contain it. Elsewhere in North America, the lack of troops stemming from the concentration on Boston ensured that British authority was overthrown in the other twelve rebellious colonies, while the Patriots were able to mount an invasion of Canada that achieved initial success, bottling up the British in Québec.[6] Thus, the original geography of the revolution was very important. The British decision to focus on Massachusetts reflected the political perception that it was the core of the revolution and that successful action there would deter opposition elsewhere, but this proved an erroneous assumption, although one that was understandable given the troop numbers available. The flaw in the British assessment in part arose due to the development in American politics in recent years, a development toward trans-colonial activism that tested existing political structures and assumptions, both on the part of Britain and within America itself. The revolution was cause, context and consequence of this development.

As a result of the events in the first stage, the second stage of the war, a stage expected neither by most of the Patriots nor by the British government, led to a major British effort to regain control. This policy entailed both a formidable military effort and peace-making proposals, although the extent to which these cold be brought into line, and, if so, on what basis, were unclear. Here, again, it is necessary to look at the military options in terms of the political situation. The end of the rebellion/revolution could not readily be achieved by reconquering the Thirteen Colonies (and driving the Patriots from Canada). The task of such a reconquest was too great unless there was a collapse in Patriot resolve, while the Declaration of Independence altered the situation because it ensured that the conflict ceased to be a rebellion and, instead, became a move intended as irreversible. This step was taken in order to encourage foreign support by making it less likely that the conflict would end in a reconciliation within the British empire that left the supporting power exposed. This outcome made foreign support more worthwhile, both to the foreign powers and to the Patriots.[7]

It became necessary, in response, for the British to secure military results that achieved the political outcome of an end to rebellion, an outcome that was likely to require both a negotiated settlement and, linked to this, acquiescence in the return to loyalty and in subsequently maintaining obedience. This outcome rested on a different politics to that of the conquest of New France (Canada) during the Seven Years' War, a step secured by the Governor's surrender in 1760 and the subsequent peace negotiations in 1762–3. The possibility of such an outcome raises questions focused on the possible response of reconquered colonies to events that were to occur in 1784–1815, notably the outbreak of war with France and the abolition of the slave trade, and those that might have occurred. It is interesting to note the issues the British faced with the Quebecois after 1775, but also the extent to which most accepted British rule.

The determination of the Patriots to have relations with the European states was significant as it entailed not only a striving for legitimacy seen in asserting a right to statehood among other states, but also a practical desire to acquire resources. In particular, France and Spain were key sources of arms and funds, while America came to play a role in public politics in France. This role focused the interest in geographical information about America that stemmed from the war and that was also seen in the individual American colonies. Atlases and maps depicting North America were produced in considerable numbers.[8] War ensured a particular interest in accurate maps. Although combatants, the French, ironically, including the navy, in order to make up for their lack of knowledge and access to the North American shoreline, relied on the availability of British printed maps sold through the map trade.[9] What was unclear for all participants was which military results would best secure the desired outcomes, a question that went back to the beginning of the Revolution when British ministers had debated whether they could rely on naval power alone, or whether it would be necessary to deploy an army large enough to defeat opposition.[10] A key factor encouraging the latter was the conviction that it was vital, practically and morally, not to abandon the Loyalists and the related belief that there were large numbers of them, an assessment that reflected confirmation bias.

This was true also for the French. How they should respond to war was uncertain. The context was different to that in 1756–63. The French revival in India, as in the Western Hemisphere, during the war was a product of France not being at war in Europe and of Britain being stretched. As in North America, the situation for France in India was very different to that in the Seven Years' War, which provides a valuable comparative context for the American Revolution, as well as underlines the growing interconnectedness of war around the world. It is instructive that the French did well in North America in 1754–6 when fighting the British alone, but that also arose from the nature of the conflict then, for it was concentrated on the interior. Whereas in 1758–60, the British were able to focus on the linkage of army and naval power, and to make the St. Lawrence at once interior, and an interior reached by a naval power operating along a river axis. The latter was not seen in the case of the war in 1775–83, other than in Canada in 1776. In contrast, Burgoyne could not use this factor in 1777.

Even sending a large army in 1776 left policy unclear for the British. Was the priority for the British the defeat, indeed destruction, of the Continental Army, as it represented the Revolution, not least its unity? Or was it the capture of key American centers? Each goal appeared possible, and there was a mutual dependence between them (one that was different to the situation during the Civil War). The British would not be able to defeat the Patriots unless they could land and support troops. For this capability to be maintained it was necessary to secure port cities. In contrast, the Champlain-Hudson axis could be invaded overland from Canada, but in 1777 and 1814 these invasions were unsuccessful, and in any event only affected a limited part of America. In contrast, amphibious forces could address the centers of American power, and both in this conflict and in the War of 1812. The geopolitical changes that were to be facilitated by the development of a rail system had not yet occurred.

Yet, as for the Union in the Civil War, captured port cities could best be held only if opposing field forces were defeated. The equations of troop numbers made this clear, not least the problems posed for finite military resources by maintaining large garrison forces. Indeed, the latter issue lent further military point to the political strategy of pacification, as such a strategy would produce local Loyalist forces as well as diminish the number of Patriots.

The British emphasis possibly should have been on destroying the Continental Army, which was definitely a prospect in 1776–7. It was unclear how far this would lead to a comparable collapse of the militia, but there would probably have been a major consequence not least in fracturing and, in part, atomizing the military resistance. Repeatedly, the Patriot riposte depended on the Continental Army and not the militia, for example at Trenton and Germantown. The crushing of the Continental Army would also have affected the views of European powers as well as opinion in Britain, North America, and more generally, from settlers in the West Indies to Native Americans. One consequence would have been the lessening, if not severing, of the supply of military *matériel.*

Instead of destroying the Continental Army, a goal that in large part depended on being able to force it to fight, the British focused on regaining key centers. This was not least as this policy was seen as a way of demonstrating the return of royal authority, notably by ensuring that large numbers of Americans again came under the Crown. Indeed, from the period when the Empire struck back, the summer of 1776, the British gained control of most of the key American points, either for much of the war (New York from 1776, Savannah from 1778, Charleston from 1780), or, as it turned out, temporarily (Newport from 1776 and Philadelphia from 1777), although such an outcome was far from inevitable. Nevertheless, this policy faced difficulties, with Charleston falling neither when attacked in 1776 nor in 1779, and it still left important centers, most obviously Boston from 1776 and Philadelphia from 1778, that were not under British control. This point indicated the fundamental political problem facing the British, and something more generally true in military history: Whatever is achieved in the field, it would still be necessary to secure a political settlement, at least in the form of a return to loyalty. The understanding of this issue was an achievement for the British, but also posed a problem; whereas, correspondingly, this understanding was also both achievement and problem for the Patriots.

This point helps explain the attention devoted by Patriot leaders throughout the war to politics, essential to secure the persistence and coherence of the war effort. Political engagement entailed support for independence but also an opposition to Britain that drew part of its vigor from a paranoia that saw British policy as directed to a new ethnic prospectus and geography. Pre-war anxieties about Native Americans and Blacks were given renewed energy by the war and indeed in 1776–8 the Creek killed more Georgia Patriots than British troops did.[11] In South Carolina, as in Virginia, although not only there, the cause of liberty was advanced with a clear racist inflection. Thus, in 1775, Thomas Jeremiah, a harbor pilot in Charleston and a wealthy "Free Negro," was falsely accused of acting as a British agent in encouraging a slave insurrection, a charge advanced by Henry Laurens (the city's foremost Patriot and later President of the Continental Congress). Though free, Jeremiah was tried in a slave court, convicted, and hanged.[12]

In a section in the Declaration of Independence that was deleted, Jefferson accused George III of inciting a slave rebellion, and the willingness of slaves to respond to encouragement by John, 4th Earl of Dunmore, the last royal governor, made this issue particularly sensitive for Virginians, and helped ensure their more general commitment to the Patriot cause. Indeed, in the Lords, Shelburne warned that such a policy would have a comparable impact on the opinion among settlers in the West Indies. The Patriot stance was scarcely a significant example for Blacks in the Haitian Revolution of 1791.[13]

As with the Confederates in 1860–1, a paranoid sensibility contributed to Patriot resolve, as it gave meaning to more abstract feelings about liberty. This situation prefigured the outbreak of conflict in South Carolina in 1861. Yet, it was not the case that, excepting this issue, liberty was only an abstract issue. Instead, the Constitutionalism seen in the new state constitutions was linked to local struggles for power and about policy.

The British, in turn, could try, by political approaches and military efforts, to alter these political equations within the Thirteen Colonies, prefiguring Confederate attempts to affect the situation in the North during the Civil War. At times, the British succeeded in doing so, as in the New York campaign of 1776 when British victories led many of Washington's men to return home while Loyalists came forward in numbers.

Indeed, the porous nature of the allegiance of many[14] provided a clear political benefit to victory. Thus, a new political prospectus was offered in South Carolina after the successful siege of Charleston in 1780. In tidewater South Carolina more generally, British authority was swiftly recognized. These developments appeared to be a vindication of the British policy of combining military force with a conciliatory policy, offering a new imperial relationship that granted most of the Patriot demands made at the outbreak of the war.

This strategy was not to succeed, but that did not mean that it could not have succeeded. Indeed, that is the most appropriate conclusion. We know that the British failed while the Patriots won, although in neither case was this scenario complete until the British ministerial change in

1782, and the comparable change in goals in 1782, and more clearly in 1783. Yet, it was not obvious that this would be the outcome. As a result, to understand the war, its causes, and consequences, it is necessary to underline the uncertainties of contemporary contingencies, contexts, and connections.

British defeat in the war and the loss of the Thirteen Colonies led contemporaries to suspect that there had been a fundamental weakening of the empire which would be followed up by France challenging British power elsewhere, notably in India. That these gloomy predictions were to be proved wrong owed little to Shelburne's confidence in the prospect of Anglo-French cooperation despite the negotiation of a trade treaty, though he was to be proved correct about the possibility of revived Anglo-American commercial links.

As it happened, in a suspicion, and eventually confrontation, that nearly led to war in 1787, it was to be French weakness that was decisive. This weakness owed much to systemic governmental flaws and to ministerial and political issues, but the financial strains of war with Britain in 1778–83 also played a major role, not least in accentuating the other problems. In April 1784, Louis XVI told Admiral Suffren that the war in America had so hit French finances that it had not been possible to fight on in Asia.[15] Thus, to a certain extent, the French collapse in the Dutch crisis of 1787 was the last act in the American war, and, from this crisis stemmed a further crisis in politics that helped lead to the outbreak of the French Revolution two years later.

The idea that the American Revolution led to the French one is well-established. As with the first revolution on its own, this idea can be approached in a functional way alone or by paying attention as well to ideological factors. The former would present the cost of French participation in the American Revolution as helping lead to subsequent political breakdown, while the latter would emphasize more centrally the anti-authoritarian example offered by the American Revolution.

Debate on this matter is still open, but it is best to adopt a multivalent interpretation. That is an appropriate conclusion throughout for any assessment of the American Revolution, both in its military and its political aspects: In place of simple clarity should emerge a clear appreciation of complexity—a complexity in causes, course, and consequences. The understanding of the Revolution is now an aspect of American "culture wars," rather than a substitute for conflict between Britain and America, or an expression of hostility between them. Yet it is also a war that can be readily studied from and for all participants, a war that is fascinating and transitional, instructive and as ever important.

# Endnotes

## Preface Endnotes

1 BL. Add. 32413 fols 14, 16–17.
2 NAS. GD. 26/9/513/7.
3 J.R. McNeill, *Mosquito Empires: Ecology and War in the Greater Caribbean, 1620–1914* (Cambridge, 2010); V. Scribner, *Under Alien Skies: Environment, Suffering, and the Defeat of the British Military in Revolutionary America* (Chapel Hill, NC, 2024).
4 Hayes to Charles Mellish, 16 January 1781, Me 172-111/26.

## Chapter 1 Endnotes

1 French ambassador Ossun to Vergennes, French Foreign Minister, 16 Sept. 1775, AE. CP. Espagne 577 f. 287–97.
2 J. Byrd, *Sacred Scripture, Sacred War: The Bible and the American Revolution* (New York, 2013); B.E. Stewart, *Redemption from Tyranny: Herman Husband's American Revolution* (Charlottesville, VA., 2020).
3 Army surgeon John Hayes to Charles Mellish, 30 Dec. 1778, Me 172-111/9.
4 Ferguson to William Eden, 2 Jan. 1780, BL. Add. 34417 f. 5.
5 Yorke to Edward Weston, 25 Oct. 1763, BL. Add. 58213 fol. 308.
6 David, Viscount Stormont, envoy in Paris, to William, 4th Earl of Rochford, Secretary of State for the Southern Department, 7 Dec. 1774, NA. SP. 78/294 f. 166.
7 L. Vorsey, *The Indian Boundary in the Southern Colonies, 1763–1775* (Chapel Hill, NC, 1996), 162–4.
8 D.C. Lord and R.M. Calhoon, "The Removal of the Massachusetts General Court from Boston, 1769–1772," in *Journal of American History*, 55 (1969): 735–55.
9 A. Land (ed.), *Letters from America by William Eddis* (Cambridge, MA, 1969), 65.

10 George to Charles Jenkinson, Secretary at War, 8 June 1780, BL. Add. 38564.
11 Wentworth, Governor of New Hampshire, to Rockingham, 2 Nov. 1770, WW. R1-1321.
12 T.H. Breen, "Where Have All the People Gone? Reflections on Popular Political Mobilization on the Eve of American Independence," in R. Chickering and S. Förster (eds.), *War in an Age of Revolution, 1775–1815* (Cambridge, 2010), 282. See, more generally, Breen, *American Insurgents, American Patriots: The Revolution of the People* (New York, 2010).
13 James Harris, British diplomat, to Frederick Robinson, 21 July 1777, Bedford, County Record Office, Lucas papers, 30/15/26/9.
14 Anon., *Some Reflections on the Trade Between Great Britain and Sweden* (London, 1756), 17–18.
15 G. Yagi, *The Struggle for North America, 1754–1758: Britain's Tarnished Laurels* (London, 2016).
16 P.D.G. Thomas, *The Townshend Duties Crisis: The Second Phase of the American Revolution, 1767–1773* (Oxford, 1987); F. Anderson, *Crucible of War: The Seven Years' War and the Fate of Empire in British North America, 1754–1766* (London, 2000); J. Lepore, *The Whites of Their Eyes: The Tea Party's Revolution and the Battle over American History* (Princeton, NJ, 2010).
17 P.O. Hutchinson (ed.), *The Diary and Letters of His Excellency Thomas Hutchinson* (2 vols., New York, 1971) I, 159. On Hutchinson, B. Bailyn, *The Ordeal of Thomas Hutchinson* (Cambridge, MA, 1974).
18 George to William Grenville, 31 Jan. 1796, BL. Add. 58859 f. 47.
19 NA. SP. 78/291 f. 184–5.
20 D. Ammerman, *In the Common Cause: American Response to the Coercive Acts of 1774* (Charlottesville, VA, 1974).
21 Lasowski, report to François, Duke of Rochefoucauld-Liancourt, 1784, London, University of London archives, MS. 138 f. 177–82.
22 T.R. Adams, "The British Pamphlet Press and the American Controversy, 1764–1783," in *Proceedings of the American Antiquarian Society*, 89 (1979), 38.
23 Thomas, "George III and the American Revolution," in *History*, 70 (1985): 16–31, and *Tea Party to Independence: The Third Phase of the American Revolution, 1773–1776* (Oxford, 1991).
24 D. Higginbotham, *The War of American Independence. Military Attitudes, Policies, and Practices, 1763–1789* (New York, 1971), 50.
25 George to North, 11 Sept., 18 Nov. 1774, *Fortescue*, vol. 3, pp. 131, 153; R.L. Bushman, *King and People in Provincial Massachusetts* (Chapel Hill, NC, 1985).

26 J. Flavell, "British Perceptions of New England and the Decision for a Coercive Colonial Policy, 1774–1775," in Flavell and S. Conway (eds.), *Britain and America Go to War. The Impact of War and Warfare in Anglo-America, 1754–1815* (Gainesville, FL, 2005), 108–9, 99.

27 L.H. Butterfield (ed.), *Adams Family Correspondence*, 1 (Cambridge, MA, 1963), 183.

28 George to North, 18 Nov. 1774, *Fortescue*, vol 3, p. 154.

29 George to North, 4 Feb. 1774, *Fortescue*, vol. 3, p. 59.

30 R.R. Rea, "Anglo-American Parliamentary Reporting: A Case Study in Historical Bibliography," in *Bibliographical Society of America, Papers*, 49 (1955), 224–8; L.D. Campbell (eds.), *The Miscellaneous Works of Hugh Boyd* (London, 1800), I, 247–9; B. Knollenberg (ed.), *Jonathan Williams and William Pitt: A Letter of January 21, 1775* (Bloomington, IN, 1949). See, more generally, R.C. Simmons and P.D.G. Thomas (eds.), *Proceedings and Debates of the British Parliaments Respecting North America, 1754–1783* (New York, 1916), vol. 5.

31 M. Jensen (ed.), *Tracts of the American Revolution* (2nd ed., Indianapolis, IN, 2003), 274–5.

32 R.E. Tookey, *Liberty and Empire: British Radical Solutions to the American Problem 1774–1776* (Lexington, KY, 1978).

33 R.A. Ryerson, "'Like a Hare before the Hunters': John Adams and the Idea of Republican Monarchy," in *Proceedings of the Massachusetts Historical Society*, 3rd ser., 107 (1995): 16–29; R.A. Ryerson, "John Adams, Republican Monarchist," in E.H. Gould and P.S. Onuf (eds.), *Empire and Nation: The American Revolution in the Atlantic World* (Baltimore, MD, 2005), 76–7.

34 J.G.A. Pocock, "Empire, state and confederation: the War of American Independence as a crisis in multiple monarchy," in J. Robertson (ed.), *A Union for Empire: Political Thought and the Union of 1707* (Cambridge, 1995), 318–48.

35 N. York, "Federalism and the Failure of Imperial Reform, 1774–1775," in *History*, 86 (2001): 155–79.

36 M. Elliott, *Partners in Revolution: The United Irishmen and France* (New Haven, CT, 1982).

37 G.M. Ditchfield, 'The Subscription Issue in British Parliamentary Politics, 1772–1779', *Parliamentary History*, 7 (1988), pp. 62–5.

38 M. McConnell, *Army and Empire: British Soldiers on the American Frontier, 1758–1775* (Lincoln, NE, 2004).

39 George to North, 18 Aug. 1775, *Fortescue*, vol. 3, p. 248; J. Bullion, "The *Ancien Regime* and the Modernising State: George III and the American Revolution," in *Anglican and Episcopal History*, 68 (1999): 67–84.

## Chapter 2 Endnotes

1 Gage to Viscount Barrington, Secretary at War, 26 June 1775, BL. Add. 73550.
2 J.W. Hall, "An Irregular Reconsideration of George Washington and the American Military Tradition," in Journal *of Military History*, 78 (2014): 961–93.
3 S. Brumwell, *George Washington: Gentleman Warrior* (London, 2012).
4 C. Cox, *A Proper Sense of Honor: Service and Sacrifice in George Washington's Army* (Chapel Hill, NC, 2004).
5 D.E. Lapp, "Did They Really 'Take None but Gentlemen'? Henry Hardman, the Maryland Line, and a Reconsideration of the Socioeconomic Composition of the Continental Officer Corps," in *Journal of Military History*, 78 (2014): 1239–61.
6 "Capt. Ephraim" [1776], Exeter, Devon RO. 997Z/Z12.
7 R.A. Herrera, "'The zealous activity of Capt. Lee': Light-Horse Harry Lee and *Petite Guerre*," in *Journal of Military History*, 79 (2015): 9–36.
8 D. Murphy, *William Washington, American Light Dragoon: A Continental Cavalry Leader in the War of Independence* (Yardley, PA, 2014).
9 Anon., *A Letter to the People of England, Upon the Militia* (London, 1757).
10 Memoranda of James Harris MP, Jan. 1779, London, History of Parliament transcripts.
11 M.S. Adelberg, *The American Revolution in Monmouth County: The Theatre of Spoil and Destruction* (Charleston, SC, 2010).
12 Napier to Earl of Dalhousie, Governor-General of India, 27 June 1849, BL. Add. 49106 fols 1–4.
13 Major-General James Pattison to Amherst, 9 June 1779, NA. WO. 35/115 f. 65–6.
14 T. W. Braisted, *Grand Forage 1778: The Battleground around New York City* (Yardley, PA, 2016).
15 Rainsford to Amherst, 4 Aug. 1779, NA. WO. 34/117 fols 27–8; Anon, undated memorandum, NA. PRO. 30/11/258 fols 7–8.
16 NA. WO. 34/125 fol. 10.
17 M.H. Spring, *With Zeal and With Bayonets Only: The British Army on Campaign in North America, 1775–1783* (Norman, OK, 2008).
18 S. Brumwell, *Redcoats: The British Soldier and War in the Americas, 1755–1763* (Cambridge, 2002).
19 D. Hagist, *Noble Volunteers: The British Soldiers Who Fought the American Revolution* (Yardley, PA, 2020).
20 J. Piecuch (ed.), *Cavalry of the American Revolution* (Yardley, PA, 2012).
21 A. Bruce to Henry, 2nd Duke of Newcastle, 7 Oct. 1780, NeC 2600.

22 L. Diamant, *Chaining the Hudson: The Fight for the River in the American Revolution* (New York, 1989).

## Chapter 3 Endnotes

1 S.R. Taaffe, *Washington's Revolutionary War Generals* (Norman, OK, 2019).
2 Greene to Knox, 7 Dec., Greene to Lee, 31 Dec., 1780, LC, Department of Manuscripts, Greene Letterbook.
3 P. Papas, *Renegade Revolutionary: The Life of General Charles Lee* (New York, 2014).
4 *Franklin Papers*, 22, pp. 292–3.
5 G.T. Knouff, *The Soldiers' Revolution: Pennsylvanians in Arms and the Forging of Early American Identity* (University Park, PA, 2004).
6 G.B. Nash, *The Urban Crucible: Social Change, Political Consciousness, and the Origins of the American Revolution* (Cambridge, MA, 1979); H. Ward, *The War for Independence and the Transformation of American Society* (London, 1999).
7 Sheffield, Archives, Wentworth Woodhouse papers, R1-1590, 1575.
8 W. Bellion, *Iconoclasm in New York: Revolution to Reenactment* (University Park, PA, 2019).
9 D.E.H. Smith, "Wilton's Statue of Pitt," in *South Carolina Historical and Genealogical Magazine*, 15 (1914): 18–38.
10 S. Carpenter, K. Delamer, J. McIntyre and A. Zwilling, *The War of American Independence, 1763–1783: Falling Dominoes* (New York, 2023).
11 Anon., *Reflections on the Present State of the American War* (London, 1776), 5.
12 *Annual Register*, 19 (London, 1776), 2.
13 PCC, vol. 58.
14 BL. Add. 21687 fol. 245.
15 BL. Add. 34416 fol. 273.
16 *Franklin Papers*: 22, p. 438.
17 Howe to Lord George Germain, Secretary of State for America, 30 Nov. 1777, NA. PRO. 30/8/7.
18 HMC., *Lothian*: p. 300.
19 J. Huston, *Logistics of Liberty. American Services of Supply in the Revolutionary War and After* (Newark, NJ, 1991).
20 P. Nelson, *Anthony Wayne* (Bloomington, IN, 1985), 75–6.
21 P.H. Smith (ed.), *Letters of Delegate to Congress, 1774–1789*, vols 10–11 (Washington, 1983–4).
22 Greene to Morgan, 16 Dec. 1778, T.B. Myers (ed.), *Cowpens Papers* (Charleston, SC, 1881): 9–10.

23 J.B. Harley, "Contemporary Mapping of the American Revolutionary War," in Harley, B. Petchenik, and L. Towner (eds.), *Mapping the American Revolutionary War* (Chicago, IL, 1978), 1–44.
24 S. Wilkinson, *The Defense of Piedmont, 1742–1748: A Prelude to the Study of Napoleon* (Oxford, 1927); P. Bianchi, "La guerra franco-piemontese e le Valli valdesi (1792–1779)," in G.P. Romagnani (ed.), *La Bibbia, la coccarda e il tricolore. I Valdesi fra due emancipazioni, 1798–1848* (Turin, 2001), 72–117; J.R. McIntyre, "Pandours, Partisans and Freikorps: The Development of Irregular Warfare and Light Troops across the Eighteenth Century," in A. Burns (ed.), *The Changing Face of Old Regime Warfare* (Warwick, 2033), 161–80.
25 Rockingham to Pemberton Milnes, 15 Feb. 1775, WW R1-1553.
26 D.F. Johnson, *Occupied America: British Military Rule and the Experience of Revolution* (Philadelphia, PA, 2020).
27 Eden to Francis, Marquess of Carmarthen, Foreign Secretary, 6 June 1786, NA. FO. 27/19 fol. 116.
28 P.P. Hill, *French Perceptions of the Early American Republic, 1783–1793* (Philadelphia, PA, 1988).

## Chapter 4 Endnotes

1 L.E. Horgan, *Forged in War: The Continental Congress and the Origin of Military Supply and Acquisition Policy* (Westport, CN, 2002).
2 *Annual Register*, 19 (1776), 2.
3 NRO. 1314/6.
4 NRO. 1314/7.
5 Halifax, SH 7/JL/1, p. 15.
6 Evelyn to Sir Frederick Evelyn, 23 April, 19 Aug. 1775, BL. Evelyn papers, LE1.
7 W.H. Moomaw, "The British Leave Colonial Virginia," in *Virginia Magazine of History and Biography*, 66 (1958): 147–60.
8 M. Lurie, *Taking Sides in Revolutionary New Jersey: Caught in the Crossroads* (New Brunswick, NJ, 2022).
9 K. Roberts, *March to Quebec: Journals of the Members of Arnold's Expedition* (New York, 1940).
10 H. Mayer, "Canada, Congress, and the Continental Army: Strategic Accommodations, 1774–1776," in *Journal of Military History*, 78 (2014): 503–35.
11 M.R. Anderson, *The Battle for the Fourteenth Colony: America's War of Liberation in Canada, 1774–1776* (Lebanon, NH, 2013).

## Chapter 5 Endnotes

1 P. Papas, *"That Ever Loyal Island": Staten Island and the American Revolution* (New York, 2007).
2 F. Baer, "Britain's Decision To Hire German Troops in the War for American Independence," in The Hessians, 15 (2012): 45–51.
3 George to John Robinson, Secretary to the Treasury, 26, 3 Oct. 1776, BL. Add. 37833 f. 99, 71.
4 Clinton to his cousin, the Duke of Newcastle, 18 May 1776, NeC 2330.
5 George to Lord North, 16 Oct. 1775, Fortescue, vol. 2, p. 270.
6 D.K. Wilson, *The Southern Strategy: Britain's Conquest of South Carolina and Georgia, 1775–1780* (Columbia, SC, 2005).
7 P. Chase (ed.), *Papers of George Washington*, Revolutionary War Series, vol. 5 (Charlottesville, VA, 1993), 293, 631–2.
8 Congreve to Reverend Richard Congreve, 4 Sept. 1776, Stafford, Staffordshire CRO, D1057/M/F/30.
9 D. McCullough, "What the Fog Wrought: The Revolution's Dunkirk, August 29, 1776," in R. Cowley (ed.), *What If? America: Eminent Historians Imagine What Might Have Been* (London, 2004), 43–54.
10 NAS. GD. 26/9/513/15.
11 D. Twohig (ed.), *Papers of George Washington*, 6 (1994).
12 B.L. Carp, *The Great New York Fire of 1776: A Lost Story of the American Revolution* (New Haven, CT, 2023).
13 Clinton to Newcastle, 20 Sept. 1776, NeC 2323.
14 D. Smith, *William Howe and the American War of Independence* (London, 2015).
15 R.F. Smith, *Manufacturing Independence: Industrial Innovation in the American Revolution* (Yardley, PA, 2016).
16 M. Cecere, *March to Independence: The American Revolution in the Southern Colonies, 1775–1776* (Yardley, PA, 2021).
17 J.R. Maass, "'Too Grievous for a People to Bear': Impressment and Conscription in Revolutionary North Carolina," in *Journal of Military History*, 73 (2009): 1091–15.
18 M.P. Gabriel (ed.), *Quebec During the American Invasion, 1775–1776: The Journal of François Baby, Gabriel Taschereau, and Jenkin Williams* (East Lansing, MI, 2005).
19 E.A. Fenn, *Pox Americana: The Great Smallpox Epidemic of 1775–82* (NY, 2001); A. Becker, *Smallpox in Washington's Army. Disease, War, and Society during the Revolutionary War* (Lanham, MD, 2022).
20 BL. Add. 32413 fol. 12.
21 George to North, 13 Dec. 1776, Fortescue, vol. 3, p. 406.

22 C.P. Neimeyer, "The British Occupation of Newport, Rhode Island, 1776–1779," in *Army History* (Winter 2010): 35; M.S. Adelberg, "An Evenly Balanced County: The Scope and Severity of Civil Warfare in Revolutionary Monmouth County, New Jersey," in *Journal of Military History*, 73 (2009): 9–47.
23 J.L. Van Buskirk, *Generous Enemies: Patriots and Loyalists in Revolutionary New York* (Philadelphia, PA, 2002).
24 Savile to Rockingham, 15 Jan. 1777, Sheffield, City Library, Wentworth Woodhouse Mss. RI-1705.
25 J.M. Wendel, "Turgot and the American Revolution," in *Modern Age*, 23 (1979): 282–9.
26 BL. Add. 24162 f. 144.

## Chapter 6 Endnotes

1 P.D. Chase (ed.), *The Papers of George Washington: Revolutionary War Series*, vol. 10 (Charlottesville, VA, 2000), p. 507.
2 NAS. GD. 26/9/513/8.
3 Mellish to Newcastle, 5 May 1777, NeC 2815.
4 Duff to Dorothea, Countess of Fife, 23 Jan. 1777, Aberdeen, University Library, Duff of Braco papers, 2727/1/88. See also, Sir George Savile to Rockingham, 15 Jan. 1777, WW R1-1705.
5 North to Francis, 1st Earl of Guildford, 16 Aug. 1777, Bodleian Library, Oxford, MS North adds C4 f. 179.
6 Lord Robert Spencer to Thomas, 2nd Lord Grantham, envoy to Spain, 16 May 1777, Bedford, County Record Office, Lucas papers, 30/14/361[or 301] f. 13; Baron Beckers, Palatine minister, to Haslang, 31 May 177, Munich, 255.
7 George to North, 31 May 1777, Fortescue, III, 449.
8 NA. PRO. 30/8/5.
9 R.M. Dunkerly, *Decision at Brandywine: The Battle on Birmingham Hill* (Yardley, PA, 2021).
10 D. Twohig, *The Papers of George Washington: Revolutionary War Series*, VIII (Charlottesville, VA, 1998), 182, 238, IX (1999), 317, 561.
11 S.R. Taaffe, *The Philadelphia Campaign, 1777–1778* (Lawrence, KS, 2003).
12 G.S. Brown, *The American Secretary. The Colonial Policy of Lord George Germain, 1775–1778* (Ann Arbor, MI, 1963), 101–15.
13 Clinton, 9 Oct. 1777, NeC 2357/1.
14 Major-General William Phillips, who served under Burgoyne, to Duke of Newcastle, 10 July 1777, NeC 2810.

15 D.R. Cubbison, *Burgoyne and the Saratoga Campaign: His Papers* (Norman, OK, 2012).
16 Elliot to Eden, 1 Jan. 1778, BL. Add. 34415 f. 4–5.
17 Clinton, 13 Oct. 1777, NeC 2344/1.
18 Clinton, 13 Oct. 1777, NeC 2344/1.
19 T. Corbett, *No Turning Point: The Saratoga Campaign in Perspective* (Norman, OK, 2012);W. Griswold and D. Linebaugh (eds.), *The Saratoga Campaign: Uncovering an Embattled Landscape* (Lebanon, NH, 2016); K.J. Weddle, *The Compleat Victory. Saratoga and the American Revolution* (Oxford, 2021).
20 T. Corbett, *No Turning Point: The Saratoga Campaign in Perspective* (Norman, OK, 2012).
21 R.A. Bowler, *Logistics and the Failure of the British Army in America 1775–1783* (Princeton, NJ, 1975), 231–4.
22 C. Boutin, "Adversary and Ally: The Role of Weather in the Life and Career of George Washington," in *Journal of Military History*, 81 (2017): 708.
23 Washington to Hamilton, 30 Oct. 1777, *Hamilton*, vol. 1, p. 347.
24 W. Bodle, *The Valley Forge Winter: Civilians and Soldiers in War* (University Park, PA, 2002); J. Buchanan, *The Road to Valley Forge: How Washington Built the Army That Won the Revolution* (Hoboken, NJ, 2004); J.R. Maass, *From Trenton to Yorktown. Turning Points of the Revolutionary War* (Barnsley, 2025).
25 Clinton to Newcastle, 5 Dec. 1777, NeC 2337.
26 George to Henry Dundas, 9 Oct. 1799, BL. Add. 40100 f. 235.
27 Frederik Hannecken, Danish Secretary of Legation, report, 13 Sept. 1776, Copenhagen, Danske Rigsarkivet, Department of Foreign Affairs, vol. 1957.
28 George to Robinson, 27 Sept. 1776, BL. Add. 37833 f. 51.
29 Hannecken, 27 Sept. 1776, Rigs 1957.
30 Yorke to Eden, 8 April 1777, BL. Add. 34413 f. 387.
31 American Commissioners in France to Vergennes, and enclosed memorandum, 5 Jan. 1777, *Franklin*, vol. 23, pp. 120–3.
32 Noailles, French envoy in London, to Vergennes, Foreign Minister, 11, 18 Ap., Vergennes to Noailles, 8, 22, 29 Mar., 12 Ap. 1777, AE. CP. Ang. 522 f. 117, 119–21, 386, 441, 50–1, 133–4, 162–3, 401.
33 Commissioners to Committee of Secret Correspondence, 17 Jan. 1777, *Franklin*, vol. 23, p. 196.
34 N. Desmarais, *America's First Ally: France in the Revolutionary War* (Havertown, PA, 2019).
35 Stormont to Thomas, 2nd Lord Grantham, envoy to Spain, 26 Ap. 1777, BL. Add. 24163 f. 93.

36 T.E. Cháve z, *Spain and the Independence of the United States* (Albuquerque, NM, 2002).
37 Noailles to Vergennes, 25 Ap. 1777, Ae. CP. Ang. 522 f. 487.
38 Stormont to Grantham, 18 June 1777, BL. Add. 24163 f. 172.
39 George to Robinson, 7 Sept. 1777, BL. Add. 37834 f. 3.
40 BL. Add. 37833.
41 I. Gruber, *The Howe Brothers and the American Revolution* (New York, 1972).
42 *Sarah Farley's Bristol Journal*, 2 Jan. 1779.

## Chapter 7 Endnotes

1 RA. GEO/3094.
2 D.K. Allison and L.D. Ferreiro (eds), *The American Revolution: A World War* (Washington, 2017).
3 AE. CP. Ang. 528 f. 289–90.
4 Vergennes to Noailles, 28 Feb. 1778, AE. CP. Ang. 528 f. 478
5 Stormont to Eden, 7 Jan. 1778, BL. Add. 34415 f. 45.
6 N. Baker, *Government and Contractors: The British Treasury and War Supplies, 1774–1783* (London, 1971).
7 Vergennes to Ossun, envoy in Madrid, 29 Aug. 1775, AE. CP. Espagne 577 f. 180.
8 Nicholas Rodger, *The Insatiable Earl. A life of John Montagu, 4th Earl of Sandwich* (London, 1993), 365–77.
9 Rodger, *Sandwich*, 221–3, 266–9.
10 D. Syrett, "Home waters or America? The dilemma of British Naval Strategy in 1778," in *MM*, 77 (1991): 365–77.
11 *London Evening Post*, 17 Jan. 1778.
12 *Keppel*, vol. 2, pp. 19–20, 23.
13 Cobbett, vol. 20, col. 340–1.
14 Cobbett, vol. 20, col. 392.
15 Cobbett, vol. 20, col. 332.
16 NeC, 2, 614; HMC *Carlisle*, pp. 387–8.
17 R.P. Multhauf, "The French Crash Program for Saltpeter Production, 1776–94," in *Technology and Culture*, 12 (1971): 163–81.
18 AE. CP. Ang. 522, f. 50, 117–22, 134, 63, 401.
19 Vergennes to Noailles, 17 Jan. 1778, AE. CP. Ang. 528 f. 125.
20 Joseph Yorke to William Eden, North to Eden, [Jan.], 16. Jan. 1778, BL. Add. 34415 f. 75, 92.
21 D. Syrett, *The Royal Navy in European Waters during the American Revolutionary War* (Columbus, SC, 1998).

22 Fitzwilliam to Rockingham, 3 Aug. 1778, WW R140–6.

23 George to North, 12 Nov. 1778, RA. GEO/3114.

24 Townshend to his wife, Anne, 28 Jan. 1778, Manchester, John Rylands Library, Eng Mss 940.

25 Fortescue, IV, 54–88.

26 T. Shadwell to Thomas, 2nd Lord Grantham, 9 June 1778, Bedford, County Record Office, Lucas papers 30/14/353/27.

27 Cobbett, vol. 19, col. 1163.

28 Cobbett, vol. 19, col. 743.

29 Cobbett, vol. 19, col. 740.

30 Mellish to his patron, Henry, 2nd Duke of Newcastle, 24 March 1778, NeC 4219.

31 George to North, 12 Nov. 1778, RA. GEO/3114.

32 K.J. Weddle, "'A Change of Both Men and Measures': British Reassessment of Military Strategy after Saratoga, 1777–1778," in *Journal of Military History*, 77 (2013): 837–65.

33 C.T. Atkinson, "British Forces in North America, 1774–1781: Their Distribution and Strength," in *Journal of the Society for Army Historical Research*, 16 (1937): 14.

34 R.A. Herrara, *Feeding Washington's Army: Surviving the Valley Forge Winter of 1778* (Chapel Hill, NC, 2022).

35 A. Sullivan, *The Disaffected: Britain's Occupation of Philadelphia during the American Revolution* (Philadelphia, PA, 2019).

36 Richard Henry Lee to Jefferson, 23 June 1778, *Jefferson*, vol. 2, p. 201.

37 W. Bodle, *Valley Forge Winter: Civilians and Soldiers in War* (University Park, PA, 2002).

38 M.E. Lender and G.W. Stone, *Fatal Sunday: George Washington, the Monmouth Campaign, and the Politics of Battle* (Norman, OH, 2016).

39 C. Toth, *The American Revolution and the West* (Port Washington, NY, 1975).

40 D.K. Wilson, *The Southern Strategy: Britain's Conquest of South Carolina and Georgia, 1775–1780* (Columbia, SC, 2005); J. Piecuch, *Three Peoples, One King: Loyalists, Indians, and Slaves in the Revolutionary South, 1775–1782* (Columbia, SC, 2008).

41 Tonyn to Amherst, 14 Nov. 1778, NA. WO. 34/111, f. 184

42 J. Tiedemann, E. Fingerhut, and R. Venables (eds.), *The Other Loyalists: Ordinary People, Royalism, and the Revolution in the Middle Colonies, 1763–1787* (Albany, NY, 2009); T.C. Jones, "'The rage of Tory-hunting': Loyalist Prisoners, Civil War, and the Violence of American Independence," in *Journal of Military History*, 81 (2017): 719–46.

43 F. Cook (ed.), *Journals of the Military Expedition of Major-General John*

*Sullivan* (Auburn, NY, 1887); C. Calloway, *The American Revolution in the Indian Country* (Cambridge, 1995).

44 Clinton to Newcastle, 22 Mar. 1778, NeC 2374.

45 BL. Add. 34416 fols 155–6, 271.

46 NA. WO. 34/112 f. 41. For 4 December 1778 figures WO. 34/111 f. 37.

47 Yorke to Amherst, 13 Nov. 1778, NA. WO. 34/111 f. 183.

48 Notes of Sir H. Clinton relative to the campaign of 1778, BL. Add. 34416 f. 154–5.

49 NA. WO. 34/112 f. 3–4.

50 Germain to Clinton, Carlisle and Eden, 4 Nov. 1778, BL. Add. 34416 f. 68; BL. Add. 34416 f. 67–9.

51 NeC, 2, 618.

52 Cobbett, vol. 20, cols 87–8.

53 B. Oberg (ed.), *The Papers of Benjamin Franklin* (New Haven, CT, 1991).

54 *Ibid.* vol. 29 (1992).

55 J.H. Hutson, *John Adams and the Diplomacy of the American Revolution* (Lexington, KY, 1980); J.R. Dull, "Benjamin Franklin and the Nature of American Diplomacy," in *International History Review*, 5 (1983): 351–5, and *A Diplomatic History of the American Revolution* (New Haven, CT, 1985).

56 Cobbett, vol. 20, col. 945.

## Chapter 8 Endntoes

1 NA. WO. 34/115 f. 71.

2 W. Willcox, *Portrait of a General. Sir Henry Clinton in the War of Independence* (New York, 1964), 260.

3 Germain to Clinton, 23 Jan. 1779, NA. WO. 34/112.

4 Keith to his cousin Frances Honour, 27 Oct. 1779, HM. 18940, p. 155.

5 Clinton to William Eden, 14 Feb. 1779, BL. Add. 34416 f. 271.

6 Clinton to Major Drummond, 2, 10 Mar. 1779, NeC 2604.

7 A.T. Patterson, *The Other Armada. The Franco-Spanish Attempt To Invade Britain in 1779* (Manchester, 1960).

8 D. Stoker, K. Hagan and M. McMaster (eds.), *Strategy in the American War for Independence: A Global Approach* (Abingdon, 2010).

9 Baron Seinsheim, Wittelsbach minister, to Baron Haslang, Wittelsbach envoy in London, 18 April 1779, Munich, 434.

10 WW. R1-1844.

11 HM. 18940, p. 151. See Keith's hopes, p. 149.

12 Ossun to Vergennes, 4 Sept. 1775, AE. CP. Espagne 577 f. 211–12.

13 *Bonner and Middleton's Bristol Journal*, 18 Sept. 1779.

14 Cobbett, vol. 20, col. 162.
15 Keppel to Rockingham [July/Aug.] 1799, *Keppel* vol. 2 p. 248.
16 W. Eden, *Four Letters to the Earl of Carlisle* (2nd ed., London, 1779), p. 53.
17 Germain to Clinton, 23 Jan. 1779, NA. WO. 34/112 f. 165–66.
18 Campbell to Eden, 19 Jan. 1779, BL. Add. 34416 f. 241.
19 Campbell to Eden, 19 Jan. 1779, BL. Add. 34416 f. 247.
20 Prévost to Amherst, 18 Jan. 1779, NA. WO. 34/112.
21 Lincoln, journal, 5 Sept.–8 Oct. 1779, LS.
22 L.V. Füser to Amherst, 30 Oct. 1779, NA. WO. 34/119 f. 248–9.
23 W. Ferraro (ed.), *The Papers of George Washington* 21 (Charlottesville, VA, 2012); B.L. Huggins, *Washington's War, 1779* (Yardley, PA, 2018).
24 Brigadier-General James Pattison to Amherst, 26 July 1779, NA. WO. 34/118 f. 171.
25 Clinton to Eden, 19 Nov. 1779, BL. Add. 34416 f. 479.
26 Pattison to Amherst, 8 Oct. 1779, NA. WO. 34/119 f. 66.
27 WO. 34/119 f. 66; Arbuthnot to Clinton, 23, 24 Oct. 1779, BL. Add. 34416 f. 452–5; NeC, 2634.
28 Clinton to Newcastle, 18 Oct. 1779, NeC 2634.
29 Lieutenant-Colonel John Leland to Amherst, 20 Aug., Pattison to Amherst, 25 Sept. 1779, NA. WO. 34/117 f. 109, 34/118 f. 170.
30 George to North, 22 June 1779, *Fortescue*, vol. 4, p. 369.
31 George to North, 27 June 1779, *Fortescue*, vol. 4, p. 379.
32 George to Charles Jenkinson, Secretary at War, 2 Aug. 1779, BL. Loan 72/1 f. 15.
33 George to Jenkinson, 7, 12, 20 Nov., 9 Dec. 1779, BL. Loan 72/1 f. 17–19, 23, 31.
34 George to North, 22 June 1779, 3 July 1780, George to Lord Thurlow, Lord Chancellor, 16 Oct. 1779, George to Jenkinson, 16 Oct. 1779, *Fortescue*, vol. 4, p. 370, vol. 5, pp. 96–7, vol. 4, pp. 458, 477; I.R. Christie, "The Marquess of Rockingham and Lord North's Offer of a Coalition, June–July 1780," in Christie, *Myth and Reality in Late-Eighteenth-Century British Politics and Other Papers* (London, 1970): 109–32.
35 George to Robinson, 29, 30 Aug., 8 Sept. 1778, 28 June 1779, BL. Add. 37833 fols 236, 240, 37834 fols 5, 99.
36 Skinner to Amherst, 4 May 1779, NA. WO. 34/114 f. 104; Clinton to Eden, 10 Nov. 1779, BL. Add. 34416 f. 479.
37 NA. WO. 34/112 fols 164–6.
38 Clinton to Newcastle, 14, 21 Aug. 1779, NeC 2633.
39 Clinton to Germain, 13 May 1779, BL. Add. 34416 f. 349.
40 Robert Fallaw and Marion West Stoer, "The Old Dominion under fire: The Chesapeake Invasions, 1779–1781," in E. Eller (ed.), *Chesapeake Bay in the American Revolution* (Centerville, MD, 1981), 443–51.

41 W.M. Fowler, *Rebels Under Sail: The American Navy during the Revolution* (New York, 1976); S. Cohen, *Commodore Abraham Whipple of the Continental Navy: Privateer, Patriot, Pioneer* (Gainesville, FL, 2010).
42 C. Smith, *Marines in the Revolution: A History of the Continental Marines in the American Revolution 1775–1783* (Washington, 1975).
43 J. Calef, *The Siege of Penobscot by the Rebels* (London, 1781); For a defense of Saltonstall, see G.E. Buker, *The Penobscot Expedition: Commodore Saltonstall and the Massachusetts Conspiracy of 1779* (Annapolis, MD, 2002).
44 J.R. Fischer, *A Well-Executed Failure: The Sullivan Campaign Against the Iroquois, July–September 1779* (Columbia, SC, 1997).
45 Samuel Tenny to Joseph Gilman, 29 Nov. 1779, LC, series 7E. Peter Force transcripts, item no. 49.
46 Colden to Amherst, 28 Oct. 1779, NA. WO. 34/119 f. 228.
47 *Cobbett*, vol. 20, cols. 1243–9.
48 *Cobbett,* vol. 20 col. 1151.
49 Portland, Maine; Maine Historical Society, Reidhead Journal.

## Chapter 9 Endnotes

1 Chesney journal, BL. Add. 32627 f. 16.
2 George to North, 12 November 1778, RA. GEO/314.
3 *Portsmouth History Notes*, citing an item in recent acquisitions by William Reese Company.
4 Alleyne Fitzherbert, British envoy in Brussels, to Keith, 7 Sept. 1779, BL. Add. 35517 f. 145.
5 Clinton to Lord John Clinton, 5 May 1781, NeC 2291.
6 Clinton to Newcastle, 21 Aug. 1779, NeC 2633.
7 Nottingham, UL., Mellish papers, 172-111/21.
8 G.F. Jones, "The 1780 Siege of Charleston as Experienced by a Hessian Officer," in *South Carolina Historical Magazine*, 88 (1987): 27, 30, 32.
9 G.F. Jones, "The 1780 Siege of Charleston as Experienced by a Hessian Officer," in *South Carolina Historical Magazine*, 88 (1987): 64.
10 C.P. Borick, *Relieve Us of this Burthen: American Prisoners of War in the Revolutionary South, 1780–1782* (Columbia, SC, 2012).
11 Clinton to Newcastle, 12 May 1780, NeC 2598.
12 C.P. Borick, *A Gallant Defense: The Siege of Charleston, 1780* (Columbia, SC, 2003).
13 J. Piecuch, *Three Peoples, One King: Loyalists, Indians, and Slaves in the Revolutionary South, 1775–1782* (Columbus, SC, 2008).

14 Journal of Captain Alexander Chesney, a Loyalist, Sept. 1780, BL. Add. 32627 f. 13.
15 J.S. Tiedemann, "Patriots by Default: Queens County, New York, and the British Army, 1776–1783," in *William and Mary Quarterly*, 43 (1986): 63.
16 Washington to Steuben, 8 Feb. 1780, *Hamilton*, vol. 2, p. 265.
17 Dearborn to Board of War, 30 June 1780, LC. Series 7E. Peter Force Transcripts.
18 R. Buel, *Dear Liberty: Connecticut's Mobilization for the Revolutionary War* (Middletown, CT, 1980); R.K. Snowman et al. (eds.), *The Papers of General Nathanael Greene* (Chapel Hill, NC, 1991).
19 Hamilton to Lieutenant-Colonel John Laurens, 30 Mar. 1780, *Hamilton*, vol. 2, p. 303.
20 Clinton to Newcastle, 4 July 1780, NeC 2625.
21 E.G. Lengel, *The Battles of Connecticut Farms and Springfield, 1780* (Yardley, PA, 2020).
22 Clinton to Eden, 14, 26 Aug., Clinton to Newcastle, 6 Aug. 1782, NeC 2623–4.
23 Cornwallis to Germain, 21 Aug. 1780, NA. PRO. 30/11/76 f. 12.
24 Hayes to Charles Mellish, 22 Aug. 1780, Me 172-111/23.
25 Williams to Hamilton, 30 Aug. 1780, *Hamilton* vol. 2, p. 385.
26 Germain to Amherst, 25 Sept. 1780, NA. WO. 34/127 f. 82.
27 Cornwallis to Clinton, 23 Aug. 1780, NA. PRO. 30/11/72 f. 44.
28 Chesney's Journal, BL. Add. 32627 f. 15–16.
29 James Hunter to Amherst, 12 July 1779, NA. WO. 34/1/6 f. 89.
30 Clinton to Newcastle, 1, 11 Nov. 1780, NeC 2609–10.
31 W.B. Willcox (ed.), *The American Rebellion: Sir Henry Clinton's Narrative of His Campaigns, 1775–1782*, pp. 226–7.
32 L.E. Babits, *Devil of a Whipping: The Battle of Cowpens* (Chapel Hill, NC, 1998).
33 J. Buchanan, *The Road to Charleston: Nathanael Greene and the American Revolution* (Charlottesville, VA, 2019).
34 Cornwallis to Clinton, 29 Dec. 1780, NA. PRO. 30/11/72.
35 Greene to Colonel Edward Carrington, 4 Dec. 1780, R.K. Showman (ed.), *The Papers of General Nathanael Greene*, VI (Chapel Hill, NC, 1991), 517.
36 Jenkinson to Amherst, 24 Oct. 1780, NA. WO. 34/127 f. 155.
37 S. Sommers, *Parliamentary Politics of a County and Its Town: General Elections in Suffolk and Ipswich in the Eighteenth Century* (Westport, CT, 2002), 178; S. Conway, *The British Isles and the War of American Independence* (Oxford, 2000).
38 George to John Robinson, Joint-Secretary to the Treasury, 6 Sept. 1780, BL. Add. 70990.

39 P.K. O'Brien, "The Political Economy of British Taxation, 1660–1815," in *Economic History Review*, 41 (1988): 1–32.
40 Mount Stuart to General Murray, 2 June 1781, BL. Add. 36803 f. 81.
41 Liston to Keith, 23 Oct. 1779, BL. Add. 35517 f. 224.
42 Jenkinson to Amherst, 24 Oct. 1780, NA. WO. 34/127 f. 152–4.
43 Vieregg to Haslang, 7 Jan. 1781, Munich 259.
44 Clinton to Newcastle, 16 Sept. 1780, NeC 2612.
45 Count Lusi, Prussian envoy in London, to Frederick II, 13 July 1781, *Polit. Corr.* Vol. 46 (1939), p. 59.
46 Stormont to Keith, 9 Jan., 16 March 1781, NA. FO. 7/1, nn. 7, 61–2.
47 Noailles to Vergennes, 21 March 1777, AE. CP. Ang. 522 f. 122.
48 S.D.M. Carpenter, *Southern Gambit: Cornwallis and the British March to Yorktown* (Norman, OK, 2019).
49 M. Cecere, *The Invasion of Virginia, 1781* (Yardley, PA, 2017).
50 Knox to Amherst, 6 Sept. 1780, NA. WO. 34/127 f. 29.

## Endnotes Chapter 10

1 Clinton to Newcastle, 28 Jan. 1781, NeC 2335, cf. 14 Jan. 1780.
2 George to Richard Grenville, 23 Nov. 1781, BL. Add. 70956.
3 Stormont to Sir Robet Murray Keith, envoy in Vienna, 16 Mar. 1781, NA. FO. 7/1, no. 61.
4 Cornwallis to Clinton, 10 Aug. 1780, NA. PRO. 30/11/72.
5 Lieutenant James Hadden to Charles Mellish, 11 May 1781, Me 172-111/47.
6 J. Boyd et al, eds, *The Papers of Thomas Jefferson* (Princeton, NJ, 1950– ), IV, 312.
7 Hadden to Mellish, 27 May 1781, Me 172-111/48.
8 J.A. Nagy, *Rebellion in the Ranks: Mutinies of the American Revolution* (Yardley, PA, 2008).
9 D. Stoker and M.W. Jones, "Colonial military strategy," in Stoker, K.J. Hagan and M.T. McMaster (eds.), *Strategy in the American War of Independence* (Abingdon, 2010), 5–34.
10 Clinton to Cornwallis, 11 June 1781, NA. PRO. 30/11/68 f. 15–18.
11 Clinton to Cornwallis, 28 June 1781, NA. PRO. 30/11/68 f. 28.
12 Clinton to Cornwallis, 8, 11 July 1781, NA. PRO. 30/11/68 f. 33–4, 38–40, 44.
13 Cornwallis to Clinton, 23 Aug. 1780, NA. PRO. 30/11/72.
14 Balfour to Captain John Saunders, 24 Ap. 1781, Gilder Lehrman Institute of American History.
15 Balfour to Clinton, 6 May 1781, Colonial and State Records of North Carolina, vol. 17, p. 1029.

16 Balfour to Germain, letter book of Nisbet Balfour, The American Revolution Institute of the Society of the Cincinnati, Anderson House, Washington, MSS L2001F617.
17 Cornwallis to Germain, 17 March 1781, NA. PRO. 30/11/76.
18 A. Waters, *To the End of the World: Nathanael Greene, Charles Cornwallis, and the Race to the Dan* (Yardley, PA, 2021).
19 Clinton to Cornwallis, 30 April 1781, NeC 2335.
20 Cornwallis to Francis, Lord Rawdon, 20 May 1781, NA. PRO. 30/11/86 f. 41.
21 Rodney to Sandwich, 13 Nov. 1789, *Life and Correspondence ... Rodney* (2 vols., London, 1830), vol. 1, p. 431.
22 M.E. Lender, *Fort Ticonderoga, the Last Campaigns: The War in the North, 1777–1783* (Yardley, PA, 2022).
23 Martin to Amherst, 26 July 1781, NA. WO. 34/135 f. 220.
24 Ibid., 19 Aug., f. 240.
25 Clinton to Newcastle, 1 Nov. 1780, NeC 2609.
26 NA. PRO. 30/11/68 f. 11–18.
27 Willcox (ed.), *Rebellion*, pp. 532–3.
28 Clinton to Cornwallis, 11 July 1781, NA. PRO. 30/11/74 f. 43.
29 Cornwallis to Clinton, 8 July 1781, NA. PRO. 30/11/68 f. 53–5.
30 Anonymous, *An Answer to that part of the Narrative of Lieutenant General Sir Henry Clinton which relates to the conduct of Lieutenant General Earl Cornwallis* (London, 1783), 110.
31 R. Kaplan, "The Hidden War: British Intelligence Operations during the American Revolution," in *William and Mary Quarterly*, 47 (1990): 135.
32 Marquis de Lafayette to Alexander Hamilton, 9 Dec. 1780, *Hamilton papers*, vol. 2, pp. 520–1.
33 Claude d'Albon, "Discours Politique sur l'Etat actuel de la Grande Bretagne," presented to Vergennes, [1781], AE. Memoires et Documents Ang. 2 f. 47.
34 J. Rice and A. Brown, *The American Campaigns of Rochambeau's Army* (2 vols, Princeton, NJ, 1972); J.D. Grainger, *The Battle of Yorktown, 1781: A Reassessment* (Woodbridge, 2005).
35 NeC, 2, 287–8, 290, 297, 303, 599.
36 J.A. Greene, *The Guns of Independence: The Siege of Yorktown, 1781* (New York, 2005).
37 R.M. Dunkerly and I.B. Boland, *Eutaw Springs: The Final Battle of the American Revolution's Southern Campaign* (Columbia, SC, 2017).
38 J. Buchanan, *The Road to Charleston: Nathanael Greene and the American Revolution* (Charlottesville, VA, 2019); J. Piecuch and J.H. Beakes, *"Cool Deliberate Courage": John Eager Howard and the American Revolution* (Charleston, SC, 2009).

39 D. Conrad (ed.), *The Papers of General Nathanael Greene*, vol. 8 (Chapel Hill, NC, 1995).
40 Robertson to Amherst, 27 Dec. 1781, NA. WO. 34/142 fol. 48. See also M.M. Klein and R.W. Howard (eds.), *The Twilight of British Rule in Revolutionary America: The New York Letter Book of General James Robertson, 1780–1783* (Cooperstown, NY, 1983).
41 AE. CP. Ang. 538 f. 203.
42 Clinton to Newcastle, 28 Dec. 1781, NeC 2287.
43 Greene to Governor Nash, 7 Jan. 1781, LC Greene Letterbook.
44 Greene to Morgan, 7, 16 December 1778, PCC vol. 172; T.B. Byers (ed.), *Cowpens Papers* (Charleston, SC, 1881), 9–10.
45 Greene to Sumter, 8 Jan. 1781, LC Greene Letterbook.
46 S.D. Aiken, *The Swamp Fox: Lessons in Leadership from the Partisan Campaigns of Francis Marion* (Annapolis, MD, 2012).
47 J. Hall, "An Irregular Reconsideration of George Washington and the American Military Tradition," in *Journal of Military History*, 78 (2014): 901–93.
48 G.Q. Saravia, *Bernardo de Gálvez: Spanish Hero of the American Revolution* (Chapel Hill, NC, 2018).
49 M.D. Green, "The Creek Confederacy in the American Revolution: Cautious Participants," in W.S. Coker and R.R. Rea (eds.), *Anglo-Spanish Confrontation on the Gulf Coast during the American Revolution* (Pensacola, FL, 1882), p. 72.
50 F. de Borja Medina Rojas, "José de Ezpleta and the Siege of Pensacola," in *ibid.*, p. 118.
51 Campbell to Amherst, 12 Aug. 1781, NA. WO. 34/136 f. 74.
52 Cornwallis to Clinton, 14 July 1780, NA. PRO. 30/11/72 f. 26.

## Chapter 11 Endnotes

1 Major-General Edward Mathew to Thomas Townshend, 25 Oct. 1782, Home Secretary, Durham Papers of the 1st Earl Grey, vol. 62.
2 J.A. Lewis, *the Final Campaign of the American Revolution: Rise and Fall of the Spanish Bahamas* (Columbia, SC, 1990).
3 Vieregg to Haslang, 6 May 1781, Munich 259.
4 T.E. Chávez, *Spain and the Independence of the United States: An Intrinsic Gift* (Albuquerque, NM, 2002).
5 Townshend to his wife, Anne, 28 Nov. 1781, Manchester, John Rylands Library, Eng. M. 940.
6 Crespigny to Robert Ellison, 30 Nov. 1781, Gateshead Public Library, Ellison MSS. A. 63 no. 41.

7 George to North, 21 Jan. 1782, *Fortescue*, vol. 5, pp. 334–5.

8 North to George, 18 Mar. 1782, *Fortescue*, vol. 5, p. 395.

9 George to Thurlow, 28 Feb. 1782, R. Gore-Browne, *Chancellor Thurlow* (London, 1953), 173.

10 *Morning Chronicle*, 11 Jan., 4 Sept. 1782.

11 Piers Mackesy, "British Strategy in the War of American Independence," in *Yale Review*, 52 (1963): 539–57.

12 Mount Stuart to General Murray, 2 June 1781, BL. Add. 36803 f. 78–9.

13 John Hayes to Mellish, 13 Jan. 1782, Me 172-111/33.

14 T. Fleming, *The Perils of Peace: America's Struggle for Survival after Yorktown* (London, 2007).

15 O.T. Murphy, *Charles Gravier, Comte de Vergennes. French Diplomacy in the Age of Revolution, 1719–1787* (Albany, NY, 1982), 252–60.

16 Stormont to Keith, 12 Feb. 1782, NA. FO. 7/4.

17 Fox to Keith, 10 May 1782, NA. FO. 7/4.

18 E. Jones, "The British Withdrawal from the South, 1781–1785," in W.R. Higgins (ed.), *The Revolutionary War in the South* (Curham, NC, 1979), 263.

19 D. Gregory, *Minorca, the illusory prize* (London, 1990), 182–95.

20 Coote to Macartney, 1 May 1782, BL. Add. 22440 f. 16.

21 J.G. Droysen et al., *Politische Correspondenz Friedrichs des Grossen* (46 vols, Berlin, 1879–1939), 46, 538.

22 NA. FO. 27/2 f. 43.

23 NA. FO. 27/2 f. 60–1.

24 Thomas Walpole to 3rd Duke of Grafton, 16 July 1782, Bury St. Edmunds, West Suffolk CRO. Grafton papers 423/838.

25 George to Shelburne, 7 May, George to Fox, 18, 22 May 1782, *Fortescue*, vol. 6, pp. 10, 34, 41.

26 George to Shelburne, 1 July 1782, *Fortescue*, vol. 6, p. 70.

27 Shelburne, 7 Dec. 1778, Cobbett, vol. 20 cols. 30–40.

28 N. Aston, "Lord Grantham and the Foreign Secretaryship, 1782–83: Personalities and peace making during the "Crisis of the Constitution,"" in R. Berman and W. Gibson (eds.), *Lantern of History* (Goring Heath, 2020), 67–85.

29 NA. FO. 27/2 f. 72.

30 NA. FO. 27/2 f. 132.

31 Fitzherbert to Grantham, 7 Aug. 1782, NA. FO. 27/3 f. 54.

32 Bedford, Bedfordshire County Record Office, Lucas papers, 30/14/306/36.

33 Cobbett, vol. 23, col. 204.

34 D. Richards, *Swords in Their Hands: George Washington and the Newburgh Conspiracy* (Chandler, NV, 2013).

35 Alexander Straton to Sir Robert Murray Keith, envoy in Vienna, 25 Mar. 1783, BL. Add. 35528 f. 133.

36 *Parliamentary Register*, vol. 9, pp. 297–302.
37 Raynel, report, 18 Sept. 1782, AE. CP. Ang. 538 f. 203.
38 George to Shelburne, 1 July 1782, *Fortescue*, vol. 6, p. 70.
39 *Cobbett*, vol. 23, col. 204.
40 BL. Add. 35528 f. 27.
41 Grantham to Keith, 22 Feb. 1783, BL. Add. 35528 f. 22.
42 *Cobbett*, XXIII, 519–20; G.C. Gibbs, "Laying Treaties Before Parliament in the Eighteenth Century," in R.M. Hatton and M.S. Anderson (eds.), *Studies in Diplomatic History* (London, 1970), 124; P. Mansel, *Prince of Europe. The Life of Charles-Joseph de Ligne 1735–1814* (London, 2003), 105.
43 A. Stockley, *Britain and France at the Birth of America: The European Powers and the Peace Negotiations of 1782–1783* (Exeter, 2001).
44 S.R. Frey, "Between Slavery and Freedom: Virginia Blacks in the American Revolution," in *Journal of Southern History*, 49 (1983): 396–8; J. Nagler, "Achilles' Heel. Slavery and War in the American Revolution," in R. Chickering and S. Förster (eds.), *War in an Age of Revolution, 1775–1815* (Cambridge, 2010), 285–97.
45 P. Griffin, *American Leviathan: Empire, Nation and Revolutionary Frontier* (New York, 2007).
46 G.F. Williams, *Year of the Hangman: George Washington's Campaign Against the Iroquois* (Yardley, PA, 2005); C. Saunt, *A New Order of Things: Property, Power, and the Transformation of the Creek Indians, 1733–1816* (New York, 1999).
47 E.J. Cashin, *Laclan McGillivray, Indian Trader. The Shaping of the Southern Colonial Frontier* (Athens, GA, 1992).
48 G.S. McCowen, *The British Occupation of Charleston, 1780–1782* (Columbia, SC, 1972), 10–13.
49 Rebecca Brannon, *From Revolution to Reunion: The Reintegration of the South Carolina Loyalists* (Columbia, SC, 2016).
50 For a report of September 1814 to the British government on American views on these lines, BL. Add. 38259 f. 93–4.

## Chapter 12 Endnotes

1 J.G. Marston, *King and Congress. The Transfer of Political Legitimacy, 1774–1776* (Princeton, NJ, 1987); N.L. York, *Turning the World Upside Down. The War of American Independence and the Problem of Empire* (Westport, CT, 2003).
2 J.M. Black, *George III, America's Last King* (New Haven, CT, 2006).
3 K.A. Yokota, *Unbecoming British: How Revolutionary America Became a Postcolonial Nation* (Oxford, 2011).

4 K. Burk, *Old World, New World: The Story of Britain and America* (London, 2007).
5 S.J. Purcell, *Sealed with Blood: War, Sacrifice, and Memory in Revolutionary America* (Philadelphia, PA, 2002); T.A. Chambers, *Memories of War: Visiting Battlegrounds and Bonefields in the Early American Republic* (Ithaca, NY, 2012).
6 S. Conway, *The British Army: 1714–1783, An Institutional History.*
7 J. Lepore, *The Whites of Their Eyes: The Tea Party's Revolution and the Battle over American History* (Princeton, NJ, 2010).
8 J. Seed, *Dissenting Histories. Religious Division and the Politics of Memory in Eighteenth Century England* (Edinburgh, 2008), 62–3.
9 B.A. Mann, *George Washington's War on Native America* (Westport, CT, 2005).
10 S. Conway, "'A Joy Unknown for Years Past': The American War, Britishness and the Celebration of Rodney's Victory at the Saints," in *History*, 86 (2001): 180–99.
11 J. Bannister and L. Riordan (eds.), *The Loyal Atlantic in the Revolutionary Era* (Toronto, 2010).
12 M. Meranze and S. Makdisi (eds.) *Imagining the British Atlantic after the American Revolution* (Toronto, 2015); P. Stock, "America and the American Revolution in British Geographic Thought, c.1760–1840," in *English Historical Review*, 131 (2016): 64–9.
13 Eden to Carmarthen, 6 June 1786, NA. FO. 27/19 fol. 116.
14 BL. Add. 57315 fol. 39.
15 J.B. Hattendorf, "The Formation and the Roles of the Continental Navy, 1775–1785," in J.B. Hattendorf, *Talking about Naval History* (Newport, RI, 2011), 200.
16 F.C. Leiner, *Millions for Defense: The Subscription Warships of 1798* (Annapolis, MD, 2000).
17 C. Murphy, "Jacobin History: Charlotte Smith's *Old Manor House* and the French Revolution Debate," in *Romanticism*, 20 (2014): 271.

## Chapter 13 Endnotes

1 There is a copy in the Library of Congress.
2 Pitt, now Earl of Chatham, to Charles, 2nd Marquess of Rockingham, leader of the Rockinghamite Whigs, 18 Nov. 1777, WW R151–6.
3 M. Roberts, *Splendid Isolation, 1763–1780* (Reading, 1970); H.M. Scott, *British Foreign Policy in the Age of the American Revolution, 1763–83* (Oxford, 1990).
4 Cobbett, vol. 20, col. 162.

5 B. Simms, *Three Victories and a Defeat: The Rise and Fall of the First British Empire, 1714–1783* (London, 2007), 677.
6 H.T. Shelton, *General Richard Montgomery and the American Revolution* (New York, 1994).
7 J.R. Dull, *A Diplomatic History of the American Revolution* (New Haven, CT, 1985).
8 K. Nebenzahl, *A Bibliography of Printed Battle Plans of the American Revolution, 1775–1795* (Chicago, IL, 1975).
9 M.S. Pedley, *The Commerce of Cartography, Making and Marketing Maps in Eighteenth Century France and England* (Chicago, IL., 2005).
10 G.S. Brown, *The American Secretary: The Colonial Policy of Lord George Germain, 1775–1778* (Ann Arbor, MI, 1963).
11 M. Searcy, *The Georgia-Florida Contest in the American Revolution, 1776–1778* (Tuscaloosa, AL, 1985), 177.
12 J.W. Harris, *The Hanging of Thomas Jeremiah. A Free Black Man's Encounter with Liberty* (New Haven, CT, 2010).
13 W. Holton, "Rebel Against Rebel: Enslaved Virginians and the Coming of the American Revolution," in *Virginia Magazine of History and Biography*, 105 (1997): 157–92.
14 J.L. Van Buskirk, *Generous Enemies: Patriots and Loyalists in Revolutionary New York* (Philadelphia, PA, 2002).
15 M. Bertrand, *Suffren. De Saint-Troez aux Indes* (Paris, 1991), 311–12.

# Index

*When entries include a geographical reference in their titles, one will find them in the country or state named. All bodies of water are listed independently. Battles, forts, and wars are all listed independently.*